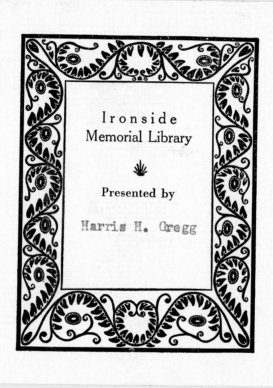

STUDIES IN JUDAISM

SECOND SERIES

STUDIES IN JUDAISM

SECOND SERIES

BY

S. SCHECHTER, M.A., Litt. D.

Philadelphia

The Jewish Publication Society of America

1908

18678

TO MY WIFE
IN DEVOTION AND GRATITUDE

PREFACE

The volume presented herewith to the public, under the title, "Studies in Judaism, Second Series," forms, like the preceding series published some ten years ago, a collection of detached essays and articles written at long intervals and called forth by various occasions.

The first two essays, "A Hoard of Hebrew Manuscripts," were written shortly after my return from Egypt, when the examination of the contents of the Genizah was still in its initial stage. Since then, the Genizah has been constantly revealing treasures to the world, to which only volumes of description could do justice. The publications containing matter coming from this treasure-trove would by this time make a little library, whilst the editions of Sirach fragments and the literature of controversies provoked by the publication of the original of this Apocryphal book might fill a fair-sized shelf in themselves. But the work is only just beginning; and as the field is so large and the workers so few, I confess that I look with envy upon the younger students who may one day, at least in their old age, enjoy the full and ripe fruit of these discoveries in all their various branches and wide ramifications.

The third and fifth essays, " The Study of the Bible " and " On the Study of the Talmud," were called forth by my appointment as Professor of Hebrew in the University College, London. The one on " The Study of the Bible " was intended to explain my attitude toward a problem closely connected with a subject I was called upon to expound to my class. The views I expressed on that occasion were described by a friend as " rank scepticism," doubting an interpretation of Jewish history now generally accepted as the final truth, and by men of a younger generation looked upon even as an ancient tradition. To this accusation I must plead guilty, and even confess that my scepticism has kept pace with the advance of years. The one " On the Study of the Talmud " was meant to give some directions to theologians attending my class, as to the way they might best profit by their Rabbinic studies. The essay being practically a plea for a scientific study of the Talmud, it was thought that it might be profitably read by wider circles.

The fourth essay, " A Glimpse of the Social Life of the Jews in the Age of Jesus the Son of Sirach," was suggested by my work, " The Wisdom of Ben Sira," when preparing the finds of the Hebrew originals of Ecclesiasticus for the press. It assumes, with many writers, that the Synagogue in the time of Sirach was, in most of its important features, already fairly developed, and that as a consequence the religious life, at 200 B. C. E. or thereabouts, did not greatly differ from what we know it to have been at 60 B. C. E.; though, of course, the Hellenistic persecutions must have greatly contributed toward emphasizing and intensifying it in various respects. The essay in question is, however, mostly devoted to the social life of the Jews, and tries to show how little such generalities as the common conception of the conversion of a Nation into a Church, answer the real facts. The Synagogue became a part of the Nation, not the Nation a part of the Synagogue.

The sixth essay, " The Memoirs of a Jewess of the Seventeenth Century," forms a review of the well-known diary of the Jewess Glückel von Hameln (1645-1719). I found much pleasure in writing it, as the diary is quite unique as a piece of literature, and bears additional testimony to the fact that our grand-mothers were not devoid of religion, though they prayed in galleries, and did not determine the lan-guage of the ritual. Theirs was a real, living re-ligion, which found expression in action and in a sweet serenity.

The eighth essay, "Four Epistles to the Jews of England," was published as a protest against the appearance on English soil of certain theological catchwords, which struck me as both misleading and obsolete. It is only fair to state that the writer's opinions did not pass unchallenged, and provoked much controversy at the time.

The seventh and ninth essays are closely connected; but while "Saints and Saintliness" deals more with the thing "saintliness," "Safed" treats more of saints, and the two are intended to complement each other in various ways.

A prominent English writer in a moody moment remarked, that one would love to be a saint for at least six months. I do not think that there are many who cherish a similar desire, but there may be some few who would not object to an opportunity of observing or dwelling with a saint for a few moments. They may perhaps learn that there is something better even than "modernity"—which is, eternity.

For the rest, these essays written in a popular style, all technicalities being strictly excluded, need no further comment. The authorities for my statements in the text are given at the end of the book in a series of notes, while the essay on Safed is accompanied by two appendixes, giving, especially in Appendix A, new matter from manuscripts upon which I have largely drawn in the text.

My thanks are due to the editors of The London Times, The Sunday School Times (Philadelphia), The Jewish Quarterly Review, and The Jewish Chronicle (London), in which periodicals some of these essays appeared for the first time. I am also indebted to Mr. I. George Dobsevage, of New York, who was always at my call during the progress of the work. My thanks are furthermore due to Rabbi Charles Isaiah Hoffman, of Newark, N. J., and Dr. Alexander Marx, Professor of History in The Jewish Theological Seminary of America, who helped me in various ways in the revision of the proofs. But I am under special obligations to my friend Miss Henrietta Szold, the able Secretary of The Jewish Publication Society of America, not only for the Index, but also for her painstaking reading of the proofs, and for ever so many helpful suggestions by which this volume has profited.

S. S.

January, 1908.

CONTENTS

A HOARD OF HEBREW MANUSCRIPTS[1]

I

The Genizah, to explore which was the object of my travels in the East (1896–1897), is an old Jewish institution. The word is derived from the Hebrew verb *ganaz*, and signifies treasure-house, or hiding-place. When applied to books, it means much the same thing as burial means in the case of men. When the spirit is gone, we put the corpse out of sight to protect it from abuse. In like manner, when the writing is worn out, we hide the book to preserve it from profanation. The contents of the book go up to heaven like the soul. "I see the parchment burning, and the letters flying up in the air," were the last words of the martyr R. Chanina ben Teradyon, when he went to the stake wrapped in the scrolls of the Law. The analogy of books with men was so strongly felt that sometimes the term "hide" was used even in epitaphs : "Here was hidden (*nignaz* or *nitman*) this man." When R. Eliezer the Great was buried, they said, "a scroll of the Law was hidden." It was probably this feeling that suggested the injunction to hide worn-out copies of the Pentateuch in the grave of a scholar. More often, however, they dug a grave for the dead books themselves in the cemetery, or hid them in some sort of shed adjoining the synagogue.

Happily for us, this process of "hiding" was not confined to dead or worn-out books alone. In the course of time the Genizah extended its protection to what we may call (to carry on the simile) invalid books ; that is, to books which by long use or want of care came to be in a defective state, sheets being missing at the beginning, in the middle, or at the end, and which were thus disqualified for the common purposes of study. Another class of works consigned to the Genizah were what we may call disgraced books, books which once pretended to the rank of Scriptures, but were found by the authorities to be wanting in the qualification of being dictated by the Holy Spirit. They were "hidden." Hence our term "Apocrypha" for writings excluded from, or never admitted into, the Canon. Of course, such books came into the Genizah in a sound condition ; but the period at which synods and councils were able to test the somewhat indefinable quality of inspiration is now so remote that these "external works" have met, by reason of long neglect, with the same fate of decomposition that awaited sacred books, by reason of long and constant use.

Besides these sacred and semi-sacred books the Genizah proved a refuge for a class of writings that never aspired to the dignity of real books, but are none the less of the greatest importance for Jewish history. As we know, the use of the sacred language

was, among the Jews, not confined to the sacred literature. With them it was a living language. They
wrote in it their letters, kept in it their accounts, and
composed in it their love-songs and wine-songs. All
legal documents, such as leases, contracts, marriage
settlements, and letters of divorce, and the proceed-
ings as well as the decisions of the courts of justice,
were drawn up in Hebrew, or, at least, written in
Hebrew letters. As the Jews attached a certain
sacredness to everything resembling the Scriptures,
either in matter or in form, they were loth to treat
even these secular documents as mere refuse, and
when they were overtaken by old age, they disposed
of them by ordering them to the Genizah, in which
they found a resting-place for centuries. The Genizah of the old Jewish community thus represents a
combination of sacred lumber-room and secular record
office.

It was such a Genizah that I set out to visit in the
middle of December, 1896. My destination was Cairo.
The conviction of the importance of its Genizah had
grown upon me as I examined the various manuscripts
which had found their way from it into English private and public libraries, and which had already led
to important discoveries. I therefore determined to
make a pilgrimage to the source whence they had
come. My plan recommended itself to the authorities of the University of Cambridge, and found warm
supporters in Professor Sidgwick, Dr. Donald Mac-
Alister, and especially Dr. Taylor, the Master of St.

John's College. To the enlightened generosity of this
great student and patron of Hebrew literature it is due
that my pilgrimage became a regular pleasure trip to
Egypt, and extended into the Holy Land.

Now that the sources of the Nile are being visited
by bicycles, there is little fresh to be said about Cairo
and Alexandria. The latter, at which I landed, is
particularly disappointing to the Jewish student.
There is nothing in it to remind one of Philo, whose
vague speculations were converted into saving dogmas,
or of the men of the Septuagint, whose very blunders
now threaten to become Scripture. Nor is any trace
left of the principal synagogue, in whose magnificent
architecture and tasteful arrangements the old Rabbis
saw a reflex of "the glory of Israel." Cairo is not
more promising at the first glance that one gets on
the way from the station to the hotel. Everything in
it calculated to satisfy the needs of the European
tourist is sadly modern, and my heart sank within me
when I reflected that this was the place whence I was
expected to return laden with spoils, the age of which
would command respect even in our ancient seats of
learning. However, I felt reassured after a brief inter-
view with the Reverend Aaron Bensimon, the Grand
Rabbi of Cairo, to whom I had an introduction from
the Chief Rabbi, the Very Reverend Doctor Herman
Adler. From him I soon learnt that Old Cairo would
be the proper field for my activity, a place old enough
to enjoy the respect even of a resident of Cambridge.

I must remark here that the Genizah, like the rest

of the property of the synagogue in Cairo, is vested
in the Rabbi and the wardens for the time being.   To
this reverend gentleman and to Mr. Youssef M. Cat-
taui, the President of the Jewish Community, my best
thanks are due for the liberality with which they put
their treasures at my disposal, and for the interest
they showed, and the assistance they gave me in my
work.

I drove to this ancient Genizah accompanied by
the Rabbi.   We left our carriage somewhere in the
neighbourhood of the "Fortress of Babylon," whence
the Rabbi directed his steps to the so-called Synagogue
of Ezra the Scribe.   This synagogue, which in some
writings bears also the names of the prophets Elijah
and Jeremiah, is well known to old chroniclers and
travellers, such as Makreese, Sambari, and Benjamin
of Tudela.   I cannot here attempt to reproduce the
legends which have grown up around it in the course
of time.   Suffice it to say that it has an authentic
record extending over more than a thousand years,
having served originally as a Coptic Church (St. Michael's), and been thereafter converted into a synagogue soon after the Mohammedan conquest of
Egypt.   Ever since that time it has remained in the
uninterrupted possession of the Jews.   The Genizah,
which probably always formed an integral part of the
synagogue, is now situated at the end of the gallery,
presenting the appearance of a sort of windowless and
doorless room of fair dimensions.   The entrance is on
the west side, through a big, shapeless hole reached

by a ladder. After showing me over the place and
the neighbouring buildings, or rather ruins, the Rabbi
introduced me to the beadles of the synagogue, who
are at the same time the keepers of the Genizah, and
authorised me to take from it what, and as much as,
I liked.

Now, as a matter of fact, I liked all. Still, some
discretion was necessary. I have already indicated
the mixed nature of the Genizah. But one can hardly
realise the confusion in a genuine, old Genizah until
one has seen it. It is a battlefield of books, and the
literary productions of many centuries had their share
in the battle, and their *disjecta membra* are now
strewn over its area. Some of the belligerents have
perished outright, and are literally ground to dust in
the terrible struggle for space, whilst others, as if
overtaken by a general crush, are squeezed into big,
unshapely lumps, which even with the aid of chemical
appliances can no longer be separated without serious
damage to their constituents. In their present condition these lumps sometimes afford curiously suggestive combinations ; as, for instance, when you find a
piece of some rationalistic work, in which the very
existence of either angels or devils is denied, clinging
for its very life to an amulet in which these same
beings (mostly the latter) are bound over to be on
their good behaviour and not interfere with Miss Jair's
love for somebody. The development of the romance
is obscured by the fact that the last lines of the amulet
are mounted on some I. O. U., or lease, and this in

turn is squeezed between the sheets of an old moralist, who treats all attention to money affairs with scorn and indignation. Again, all these contradictory matters cleave tightly to some sheets from a very old Bible. This, indeed, ought to be the last umpire between them, but it is hardly legible without peeling off from its surface the fragments of some printed work, which clings to old nobility with all the obstinacy and obtrusiveness of the *parvenu*.

Such printed matter proved a source of great trouble. It is true that it occasionally supplied us with loose sheets of lost editions, and is thus of considerable interest to the bibliographer. But considering that the Genizah has survived Gutenberg for nearly five centuries, the great bulk of it is bound to be comparatively modern, and so is absolutely useless to the student of palæography. I had, therefore, to confine my likings to the manuscripts. But the amount of the printed fragments is very large, constituting as they do nearly all the contributions to the Genizah of the last four hundred years. Most of my time in Cairo was spent in getting rid of these *parvenus*, while every piece of paper or parchment that had any claim to respectable age was packed in bags and conveyed to the forwarding agent to be shipped to England.

The task was by no means easy, the Genizah being very dark, and emitting clouds of dust when its contents were stirred, as if protesting against the disturbance of its inmates. The protest is the less to be ignored as the dust settles in one's throat,

and threatens suffocation.   I was thus compelled to
accept the aid offered me by the keepers of the place,
who had some experience in such work from their
connexion with former acquisitions (perhaps they
were rather depredations) from the Genizah.   Of
course, they declined to be paid for their services in
hard cash of so many piastres *per diem*.   This was a
vulgar way of doing business to which no self-re-
specting keeper of a real Genizah would degrade himself.   The keepers insisted the more on *bakhshish*,
which, besides being a more dignified kind of remu-
neration, has the advantage of being expected also for
services not rendered.   In fact, the whole population
within the precincts of the synagogue were constantly
coming forward with claims on my liberality—the
men as worthy colleagues employed in the same
work (of selection) as myself, or, at least, in watching
us at our work ; the women for greeting me respect-
fully when I entered the place, or for showing me
their deep sympathy in my fits of coughing caused by
the dust.   If it was a *fête* day, such as the New Moon
or the eve of the Sabbath, the amount expected from
me for all these kind attentions was much larger, it
being only proper that the Western millionaire should
contribute from his fortune to the glory of the next
meal.

All this naturally led to a great deal of haggling
and bargaining, for which I was sadly unprepared by
my former course of life, and which involved a great
loss both of money and time.   But what was worse,

was, as I soon found out, that a certain dealer in an-
tiquities, who shall be nameless here, had some mysterious relations with the Genizah, which enabled him
to offer me a fair number of fragments for sale. My
complaints to the authorities of the Jewish community
brought this plundering to a speedy end, but not before I had parted with certain guineas by way of pay-
ment to this worthy for a number of selected fragments, which were mine by right and on which he put
exorbitant prices.

The number of fragments procured by me amounts,
I think, to about a hundred thousand. The closer
examination of them has begun since my return to
England, but it will take a long time before an adequate account of them is possible. Here I can offer
only a few brief remarks about their general character,
which, of course, must be taken with due reserve.

The study of the Torah, which means the revelation of God to man, and the cultivation of prayer,
which means the revelation of man to God, were the
grand passion of old Judaism ; hence the Bible (Old
Testament) and the liturgy constitute the larger part
of the contents of the Genizah. The manuscripts of
the Bible, though offering no textual variations of
consequence, are nevertheless not devoid of points of
interest ; for some fragments go back as far as the
tenth century, and are thus of great value, if only as
specimens of writing ; others are furnished with marginal glosses, or are interspersed with Chaldaic and
Arabic versions ; whilst some are provided with quite

a new system of punctuation, differing both from the
Eastern and the Western.   Regarding the Apocrypha, I will here refer only to the fragment of the original of Ecclesiasticus, which it was my good fortune
to discover on May 13, 1896, in the Lewis-Gibson
collection of fragments.   The communications which
were then made by Mrs. Lewis to the press led to the
discovery of further fragments at Oxford.   All these
undoubtedly come from a Genizah, and justify the
hope that our recent acquisitions will yield more
remains of these semi-sacred volumes.   As to liturgy,
the Genizah offers the remains of the oldest forms of
the worship of the synagogue, and these throw much
light on the history of the Jewish prayer-book.   The
number of hymns found in the Genizah is also very
great, and they reveal to us a whole series of latter-
day psalmists hitherto unknown.

Next to these main classes come the fragments of
the two Talmuds (the Talmud of Babylon and the
Talmud of Jerusalem) and Midrashim (old Rabbinic
homilies).   They are of the utmost importance to the
student of Jewish tradition, giving not only quite a
new class of manuscripts unknown to the author of
the *Variae Lectiones*, but also restoring to us parts of
old Rabbinic works long ago given up as lost forever.   It is hardly necessary to say that both Bible
and Talmud are accompanied by a long train of commentaries and super-commentaries in Hebrew as well
as in Arabic.   It is the penalty of greatness to be in
need of interpretation, and Jewish authoritative works
have not escaped this fate.

The number of autograph documents brought to light from the Genizah is equally large. They extend over nearly seven hundred years (eighth century to the fourteenth). What a rich life these long rolls unfold to us ! All sorts and conditions of men and situations are represented in them : the happy young married couple by their marriage contract ; the marriage that failed by its letter of divorce ; the slave by his deed of emancipation ; the court of justice by its legal decisions ; the heads of the schools by their learned epistles ; the newly-appointed " Prince of the Exile " by the description of his installation ; the rich trader by his correspondence with his agents in Malabar ; the gentleman-beggar by his letters of recommendation to the great ones in Israel ; the fanatics by their thundering excommunications ; the meek man by his mild apologies ; the fool by his amulet ; the medical man by his prescriptions ; and the patient by his will. To these may be added a vast amount of miscellaneous matter, philosophical and mystical as well as controversial, which is the more difficult to identify as almost every fragment bears witness to the existence of a separate work.

All these treasures are now stored up in the Library of the University of Cambridge, where they are undergoing the slow process of a thorough examination. The results of this examination will certainly prove interesting alike to the theologian and the historian.

A HOARD OF HEBREW MANUSCRIPTS[1]

II

The examination of the contents of the Genizah is not yet concluded. " The day is short and the work is great," and the workman, if not actually " lazy," as the Fathers of the Synagogue put it, is subject to all sorts of diversions and avocations, such as lecturing, manuscript-copying, proof-correcting, and—novel reading. The numberless volumes of "fresh divinity" which an indefatigable press throws on the market daily take up also a good deal of one's time, if one would be " up to date," though many of them, I am sorry to say, prove, at best, very bad novels.

As stated in the previous article [2] on the same subject, there is not a single department of Jewish literature—Bible, Liturgy, Talmud, Midrashim, Philosophy, Apologetics, or History—which is not illustrated by the Genizah discoveries. Naturally, not all the discoveries are of equal importance, but there are very few that will not yield essential contributions to the department to which they belong. How a Weiss or a Friedmann would rejoice in his heart at the sight of these Talmudical fragments ! And what raptures of delight are there in store for the student when sifting and reducing to order the historical documents which the Genizah has furnished in abundance, including even

the remains of the sacred writings of strange Jewish
sects that have long since vanished.   Considerations
of space, however, forbid me to enter into detailed de-
scriptions; these would require a whole series of
essays.   I shall confine myself in this place to general
remarks upon the fragments in their various branches,
the trials and the surprises awaiting one in the course
of their examination, and some of the results they
have yielded up to the present.

The process of examining such a collection is
necessarily a very slow one.   In the ordinary course
of cataloguing manuscripts, you have to deal with
entire volumes, where the study of a single leaf tells
you at once the tale of hundreds and hundreds of its
neighbours and kindred.   The collections from the
Genizah, however, consist, not of volumes, but of
separate loose sheets, each of them with a history of
its own, which you can learn only by subjecting it to
examination by itself.   The identification of Biblical
fragments gives the least trouble, as they are mostly
written in large, square characters, whilst their matter
is so familiar that you can take in their contents at a
glance.   Still, a glance will not always suffice, for
these fragments are not only written in different
hands, testifying to various palæographic ages, but
many of them are also provided with Massoretic
notes, or with an unfamiliar system of punctuation.
Others are interspersed with portions of the Chaldaic
or Arabic versions.   They all have to be arranged
" after their kind," whilst as specimens of writing they

have to be sorted into some kind of chronological order. To judge by the writing—which is, I admit, not a very trustworthy test—the Genizah furnishes us with the oldest known manuscripts of any part of the Bible, older even than the Pentateuch manuscript of the British Museum (Oriental 4445), described as dating "probably" from the ninth century. On one Biblical fragment I found some gilt letters. Gold ink was well known to the Jews of antiquity. Some scholars even claim it as an invention of the People of the Book. But its use in the writing of the Scriptures was early forbidden by the Rabbis. The prohibition was meant to apply only to copies intended for public reading in the synagogue. But, as a fact, all manuscripts of the Bible are singularly free from such "ornamental aids." The fragment in question forms a rare exception, and must, therefore, date from an age when simplicity and uniformity in the materials used for writing the Bible had not yet become the rule.

Of great rarity, again, are the fragments in which all the words (except those at the beginning of the verses) are represented by a peculiar system of initials only, as, for instance, "In the beginning G. c. the h. a. the e." (Gen. 1 : 1). That such abbreviations should be employed even in copies of Holy Writ was only natural in an age when the chisel and the pen were the only means of making thought visible. On the strength of the few abbreviations they met with in Bible manuscripts, Kennicott and other scholars tried to account for certain misreadings of the Septuagint. Take your Webster's Dictionary, and look up how many hundreds of words begin, for instance, with the letter *B*, and think, on the other hand, that in the sentence before you there is room for one *B*-headed word only, and you will form some idea what a dangerous pitfall lay in every initial for the Greek translator, or even for the Jewish scribe. The Genizah has for the first time supplied us with samples proving that the abbreviation system was not limited to certain isolated words, but extended to the whole contents of the Bible. The particular system represented in the Genizah seems to have been known to the old Rabbis under the name of Trellis-writing. Dr. Felix Perles, from his acquaintance with the few specimens acquired by the Bodleian Library, at once recognised their significance for the verbal criticism of the Bible, and made them the subject of some apt remarks in a recent essay (*Analecten zur Textkritik*, etc., Munich, 1895). The Cambridge collections include such examples in far greater number, and many more may still be found. They will probably be edited in a volume by themselves, and will, I have no doubt, after careful study throw fresh light on many an obscure passage in the different versions.

While the Trellis-written Bible was undoubtedly intended for the use of the grown-up scholar, in whose case a fair acquaintance with the sacred volume could be assumed, we have another species of Biblical fragments, representing the " Reader without Tears" of the Old World. They are written in large, distinct letters, and contain, as a rule, the first verses of the Book of Leviticus, accompanied or preceded by various combinations of the letters of the alphabet, which the child had to practise upon. The modern educationalist, with his low notions of the "priestly legislation,"—harsh, unsympathetic words, indeed— would probably regard this part of the Scriptures as the last thing in the world fit to be put into the hands of children. We must not forget, however, that the Jew of ancient times was not given to analysis. Seizing upon its bold features, he saw in the Book of Leviticus only the good message of God's reconciliation with man, by means of sacrifice and of purity in soul and body. Perceiving, on the other hand, in every babe the budding minister "without taint of sin and falsehood," the Rabbi could certainly render no higher homage to childhood than when he said, " Let the pure come and busy themselves with purity." Every school thus assumed in his eyes the aspect of a holy temple, in which the child by his reading performed the service of an officiating priest.

Sometimes it is the fragments forming the conclusions of books, or, more correctly, of whole groups of books, such as the end of the Pentateuch, the end of the Prophets, and the end of the Hagiographa, that yield us important information ; for in some cases they possess appendixes or colophons that give the date of the manuscript, as well as the name of the owner and of the scribe. Occasionally we come upon a good scolding, as when the colophon runs: "This Pentateuch [or Psalter] was dedicated by N. N., in the year ——, to the synagogue ——. It shall not be sold, it shall not be removed, it shall not be pawned; cursed be he who sells it, cursed be he who removes it," etc. So far "the pious founder." It is rather disconcerting to read these curses when you happen to know something about the person who removed the manuscript, but you have to make the best of such kind wishes if you want to get at its history. Perhaps my researches may, after all, prove helpful to the feeble efforts made by the pious donor to achieve immortality, inasmuch as his name will again be given to the world in the catalogue which will one day be prepared. His chances in the dust-heap of the Genizah were certainly much poorer.

The foregoing remarks will suffice to show that even the Biblical fragments, though naturally adding to our knowledge little that is fresh in matter, are not without their points of interest, and must by no means be lightly esteemed. But this is not all. Ancient manuscripts are not to be judged by mere outward appearances; they have depths and under-currents of their own. And, after you have taken in the text, marginal notes, versions, curses, and all, there flashes upon you, from between the lines or the words, a faint yellow mark differently shaped from those in the rest of the fragment, and you discover that it is a palimpsest you have in hand. Your purely Hebrew

studies are then at an end, and you find yourself drifting suddenly into Greek, Palestinian Syriac, Coptic,
or Georgian, as the case may be.   Only in two cases
have the palimpsests turned out to be Hebrew upon
Hebrew.   A new examination then begins, and to
this you have to apply yourself the more strenuously
as the under writing is usually of more importance
than the later surface writing.

This has proved to be especially the case with the
liturgical fragments, among which the earliest, and
perhaps the most important, palimpsests have been
found.   Personally, I am quite satisfied with their
appearance.   If they restore to us the older forms of
the "original prayers," as some of them indeed do,
they need, of course, no further *raison d'être* for the
Jewish student, this being the only means of supply-
ing us with that history of our ancient liturgy which
is still a *desideratum*.   But even if they represent only
some hymn of the later Psalmists of the synagogue
(*Paitanim*), I am not, on closer acquaintance, particularly anxious to see them improved upon.   One likes
to think of the old days when devotion was not yet
procurable ready-made from hymn-books run by theological syndicates ; and many a fragment in the Genizah
headed " In thy name, Merciful One," and followed
by some artless religious lyric or simple prayer, is full
of suggestion regarding by-gone times.   You can see
by their abruptness and their unfinished state that
they were not the product of elaborate literary art,
but were penned down in the excitement of the

moment, in a "fit of love," so to speak, to express the religious aspirations of the writer. Their metre may be faulty, their diction crude, and their grammar questionable, but love letters are not, as a rule, distinguished by perfection of style. They are sublime stammering at best, though they are intelligible enough to two souls absorbed in each other. I am particularly fond of looking at the remnants of a Piyutim collection, written on papyrus leaves, with their rough edges and very ancient writing. In turning those leaves, with which time has dealt so harshly, one almost imagines one sees again the "gods ascending out of the earth," transporting us, as they do, to the Kaliric period, and perhaps even earlier, when synagogues were set on fire by the angels who came to listen to the service of the holy singers, and mortals stormed Heaven with their prayers. How one would like to catch a glimpse of that early hymnologist to whom we owe the well-known Piyut, ויאתיו, which, in its iconoclastic victory of monotheism over all kinds of idolatries, ancient as well as modern, might be best described as the Marseillaise of the people of the Lord of Hosts— a Marseillaise which is not followed by a Reign of Terror, but by the Kingdom of God on earth, when the upright shall exult, and the saints triumphantly rejoice.

These are, however, merely my personal sentiments. The majority of students would look rather askance upon the contents of the Sabbatical hymn under which the remains of Aquila were buried for nearly nine centuries. The story of Aquila, or Akylas, the name under which he passes in Rabbinic literature, is not a very familiar one to the public, and it offers so many points of interest that it is worth dwelling upon it for a while. He flourished in the first decades of the second century of the Christian Era, was a Græco-Roman by birth, and was brought up in the pagan religion of his native place, Sinope, a town in the Pontos, in Asia Minor, which acquired fresh fame as the opening scene of the Crimean War. Both Jewish and Christian legends report him to have been a kinsman of the Emperor Hadrian, but there is no historical evidence for it. It is, however, not unlikely that he had some relation with the court, as we know that Hadrian entrusted him with the restoration of Jerusalem, which he was planning at that time. Of his father we know only that he was well-off and a good orthodox heathen ; for it is recorded that Aquila, who was already professing Judaism when his father died, had great difficulties with his share in the inheritance, which included idols. In accordance with his interpretation of the Jewish law (Deut. 13 : 17), he refused to derive any profit from them, even indirectly, and threw their equivalent in money into the Dead Sea. His early training must have been that of the regular Greek gentleman, sufficiently known from Plutarch's Lives. According to one report he began life as priest in the pagan temple of his native place, in which, considering his high connexions, he probably held some rich benefice.

According to some writers Christianity formed the intermediary stage by which Aquila passed from paganism to Judaism. This would be a very natural process. But the matter, as represented by some Fathers of the Church, is not very flattering to Judaism. Their story is somewhat as follows: Aquila, abiding in Jerusalem, by the order of the Emperor, and seeing there the disciples of the Apostles flourishing in the faith, and doing great signs in healing and other wonders, became so deeply impressed therewith that he soon embraced the Christian faith. After some time he claimed the "seal in Christ," and obtained it. But he did not turn away from his former habit of believing,—to wit, in vain astronomy, of which he was an expert,—but would be casting the horoscope of his nativity every day, wherefore he was reproved and upbraided by the disciples. However, he would not mend, but would obstinately oppose to them false and incoherent arguments, such as fate and matters therewith connected; so he was expelled from the Church as one unfit for salvation. Sorely vexed at being dishonoured in this way, his mind was goaded by wanton pride, and he abjured Christianity and Christian life, became a Jewish proselyte, and was circumcised.

The best historians, however, give preference to the Jewish account, which tells us nothing about Aquila's Christian days. In this he figures as Akylas the proselyte, the disciple of R. Eliezer and R. Joshua. With the former he is said to have had a rather bad

encounter.   Perusing the passage in the Scripture,
" For the Lord your God . . . he does execute the
judgment of the fatherless and the widow, and loveth
the stranger (*Ger*) in giving him food and raiment"
(Deut. 10 : 17-18), Aquila exclaimed : "So, that is all
which God has in store for the *Ger*?   How many
pheasants and peacocks have I which even my slaves
refuse to taste " (so satiated are they with delicacies)?
To be sure, modest wants and frugal habits are no
great recommendation for a religion.   At least, it cannot under such circumstances aspire to the dignity of
the church of a gentleman.   R. Eliezer resented this
worldliness in his pupil, and rebuked him with the
words : "Dost thou, Ger, speak so slightingly of the
things for which the patriarch (Jacob) prayed so
fervently ? " (Gen. 33 : 20).   This harshness of R.
Eliezer, we are told, nearly led to a relapse of the
proselyte.   He found, however, a more patient listen-
er in the meek and gentle R. Joshua, who by his
sympathetic answer reconciled him to his new faith.

   The work which brought Aquila's name to posterity is his Greek version of the Old Testament,
which he undertook because he found the text of the
Septuagint greatly disfigured, both by wilful inter-
polations and by blundering ignorance.   It was prepared under the direction of the two Rabbis just mentioned (R. Eliezer and R. Joshua) and their fellow-
disciple R. Akiba.   The main feature of Aquila's version is an exaggerated literalism, which, as one may
imagine, often does violence to the Greek.   It is

such awkward Greek that, as somebody has said, it is almost good Hebrew. The alternative which lay before Aquila was, as it seems, between awkward Greek and bad and false renderings, and he decided for the former. One of the Church Fathers, when alluding to this version, says : "Thereupon (after his conversion to Judaism) he devoted himself most assiduously to the study of the Hebrew tongue and the elements thereof, and, when he had completely mastered the same, he set to interpreting (the Scriptures), not of honest purpose, but in order to pervert certain sayings of Scriptures, hurling his attacks against the version of the seventy-two interpreters, with a view to giving a different rendering to those things which are testified of Christ in the Scriptures."

Now, so far as one can judge from the little retained to us of his version, Aquila's perverting activity did not go much farther than that which engaged the Revision Committee for many years, who also gave different renderings, at least in the margin, to the so-called Christological passages. It is true that Jews preferred his version to the Septuagint, which at that time became the playground of theologians, who deduced from it all sorts of possible and impossible doctrines, not only by means of interpretation, but also by actual meddling with the text. One has only to read with some attention the Pauline Epistles to see with what excessive freedom Scriptural texts were handled when the severest rules of exegesis were abandoned. Some modern divines even exalt these misquotations and wrong translations as the highest goal of Christian liberty, which is above such paltry, slavish considerations as exactness and accuracy. Aquila's version may thus have interfered with theological liberty. But there is no real evidence that he entered upon his work in a controversial spirit. His undertaking was probably actuated by purely scholarly motives. As a fact, the most learned of the Church Fathers (*e. g.* St. Jerome) praise it often as a thorough and exact piece of work. As to the Rabbis, tradition records, that when Aquila put his version before his Jewish masters, they were so delighted with it that they applied to it the verse in Psalms : "Thou art fairer than the children of men, grace is poured in thy lips (45 : 3)." The Rabbis were, indeed, not entirely insensible to the grace of the Greek language, and they interpreted the verse in Genesis 9 : 27, to mean that the beauty of Japheth (the type of Greece), which is so much displayed in his language, shall, by the fact that the Torah will be rendered into the Greek tongue, find access to the tents (or synagogues) of Shem (represented by Israel.) In the case of Aquila, however, the grace admired in his version was, one must assume, the grace of truth. To the grace of an elegant style and fluent diction, as we have seen, it can lay no claim.

For most of our knowledge of Aquila we are indebted to Origen. We know his amiable weakness for universal salvation. He thought not even the devil beyond the possibility of repentance. Accordingly, he saved the "Jewish proselyte" from oblivion by inserting several of his renderings in his famous *Hexapla*, which, however, has come down to us in a wrecked and fragmentary state. The Aquila fragments discovered in the Genizah represent, in some cases, Piyutim, in others, the Talmud of Jerusalem, and the Greek under them is written in uncials, stated by specialists to date from the beginning of the sixth century. They are the first continuous pieces coming, not through the medium of quotations, but directly from Aquila's work, and must once have formed a portion of a Bible used in some Hellenistic Jewish synagogue for the purpose of public reading. The Tetragrammaton is neither translated nor transcribed, but written in the archaic Hebrew characters found in the Siloam inscription. Considering that Aquila's version is so literal that the original is always transparently visible through it, these fragments will prove an important contribution to our knowledge of the state of the Hebrew text during the first centuries of our era, and of the mode of its interpretation. A part of these fragments have been already edited in various publications, by Dr C. Taylor, the Master of St. John's College, and Mr. Burkitt, the fortunate discoverer of the first Aquila leaf. But more leaves have since come to light, which will be edited in course of time.

To return to the liturgical fragments found in the Genizah. Under this head may be included the didactic poetry of the synagogue. It is a peculiar mix-

ture of devotional passages and short epigrammatic
sentences, representing, to a certain extent, the Wisdom literature of the Synagogue in the Middle Ages.
Sometimes they are written, not unlike the Book of
Proverbs in the old Bible manuscripts, in two columns,
each column giving a hemistich. The examination of
this class of fragments requires great caution and close
attention, not so much on account of their own merits
as because of their strong resemblance to Ecclesiasticus both in form and in matter. You dare not neglect the former lest some piece of the latter escape
you. The identification of the Ecclesiasticus fragments is, indeed, a very arduous task, since our knowledge of this apocryphon has been till now attainable
only through its Greek or Syriac disguise, which
amounts sometimes to a mere defaced caricature of
the real work of Sirach. But I hardly need to point
out that the recovery of even the smallest scrap of
the original Hebrew compensates richly for all the
labor spent on it. Apart from its semi-sacred character, these Sirach discoveries restore to us the only
genuine document dating from the Persian-Greek
period (from about 450 till about 160 B. C. E.), the
most obscure in the whole of Jewish history. And I
am strongly convinced that with all his "Jewish
prejudices" he will prove a safer guide in this laby-
rinth of guesses and counter-guesses than the liberal-
minded "backward prophet" of the Nineteenth Century, whose source of inspiration is not always above
doubt.[3] I am happy to state that my labours in this

department were rewarded with several discoveries of fragments from Sirach's "Wisdom Book." They will soon be submitted to the necessary study preceding their preparation for the press, when they will appear in a separate volume.

The Rabbinic productions of the earlier sages, teachers, and interpreters, as they are embodied in the Mishnah, the Additions, and the Talmud of Jerusalem and the Talmud of Babylon, formed the main subjects of study in the mediæval schools of the Jews. It is thus only natural that the Genizah should yield a large number of fragments of the works mentioned, and they do, indeed, amount to many hundreds. Some of these are provided with vowel-points, and occasionally also with accents, and thus represent a family of manuscripts hitherto known only through the evidence of certain authorities testifying to the fact that there existed copies of early Rabbinic works prepared in the way indicated. But what the student is especially looking out for is for remainders of the Talmud of Jerusalem, which, though in some respects more important for the knowledge of Jewish history and the intelligent conception of the minds of the Rabbis than the "twin-Talmud of the East," has been, by certain untoward circumstances, badly neglected in the schools, and thus very little copied by the scribes. Its real importance and superiority above similar contemporary productions was only recognised in the comparatively modern centuries, when the manuscripts, as just indicated never

very ample, had long disappeared. The Genizah opens
a new mine in this direction, too, and the number of
fragments of the Jerusalem Talmud increasing daily,
also amounting to a goodly volume, will doubtless
be published by some student in due time.

Where the Genizah promises the largest output is
in the department of history, especially the period
intervening between the birth of Saadya (892) and
the death of Maimonides (1205). This period, which
gave birth to the greatest of the Eminences (Gaonim),
Rabbi Saadya, Rabbi Sherira, and Rabbi Hai, which
witnessed the hottest controversies between the Rab-
binites and the Karaites and other schismatics, and
which saw the disintegration of the great old schools
in Babylon, and the creation of new centres for the
study of the Torah in Europe and in Northern Africa,
forms, as is well known, one of the most important
chapters in Jewish history. But this chapter will now
have to be re-written; any number of conveyances,
leases, bills, and private letters are constantly turning
up, thus affording us a better insight into the social
life of the Jews during those remote centuries. New
letters from the Eminences addressed to their contemporaries, scattered over various countries, are daily
coming to light, and will form an important addition
to the Responsa literature of the Gaonim. Even entire
new books or fragments of such, composed by the
Gaonim, and only known by references have been
discovered. Of more significance are such documents

as those bearing on the controversy between Rabbi
Saadya and his contemporary Ben Meïr, the head of
the Jews in Palestine, which prove that even at
that time the question of authority over the whole of
Jewry, and of the prerogative of fixing the calendar,
was still a contested point between the Jews of Palestine and their brethren in the dispersion. The controversy was a bitter one and of long duration, as
may be seen from another document dating from the
Eleventh Century, the Scroll of Abiathar, which, at
the same time, reveals the significant fact that the
antagonism between the Priestly and the Kingly, or
the Aaronide and Davidic families, had not quite died
down even at this late period. Some of the documents are autograph. It is enough to mention here
the letter of Chushiel ben Elhanan (or Hananel)
of Kairowan, addressed to Shemariah ben Elhanan
of Egypt, written about the year 1000. To these two
Rabbis, legend attributes a large share in the trans-
planting of the Torah in Northern Africa, so that our
document will prove an important contribution to
the history of the rise of the Yeshiboth outside of
Babylon.

Looking over this enormous mass of fragments
about me, in the sifting and examination of which I
am now occupied, I cannot overcome a sad feeling steal-
ing over me, that I shall hardly be worthy to see all the
results which the Genizah will add to our knowledge
of Jews and Judaism. The work is not for one man

and not for one generation. It will occupy many a specialist, and much longer than a lifetime. However, to use an old adage, " It is not thy duty to complete the work, but neither art thou free to desist from it."

THE STUDY OF THE BIBLE[1]

There is a saying of an old Hebrew sage, "In a place where one is unknown, one is permitted to say, I am a scholar." Now I am, I fear, neither so humble as to think myself quite a *persona ignota*, nor am I, I trust, so arrogant as to claim, in the presence of so learned an audience, a title to deserve which I have still to do my life's work. But being about to express opinions not quite in harmony with current views, I shall avail myself of this license so far as to say what I am not: I am no partisan, I hold no brief for a particular school, and I have no cause to defend. Such a declaration, which would be entirely out of place in any other branch of human knowledge, is unfortunately still necessary in view of the particular nature of the subject which, by the courtesy of the Council and the Senate of the college, it will be my privilege to expound. My subject is the Hebrew language; and the means of acquiring it are the same as make for proficiency in any other language— sound knowledge of its grammar, wide acquaintance with its vocabulary, and, above all, real familiarity with its literature; for it is in the literature that the spirit still surviveth, even in the so-called dead languages. But the literature by which the Hebrew language is represented is a *sacred* literature; a literature which by common consent of the civilised world bears the name of a Testament. As such, every line in it claims to bear testimony to some eternal truth, to convey some moral lesson, and reveal some awful mystery. The very first text (Genesis) on which I shall have to lecture gives us an account of the Creation, whilst the verse, "And God created man in his own image," has kept busy pulpit and brush for nearly twenty centuries, and another twenty centuries may pass before humanity gets into possession of its sacred and secret *dossier*. However, this is the province of the artist and the preacher. But even in the region of mere exegesis we are confronted with two important theological schools—I say advisedly, theological schools.

For, in spite of all professions of impartiality and freedom from prejudice, each school has its own theological standpoint which greatly affects even its etymology. To give one instance: According to Wellhausen, the word Torah (תורה) meant originally the thing thrown or cast, a term borrowed from the lots or stones cast by the priests for the purpose of deciding difficult cases. On the other hand, the pure philologist Barth derives it in his *Etymologische Studien* from a root still extant in Arabic, denoting "the thing reported," or "come down by tradition," and proceeds to say, "Thus Wellhausen's hypothesis is not confirmed."[2] But Wellhausen's hypothesis is somehow strangely in harmony with Wellhausen's conception of the law, which thus would originate in a sort of priestly fetich.

However, this is a minor point. More serious is the question as to the dates at which the various books and documents of which the Old Testament is made up, were composed. When I speak of the old school, I do not refer to the class of commentators represented by Doctor Pusey in England and Professor Hengstenberg in Germany. I am rather thinking of the school led by Ewald, Bleek, Dillmann, Strack, Kittel, and many other men of prominence, none of whom could be suspected of being blind followers of tradition. They all accepted the heterogeneous composition of the Pentateuch, and cheerfully took part in the difficult task of its proper analysis. In fact, few scholars have contributed more toward this analysis than Dillmann. And even a superficial acquaintance with their works shows that not a single tradition was allowed by them to stand, in which anything that might be construed as an anachronism could be detected. When we consider that this school has furnished us with grammarians, lexicographers, and general Semitic scholars at least as eminent as those of the new school, we shall at once perceive that the arguments for settling the dates of the various documents cannot possibly have been evolved on merely philological lines. Theological considerations as to the nature of inspiration and the real functions of religion, metaphysical speculations as to the meaning and the laws of progression and development in history, and, above all, the question as to the compatibility of a real living faith with a

hearty devotion to the ceremonial law, play at least
an equal part therein.   To a certain extent it was the
supposed antagonism between religion as a social
institution, and religion as a matter personal and
inward, which, on the one hand, turned post-exilic
Judaism into a sort of "revival camp" with the whole
of the community on the mourners' bench, and, on
the other hand, converted the greatest collection of
religious lyrics into a mere hymn-book, reflecting, not
the aspirations and longings of the individual, but the
corporate utterances of the community.

Having to lecture on these sacred documents, I
may perhaps be expected to take part in this controversy.   In fact, I have already been asked the old
question, "Art thou for us or for our adversaries?"
I will, therefore, declare beforehand that, far from
being the mouthpiece of a single school, I shall,
when necessary, try to do justice to both, so far as I
understand them.   At the same time, however, I
shall beg leave to maintain a sceptical attitude toward
both schools, which will enable me to preserve my
freedom of judgment.   I say, when necessary, for, as
a rule, literary criticism will be my province, and I
shall not easily be drawn into the discussion of questions in the settling of which theology and metaphys-
ics occupy a more prominent part than philology and
exegesis.

In adopting this course, I am guided by the following reasons: First, as I understand, the traditions of
the University College of London have always tended

to exclude all controversial matter which cannot well be discussed without a certain theological bias. The fact that we now conjure with the names of the neo-Platonist Schleiermacher and the Hegelian Watke, instead of appealing to the authority of Thomas Aquinas and Albertus Magnus, has by no means cooled down our theological temperature. As in days of old, theological controversies are still wanting in "sweet reasonableness," and should, therefore, receive no encouragement from a teacher.

Another reason for reducing these discussions to a minimum is economy. The old saying, "Art is long, and Life is short," is to no subject more applicable than to the study of Hebrew. It is a strange world, both in language and in thought, quite bewildering for the beginner. It has practically no vowel-system; at least, not one which is perceivable to the European eye. The tiny little signs above and below the line proved a stumbling-block to a Goethe, and he gave up the study of Hebrew in despair. Yet how much depends on correct vocalisation. To give an example of a somewhat general character, I will only mention here two combinations of the letters *Yod*, *Zadi*, and *Resh*. Read *Yozer*, it means "he who forms, who fashions, who creates," hence "creator." Read *Yezer*, it denotes "frame, formation, imagination, desire, evil desire," developing gradually, in the later Hebrew literature, into the mysterious, unspeakable angel we know so well from Milton's "Paradise Lost." Hence the exclamation of a Rabbi in referring to the great dualism of flesh and spirit under which man is constantly labouring: "Woe unto me of my *Yezer*, and woe unto me of my *Yozer*."[3] On the other hand, the normal span of our academic life extends over the short period of nine terms, some eighteen months in all. Considering now how little preparation the student receives for this branch of study in the schools leading up to the University, it is evident that there is no time to spare for discussions lying beyond the sphere of grammar and literary criticism. The temptation to indulge in theology and metaphysical reconstructions of history is very great, indeed, but it must be resisted at this stage of the student's new life.

It may, perhaps, be objected, that in the majority of cases the student of Hebrew is less intent upon acquiring the knowledge of a Semitic language than upon gaining a fair acquaintance with the contents of the sacred volume. But I am inclined to think that even with this purpose in view I shall be more helpful to the student by lecturing *on* the Bible than by lecturing *about* the Bible. For the great fact remains that the best commentary on the Bible is the Bible itself. I remember to have read somewhere that the best commentary on the Sermon on the Mount is Lord Tennyson's "In Memoriam." This is, I am afraid, a pompous platitude. But I think that every student will agree with me that, for instance, the best exposition of the "Priestly Code" is to be found in Ezekiel, that the most lucid interpretation of Isaiah is to be sought in certain portions of the Psalms, and that, if we were to look for an illustration of the ideals of the Book of Deuteronomy, we could do no better than study the Books of Chronicles and certain groups of the Psalms. To use a quaint old expression applied to Scripture: "Turn it and turn it over again, for the All is therein," both its criticism and its history. Introductions to the Old Testament, Lives and Times of the various prophets, and histories of the Canon, are excellent things in their own way; but unless we are prepared to exchange the older blind faith for the newer parrot-like repetitions of obscure critical terms, they should not be read, and, indeed, cannot be read with profit, before we have made ourselves masters of the twenty-four books of the Old Testament in the original.

This, I should think, is an obvious truth, nay, a truism. Still, I am glad to have the opportunity to utter it for once. The dread of partiality for the Massoretic text is so great in certain circles that the notion seems to gain ground that the best qualification for writing on the Old Testament is ignorance of Hebrew. Thus we are brought face to face with the multitude of books, essays, and articles on Biblical subjects by authors who freely confess, if not boast of, the fact that they know the Old Testament only through the medium of versions, but still insist on their ability to judge upon the gravest questions of dates and authorship. Translations, some author has remarked, are the structures with which a kind Providence has over-bridged the deeps of human thought caused by the division of tongues at the Tower of Babel. The re-

mark is as humble in spirit as it is prudent in practice.
It is certainly safer to walk over the bridge than to
swim the flood.   But in this case we must be satisfied
not to express opinions about the nature of the river,
its various currents and under-currents, its depths and
shallows, and the original formation of its bed.   To
form a judgment on these and similar points, one must
learn to swim and dive, nay, one must immerse himself in the very element against whose touch the bridge
was meant to protect him.   To use a New Testament
proverb, "Wisdom is justified of her children," or, as
the Rabbis would have put it, "the sons of the Torah."
But the first duty which the loyal son performs toward his mother, is to make her language his own,
so that he may dispense with interpreter and dictionary,
and patiently listen to her tale from her own lips, told
in her own way.   She may not be always inclined toward humiliating confessions ; but a single gesture, a
single turn of phrase, a sudden stammering where flow
of speech is expected, and a certain awkwardness of
expression, will at once reveal the critical points in her
story.   To learn her story through the medium of
versions and introductions, means at best to rely on
neighbourly gossip, which, however interesting and
friendly, is never free from exaggerations and conven-
tional phrases.   It is only the knowledge of the
original mother-story which enables us to detect the
elements of truth this gossip may contain.

I will, however, confess that it was neither mere
deference to the liberal traditions of this learned Soci-

ety, nor even considerations of economy, which were decisive with me in adopting the course I have just pointed out. These reasons are weighty enough, but they would hardly justify me in assuming the sceptical position I intend to maintain. In fact, nothing is more distressing to my mind than that mental squinting which finds permanent doubt the only point on which it can rest. The force of circumstances is, however, too strong for me. For I am convinced that, at present at least, there is little positive truth to state on the great questions at issue between the various schools of Bible criticism.

That tradition cannot be maintained in all its statements need not be denied. The Second Isaiah, for instance, is a fact; not less a fact is it that Solomon cannot be held responsible for the scepticism of the Book of Ecclesiastes, nor can David claim the authorship of the whole of the Psalms for himself. The question at present, however, is not as it was with the older schools, whether tradition was not possibly mistaken in this or that respect, but whether it contains elements of truth at all. For instance, had Moses, if ever there existed such a person, any connexion with that series of books known as "the Torah of Moses?" The existence of King David is still unchallenged, but did he write or, considering the peculiar religious circumstances of the age, could he, or even his contemporaries and successors for the next four centuries, have written a single hymn of the collection which tradition attributes to him? The answers given by the modern school to these and similar questions are mostly in the negative. But it may be doubted whether its reconstruction of the history of Israel, as well as its re-arrangement of the documents included in the Canon of the Old Testament have obtained that degree of certainty which would justify a teacher in communicating them to his pupils without constantly accompanying his remarks by a note of interrogation.

In questioning the results of this school, I may premise that I am in no way opposed to criticism. Criticism is nothing more than the expression of conscience on the part of the student, and we can as little dispense with it in literature as with common honesty in our dealings with our fellow-men. Nor, I trust, have I ever given way to anybody in my respect for most of the leaders of the various schools of Bible criticism, Lower as well as Higher. The attempt at an analysis of the Bible into component elements, whether one agrees with its results or assumes a sceptical attitude towards them, is one of the finest intellectual feats of this century; though a good deal of brutal vivisection is daily done by restless spirits whose sole ambition is to outdo their masters. This, however, is not the fault of the masters. No student can read a page of Kuenen's *Historisch-Kritische Einleitung*, to the Old Testament, without doing homage to his genius as a critic and admiring his patient research and single-hearted devotion to what he considered to be the truth. But, as somebody has remarked, if tradition is not infallible, neither are any of its critics.

The difficulties presenting themselves on both sides may perhaps be summed up thus: Whilst Tradition knows too much of the earlier and earliest history of Israel, our modern schools are too prolific of their information as to the later history of Israel, that is, the greater part of what is known as the Persian-Greek period. You will at once realise this peculiar distribution of knowledge and ignorance, if you compare two chronological tables, the one appended to a Bible which appeared in 1866, and the other incorporated in the second volume of Kautzsch's *Die heilige Schrift*, published in 1894. The former is most complete in its record of events said to have taken place before 1088 B. C. E., and is almost one large blank after 450 B. C. E. In the latter the very opposite is the case, the blank being transferred to the first thousand years of Israel's history, whilst the Persian-Greek period teems with historical events and, in particular, with the chronology of the composition of various canonical writings. In the Rabbinic literature, as is well known, the whole duration of the Persian empire as contemporary with the Second Temple shrank to some fifty-two years. This, as I hardly need say, is questionable chronology. But it is wise scepticism worthy of recommendation, implying, as it does, a confession of ignorance about a period of which we know so little.

Modern learning has thus, with its characteristic *horror vacui*, peopled these very centuries with

lawgivers, prophets, psalmists, and apocalypse writers;
but every student will, I think, readily admit that
there is still many an obscure point to be cleared up.
For instance, the exact number of the Maccabæan
Psalms, which is constantly shifting; the exact date
of the composition of the Book of Ecclesiastes, which
is still a mere guess; the causes leading to the conclusion of the so-called second canon; the precise
nature of the work of creating new canons and some
clear definition of the authority of the men who pre-
sumed to execute this delicate task. Again, most of the
theories advanced as to the date and the authorship of
the group of Psalms assigned to the third century, of
the Song of Songs, and of the Book of Ruth, are, to
use a Talmudic expression, "mountains suspended on
a hair," and are in no way better than those they are
meant to replace. Altogether, the period looks to me
rather over-populated, and I begin to get anxious about
the accommodations of the Synagogue, or, rather, the
"House of Interpretation" (*Beth ha-Midrash*), which
was not a mere *Bamah*, but a thing of moment in the
religious life of those times. In its service were enlisted
whole assemblies of men, whom neither the *aperçus* of
a Wellhausen, nor the really learned researches of a
Kuenen, can argue out of existence, and whose humble
activity consisted in interpreting the law, raising up
many disciples, and making "fences" round the Torah.
But there is scarcely breathing-space left for such men
as these in an ambitious age that was absolutely bent
on smuggling its own productions into the Scriptures.

Now, neither hypothesis of the rise of the Canon —that given by tradition and that afforded by the new school—is quite free from difficulties and improbable assumptions. I cannot here enter into details, and must refer you to Kittel's "Introduction," which seems to me to be a fair exposition of the question on both sides. But I may be allowed to make one general remark, and that is, that there is no period in Jewish history which is so entirely obscure as the period extending from about 450 to 150 B. C. E. All that is left us from those ages are a few meagre notices by Josephus, which do not seem to be above doubt, and a few bare names in the Books of Chronicles of persons who hardly left any mark on the history of the times. One gets rather suspicious of a hypothesis with powers of vision which seem to grow in proportion to the increasing darkness surrounding an age. More light is wanted.

This light promises now to come from the discoveries made within the last few years. I am referring to the discovery of the original Hebrew of the apocryphal work, "The Wisdom of Ben Sira," or, as it is commonly called, "Ecclesiasticus," in contradistinction to Ecclesiastes.

There is no need to enlarge on the importance of this work for the Biblical student. It is sufficient to remind you of two facts : first, that it is the only Jewish literary production that has come down to us from those "dark ages" which can boast of something like a date. As you can see in the various Introductions to the Apocrypha, scholars are not quite unanimous as to this date. But it is certain that it cannot be placed before about 280 B. C. E., nor much later than 200 B. C. E. The second fact which I wish to recall to your minds is that the modern school has placed the greatest part of the *Kethubim*, or the Hagiographa, at just about those dates. A great part, again, of the Psalms has been placed after those dates, namely, in the Maccabæan age. The Wisdom of Ben Sira was written in Hebrew, and would thus have furnished us with an excellent test of the mode of thinking as well as of the language and style of the period in question. But the original unfortunately disappeared for many centuries. To my knowledge, Samuel David Luzzatto was the first to enlist the Wisdom of Ben Sira in the service of Bible criticism. Judging from the few quotations from Ben Sira given in the Talmud, he was led to the belief that this apocryphal work was written in New-Hebrew, the dialect in which the Mishnah and cognate Rabbinic works were compiled. This being the stage of the language about 200 B. C. E., it follows that the Maccabæan age could not have produced Psalms composed in the best classical style of an earlier age. Even more cogent was the argument of Professor Ehrt, who undertook to prove that Ben Sira had made use of Psalms supposed by the modern school to date from the Maccabæan age. He was silenced by the strange answer that his evidence had to be sifted. Perhaps what was meant was, that only the original of a work could enable us to see how far and how much the author copied from other works. But the original was then considered as lost for ever. The last Christian who made mention of it was St. Jerome in the fourth century. One of the last Jews who stated that he had seen it was the Gaon R. Saadya, who died in 942. The unexpected, however, came to pass on May 13, 1896, when it was my good fortune to discover, among the Hebrew and Arabic fragments which Mrs. Lewis and Mrs. Gibson acquired on their travels through the East, a leaf of the original Hebrew of Ecclesiasticus. Subsequently more discoveries suggested by my description of the discovered leaf were made, in Oxford, in Cambridge, and elsewhere. Of the Lewis-Gibson Fragment, together with the fragments deposited now in the Bodleian Library, there exist at present six editions: one by English scholars, two by German professors, two more by French *savants*, and one by a Russian student. The *editio princeps* of the first find was published in the July number of "The Expositor," in 1896. Of the Cambridge Fragments, covering a much larger ground than the fragments already made known, one leaf only was edited in "The Jewish Quarterly Review" of January, 1898, under the heading of "Genizah Specimens." The remaining leaves will shortly be published by the University Press of Cambridge.[4]

These discoveries when put together restore to us about twenty-five chapters of the original Hebrew of the Wisdom of Ben Sira, or about half of the whole book, consisting of fifty-one chapters. We are thus

in a position now to form a fair judgment of the state
of the Hebrew language about 200 B. C. E., or, it may
be, 280 B. C. E., as well as of the standard of authorship in that age. I am bound to say that this judgment is not flattering to our omniscience. I say it
with a certain amount of regret, as for a goodly number of years I was an ardent believer in the possibility
of Maccabæan Psalms, an hypothesis on which I built
great hopes. This is a great disappointment to me.
Alas, there is no insurance office in which students
can insure theories against the dangers resulting from
unexpected discoveries and fresh excavations. I must
reluctantly submit to a "total loss" of my hypothesis.

As regards the Ben Sira discoveries, to begin with
a concrete example, I will mention the case of the Book
of Job. The theories regarding the age in which this
book was composed range at present from about 1320
to about 200 B. C. E. With that singular capacity
for blundering which distinguishes the Greek trans-
lators, the name of Job was omitted from the list of
the heroes of Israel's past whom Ben Sira praises in
his *Hymnus Patrum*, and some bolder spirits conse-
quently felt themselves at liberty to make the writer
of Job nearly a contemporary of Ben Sira. The restored original Hebrew proves that the Greek translator mistook *Iyob*, the name of the hero of the Book
of Job, for *Oyeb*, meaning *enemy*. The Greek runs
thus: "For, verily, he remembered the enemies in the
storm," whilst the Hebrew reads, "Also he made mention of Job," a point to which several scholars, among

them Joseph Halévy, have drawn the attention of students. But Ben Sira knew more; he was, in fact, thoroughly familiar with the contents of the Book of Job. His whole cosmography is based on the last chapters of the Book of Job, from which he copied various passages.

As to the language and the style of Ben Sira, it is true that certain portions of the book, especially the just mentioned *Hymnus Patrum*, are written mostly in classical Hebrew. A careful analysis, however, will show that they are at best nothing more than a series of quotations from the canonical writings, joining verse to verse and phrase to phrase, all alike copied from the Bible. In other words Ben Sira was, like so many post-Biblical writers, an imitator of the Old Testament both in form and in matter; his model for the former being the whole of the Old Testament, whilst the matter is, as far as the gnomic part is concerned, generally borrowed from the Book of Proverbs.

But like all imitators he was not always on his guard, and, in careless moments, terms, expressions, and idioms escaped him which make it sufficiently clear that in his time the New-Hebrew dialect, both in respect of grammar and of phraseology, had reached its highest development. What is even more to our present purpose, is the fact, rendered certain by the original Hebrew, that Ben Sira was acquainted with the Psalter in all its parts, those ascribed to the Persian period as well as those ascribed to the Maccabæan and post-Maccabæan ages. He copies freely from them, in some cases he borrows whole verses, though, quite in the fashion of the Rabbis, he is rather too liberal in their application.

It would prove tedious to enter into an analysis of the Book of Ben Sira. This could not be done without giving complete lists of words, phrases, and idioms, amounting to many hundreds, but absolutely meaningless when disjoined from their context. I may, however, be permitted to reproduce a few verses from a hymn of Ben Sira which, echoing as it does the time in which it was written, lends itself best to consideration.

They are thus:

1. O give thanks unto the Lord, for he is good ;
   For his mercy endureth for ever.
2. O give thanks unto the God of praises ;
   For his mercy endureth for ever.
3. O give thanks unto him that is the guardian of Israel;
   For his mercy endureth for ever.
4. O give thanks unto him that created all;
   For his mercy endureth for ever.
5. O give thanks unto him that redeemeth Israel;
   For his mercy endureth for ever.
6. O give thanks unto him that gathereth the outcasts of
   Israel ;
   For his mercy endureth for ever.
7. O give thanks unto him that buildeth his city and his
   sanctuary ;
   For his mercy endureth for ever.
8. O give thanks unto him that maketh a horn to bud to
   the house of David ;
   For his mercy endureth for ever.

9. O give thanks unto him that chose the sons of Zadok
to be priests ;
For his mercy endureth for ever.

10. O give thanks unto the Shield of Abraham ;
For his mercy endureth for ever.

11. O give thanks unto the Rock of Isaac ;
For his mercy endureth for ever.

12. O give thanks unto the Mighty One of Jacob ;
For his mercy endureth for ever.

13. O give thanks unto him that chose Zion ;
For his mercy endureth for ever.

14. O give thanks unto the King of kings of kings ;
For his mercy endureth for ever.

15. And also exalteth the horn for his people, a praise for
all his saints ;
Even to the children of Israel, a people near unto him.
Praise ye the Lord. (51:12^1–12^{15}).

It is important to notice that the hymn is omitted
in all the versions. The reason for its omission by
the Greek translator can be easily found. Living at
a time when the house of Zadok was already super-
seded by the Maccabæan line, the grandson of Ben
Sira recoiled from publishing a hymn which claimed
that the בני צדוק (Sons of Zadok) were specially selected for the priesthood. But it is this very prominence given to the house of Zadok which establishes
its authenticity. For, after the unworthy part played
by the high priests of the house of Zadok during the
Hellenistic troubles, it is highly improbable that any
pious Jew—as the author of this hymn evidently was—
would feel so enthusiastic about this family, that their
continuation in the sacred office would form the
special topic of his thanksgiving to God. Such

enthusiasm could have been displayed only by one who knew the best of the Zadokides, namely Simon the Just, and who prayed so fervently for the perpetuation of God's grace upon the high priest and his children, that is, Ben Sira himself.

The model on which this hymn is formed is, as I hardly need say, Psalm 136. It is strongly reminiscent of certain passages in Isaiah, Jeremiah, and Zechariah. The last verse is directly copied from Psalm 148 : 14. But though Psalm-like in form, it is liturgical in spirit. And students of the Jewish prayer-book will at once recognise its influence on the so-called Eighteen Benedictions with their introductory Blessings. The hymn is at present, I am inclined to think, in a defective state, for its model, the 136th Psalm, suggests to us that originally it consisted of twenty-six verses, of which twelve are now missing. But these might easily be supplied by the original prayers of the Synagogue, which in their turn were, as already hinted, modelled after Ben Sira. Enough, however, remains of this hymn to give us some insight into the state of religious thought in the times of Ben Sira. We learn first from it that the theocratic tendency of those ages has been unduly emphasised by modern critics. At least, it never went so far as to suppress devotion to the house of David. Even with so strong a partisan of the High Priest Simon as Ben Sira was, loyalty to the descendants of Zadok went hand in hand with the hope for the restoration of the Davidic family, in which the Messianic belief was embodied. If the first was commanded by the Torah, the second was guaranteed by the Prophets, the fulfilment of whose words is a subject of prayer for Ben Sira. To the harmony of these two beliefs, antagonistic as they may appear to the modern eye, all subsequent Jewish literature bears witness, in which the restoration of the priestly order to the service in the Temple and the advent of the Messiah ben David form so prominent a part, and are equally prayed for.

We learn further from this hymn that what occupied the mind of this latter-day psalmist was the history of his own times, not the events of the remote past. Living, as it would seem, in comparatively peaceful times, which, however, were preceded by a great crisis in the history of the nation, he gives thanks for the rebuilding of the city and the Temple and for the gathering of the outcast of Israel. What he further praises God for are the two great religious institutions of his age : the priesthood as represented by the house of Zadok, and "the house of David," which, embodying the hope of Israel in the future, passed with Ben Sira for a living reality. The invocation of the God of the Fathers, though Biblical in its origin, is at the same time a characteristic feature of the Jewish liturgy. In fact, the first of the Eighteen Benedictions is called "Fathers." The expression "King of kings of kings" shows also the marked Persian influence to which Ben Sira was as much subject as any later Rabbi who uses the same appellation for God. We thus see clearly that what inspired Ben Sira was the present and the future of his people. To these he refers in plain language, and in the language of his time. Is it possible, I ask, that Psalms written about the same age or even later should have so little distinct reference to the events of their own time, that we have the greatest difficulty in recognising their allusions? Is it conceivable, I ask again, that Ben Sira, writing in comparatively uneventful times, should be entirely given over to the present, and yet the author of the 136th Psalm, writing as is alleged some fifty years later, should not have a single reference to the great events of his generation? Instead of making the Maccabæan victories the subject of his thanksgivings, he praises God for the Exodus from Egypt. Is it possible that Ben Sira should make the selection of the house of Zadok the theme of his thanks to God, and no Maccabæan writer should thank God in plain language for replacing it by the new dynasty? And quite apart from this new hymn, is there any adequate reason why Ben Sira, in celebrating his hero, should give us his name, Simon ben Johanan, whilst the Maccabæan heroes should be typified by Joshua, David, Solomon, Saul, and alluded to in all possible obscure ways, but never called by their right names? Again, is it possible that Ben Sira, with all his care as an imitator, and writing only two or three hymns, should forget himself so as to use an appellation of God in which the Persian influence is so manifest, whilst all the hosts of poets of the Persian and the Greek period, of whom the Psalter is supposed to be the work, should succeed in divesting themselves of every trace of the influences of their times?

All these considerations added to others of not less weight, which would, however, lead us too far were I to produce them here, make it clear to me that we have been taking too many liberties with tradition. Least of all were we justified in undertaking the reconstruction of a period in Israel's history of which scarcely a single historical record was left to us. Tradition had at least at its disposal legends and myths, if you prefer to call them so. We have nothing but a series of hypotheses which, in many respects, are more improbable than those they were meant to displace. It is, therefore, only with the utmost caution, doubting doubt itself, that we can at present express any positive opinions on such obscure points.

I say, at present—for a single new discovery of a book like Ben Hagla, mentioned in the Talmud in connexion with Ben Sira, but lost to us, or a single fresh excavation in the field of Egyptology and Assyriology, may settle all these questions for us. I am thinking of another possibility. "I have," once said a sage of by-gone times, "learned much from my teachers, more from my colleagues, but most from my pupils." I am quite prepared to follow this wise example. And none would be more happy than I, should I succeed in forming in this place a school of Biblical students whose zeal and devotion to Semitic studies should surpass mine, whose penetrating vision might remove all obscurities before them, so that they might disperse all doubts, allay all suspicions, and convert my cautious utterances into positive dogmatic statements.[5]

A GLIMPSE OF THE SOCIAL LIFE OF THE JEWS IN THE AGE OF JESUS THE SON OF SIRACH[1]

My object in heading this paper "A Glimpse of the Life of the Jews in the Age of Jesus, the Son of Sirach," or, as I shall call him, Ben Sira, was to indicate at once its limits and its limitations. Thus, it will be observed that I did not circumscribe the age which will occupy our attention by any exact date, and this for the simple reason that the age in which Ben Sira lived is still a controverted point amongst students, some fixing it at 280 B. C. E., others some two generations later, about 200 B. C. E. Considering, however, that in either case Ben Sira must have belonged to a generation which had already come under the Hellenistic influence under which Asia fell by the conquests of Alexander the Great, but, on the other hand, never saw the reaction brought about against it by the Maccabæan rise, the question of precise date does not seriously affect the solution of our problem.

Of more importance is the question as to the sources which should legitimately be made use of in this study. This is a case of advanced Bible Criticism versus Tradition. If we accede to the former, Ben Sira must have lived in an age when the Psalms were still in the process of composition, when "sceptical books " could still be smuggled into the Canon under an ancient, revered name, when certain Bedouins in some obscure corner of Arabia had just left off discussing the most solemn mysteries of our being, when Shulamith and her Beloved were about to set out on their symbolic career. The Bible, then, should furnish us with the material, particularly the Hagiographa, or *Kethubim.* If we accept Tradition as our guide, Biblical authorship would be, in the age of Ben Sira, a matter of a remote past, and we should have to turn to the pages of the Talmud for information bearing on our subject, especially to those portions of it recording the activity of the Great Synagogue (*Keneseth ha-Gedolah*) and the Ordinances of Ezra.

I have my serious doubts as to the soundness of the hypothesis of Maccabæan Psalms and similar theories that tend to fill the void in our knowledge of the period in question with shreds from the Bible.[2] But this scepticism by no means entirely removes our doubts in the trustworthiness of the Rabbinic records that were not reduced to writing for centuries after Ben Sira, and can thus hardly be considered as real contemporary evidence. To this description the Wisdom of Ben Sira alone can lay claim. All other works, as the Talmud, the "Chronicle of the World," and similar documents, can be regarded only as secondary sources, to be used as supplementary evidence, provided there is nothing incongruous in the nature of their statements with the times they profess to describe.

But even the use of Ben Sira is not quite free from obstacles and pitfalls. There is a passage in the "Chronicle of the World" to the effect that Elijah's occupation since his translation consists in "writing the history of all generations." I never realised the force of this legend so much as when studying Ben Sira's Wisdom. For, apart from the difficulties inherent in every author coming down to us from antiquity, such as additions, omissions, and textual corruptions, there is always with Ben Sira the question whether he really meant what he said. We have no reason to question his veracity. "Gainsay not the truth, and humble thyself before God," was an axiom of his. What impairs the value of his statements is the consideration that Ben Sira was, as proved elsewhere,[3] rather too much addicted to quoting from the Canonical Writings and giving ample extracts from them. It is, therefore, hard to decide whether his words can always be taken as stating a fact to which he was witness, or conveying a sentiment which he felt, or whether they are to be taken as mere repetitions of Scriptural phrases intended as ornamental flourishes. Thus, for instance, when we read in Ben Sira the various passages about the strange woman, we may reasonably ask, Do they describe the low state of morality in Jerusalem, or are they not bad exaggerations due to the author's thinking of similar passages in the Book of Proverbs? Again, when he devotes almost a whole chapter to a prayer for the deliverance of his people from the hands of the oppressor, does it indicate the actual hostile relations between Israel and the surrounding nations, or has it to be looked upon as being, in part at least, a mere exercise in a species of lyrics for which certain elegiac Psalms served him as models ?

Only an Elijah with his angelic gift of omniscience, and his advantage of being the contemporary of almost all times and ages, could know whether Ben Sira was in the mood for writing history or "doing composition." We poor mortals have to be on our guard not to know too much, and be satisfied with guesses and hypotheses. All that we can aspire to are mere glimpses.

Life with the Jew meant religion, and it is impossible to get a glimpse of his social life without at least throwing a glance at his spiritual life. This, indeed, was even at those remote times fully developed. For not only was the Law in full operation, but Judaism had already entered upon its course of Rabbinism, the main function of which was to bring man with all his various faculties and aspirations under the sway of the Torah. The Canon of the Prophets is also an accomplished fact, and the words of Ben Sira regarding Isaiah,

> By a spirit of might he saw the end,
> And comforted the mourners of Sion (48 : 24),

thus attributing the "comfort portions" to the same author to whom the first forty chapters are ascribed, are a guarantee also for the formation of tradition as to the rise and history of the books included in that portion of the Bible long before 200 B. C. E.

Beside these two Canons there existed also "the other Books of the Fathers," as Ben Sira's grandson expresses himself, which probably represented all the writings included in the Hagiographa (*Kethubim*), with the single exception, perhaps, of certain portions in the Book of Daniel.

The discontinuance of prophecy, however, must not be taken as proof of spiritual sterility. Prophecy might have been sorely missed by Ben Sira, but only as a means of prediction, not as a source of religious inspiration. This latter they had "in the book of the Covenant of the Most High God," or the Torah, which, in the words of Ben Sira (?), with whom she is identical with Wisdom, is "the mother of fair love, and fear, and knowledge, and holy hope." Far from causing sterility or stagnation, Wisdom, or the Torah, says of herself :

> . . . . I will water my garden,
> And will water abundantly my garden bed ;
> And, lo, my stream became a river,
> And my river became a sea.
> I will yet bring instruction to light as the morning,
> And will make these things to shine forth afar off.
> I will yet pour out doctrine as prophecy,
> And leave it unto generations of ages (24 : 31).

With such a Torah Ben Sira felt but little need for a new revelation. With the Psalmist he would pray, "Open thou mine eyes that I may behold wondrous things out of thy Torah," which wondrous things

consist mainly in divining God's will so far as it has
any bearing upon life and conduct. This brings us
to the Synagogue, or the House of Interpretation (of
the Torah), which forms so prominent a feature in the
religious life of post-exilic Judaism. With the
scanty materials at our disposal it is difficult to define
its exact position as a religious factor in those early
times. First, however, we must cast a glance at least
at the Holy Temple, which, by reason of its long historical prestige, its glorious ritual, performed by a
hereditary priesthood and presided over by a pontiff,
who not only had a seat in the councils of the nation,
but practically represented in his person the whole
legislature, must have almost monopolised the affec-
tion and the devotion the people bestowed upon their
religious institutions. The contents of Chapter 50 of
the Wisdom of Ben Sira convey to us a fair idea of
what the best of the nation felt when in the presence
of their priestly rulers, and what impression the service
in the Temple made on them.

The central figure in that chapter is Simon the son
of Johanan, "the great one of his brethren and the
glory of his people," the patriot and the leader,

> Who took thought for his people against the spoiler,
> And fortified his city against the besieger (50: 4),

whose personal appearance was so striking that Ben
Sira enthusiastically exclaims :

> How glorious was he when he looked forth from the tent ;
> At his coming forth out of the Sanctuary !
> As the morning star in the midst of a cloud,

> As the moon at the full in the days of the solemn fast :
> As the sun dawning upon the temple of the King,
> And as the rainbow seen in the cloud (50 : 5–7).

It should, however, be noticed that a good deal of this enthusiasm may have been due as much to the gorgeous attire of the pontiff as to any personal charm Simon may have possessed. At least, this is the impression we receive from a similar description of a high priest left to us by the anonymous author of the Aristeas Letter, who rather revels in the minute description of the various vestments the high•priest wore, the robes, the diamonds, the bells, and the pomegranates, and he tells us that the effect produced on him by the sight of the high priest in full canonicals as required by the service, was to feel himself transferred to another world.

In a similar strain are the lines of Ben Sira picturing his hero at the moment when he was performing the service in the Temple :

> When he ascended the altar of majesty,
> And made glorious the precinct of the Sanctuary,
> When he received the pieces out of the hand of his brethren,
> While himself standing by the altar fires :
> Round him a crown of sons
> Like cedar plants in Lebanon.
> And they compassed him about like willows of the brook :
> All the sons of Aaron in their glory
> With the fire-offerings of the Lord in their hand (50 : 12–13).

The culminating point of Ben Sira's enthusiasm is reached with the choral part of the service, in which the laity had its due share in the responses :

> Then sounded the sons of Aaron, the priests,
> With trumpets of beaten work.

And they sounded, and made their glorious voice heard
To bring to remembrance before the Most High.
All flesh together hasted,
And fell down upon their faces to the earth,
To worship before the Most High,
Before the Holy One of Israel. . . . . .
And all the people of the land chanted
In prayer before the Merciful. . . . . .
Then he came down and lifted up his hands
Over all the congregation of Israel,
And the blessing of the Lord was on his lips
And in the name of the Lord he gloried.
And they bowed again a second time,
The people all of them before him (50 : 16–22).

Thus Ben Sira. The author of the Aristeas Letter, who writes for Gentiles, and dwells at great length on the sacrificial service, remarks that it was carried out in such deep silence as to make one think that not a single human being was to be found anywhere in the place. And yet, he proceeds to say, there were present, as a rule, about seven hundred ministering priests, in addition to the great crowds of the laity who brought the sacrifices. But all this was performed in solemnity and in a manner worthy of the great Deity.

It will, however, be noticed that neither Simon nor the high functionaries surrounding him appear in the capacity of teachers or instructors of the people. The office of teaching was left, as already indicated, to the Synagogue, represented by the Scribes, or Sages, who were recruited from all classes of the people. It is impossible to define the exact relation of the Synagogue to the Temple. Some writers describe the Synagogue as the altars on the high places of post-exilic Judaism; others, again, fond of modern theological slang, as the Procathedrals of the provinces. All these names, however, are to some extent misleading, implying, as they do, a certain conscious, antagonistic attitude in the Synagogue toward the Temple, for which there is no real evidence. We know fairly that there was a synagogue within the precincts of the Temple. Had there been room for the least suspicion of schismatic tendencies, the priests would as little have allowed it accommodation within the sphere of their jurisdiction as, for instance, the dignitaries of the Vatican could be expected to grant a site for a Protestant chapel in the court of St. Peter's. Nor, indeed, is there known any conscious opposition to the Temple on the part of the Rabbis. Simon ben Shetach, Hillel, and all the other leaders of the Synagogue, were as zealous for the maintenance of the priestly order and the sacrificial worship as ever any high priest was. Some of these leaders were even priests themselves, and served in the Temple in such capacities. More appropriate, therefore, is the traditional designation *Beth ha-Keneseth* (House of Assembly), or the even more ancient and more classic name, *Beth ha-Midrash* (House of Interpretation)[4], thus confining the activity of the Synagogue mainly to instruction. Worship was only a secondary matter with it.

and stood in no competitive relation to that performed in the Temple, since no amount of prayer ever so sublime could relieve the Jew from the bringing of a meal-offering or a sin-offering when such was his duty in accordance with the injunctions of the Levitical Code. The office of the Synagogue must, therefore, have been looked upon as supplementary or auxiliary to that of the Temple, which in the age of Ben Sira was generally limited to the functions of worship.

If there was any element in the Synagogue which might have led to a rupture with the sister institution, it was not its teaching, but its democratic constitution, which, to some minds, must have contrasted favourably with the hierarchic government of the Temple. " Three crowns there are," said a Rabbi : " the crown of royalty, the crown of priesthood, and the crown of the Torah. The first two are in the exclusive possession of two families, the lineage of David and the descendants of Aaron. But the crown of the Torah is free to all, and can be acquired only by labour. He who wants to take it, let him come and take it, as it is said : ' Ho ! every one that thirsteth, come ye to the waters.' " [5] Only a few generations after Ben Sira we find Shemaiah and Abtalyon, descendants of proselytes, holding, according to tradition, the high offices of " President " and " Father of the Court of Justice " in the Sanhedrin.

But in spite of its humble claims, and notwithstanding the lowly origin of those who served in it, there can be little doubt that the influence of the

Synagogue as a religious factor even in the times of Ben Sira was more deeply felt than the scarcity of references to it in the contemporary literature would lead us to believe.   For, judged in the light of subsequent events, it is not impossible that the very darling priests whom Ben Sira admired as the " crown of sons" developed in later life into the class of traitorous prelates who headed the paganising movement preceding the Maccabæan rise, among whom Jason and the Tobiades were only the more notorious specimens. But whilst the priests, according to the Second Book of Maccabees, had no inclination to serve at the altar, but, despising the Temple and neglecting the sacrifices, hastened to be partakers of the unlawful allowance in the " place of exercise,"[6] there were, as we know from the same source, mighty men in Israel, every one who offered himself willingly for the Law. By those mighty men are meant the Scribes and the Assidæans, but they had a large following, as is clear from another passage, "in the many in Israel who chose to die that they might not profane the Holy Covenant."[7] Now, in pre-exilic times, the backslidings of the kings and the nobles as a rule involved the apostasy of the whole nation, and if the king "did that which was evil in the sight of the Lord," the people were sure to do what was worse.   But, in the age occupying our attention, we find the strange phenomenon that the bulk of the nation, far from being affected by the apostasy of their political leaders, arrayed themselves in organised resistance, determined to defend their religion against all attacks from within and without. Considering that these political leaders came mostly from the ranks of the priestly aristocracy, we must assume that there were spiritual forces at work other than the Temple, which prepared the nation for the crisis. This force was the Synagogue, which, by reason of its less elaborate service and its office of instruction, was admirably fitted to place religion within the reach of the people at large, and to teach them to consider man's relations to God as his own personal affair, not to be regulated by the conscience or caprice of either prince or priest.

This instruction was given free, without any expectation of reward, and ungrudgingly. For, as Ben Sira expresses it :

All wisdom cometh from the Lord, ...
She is with all flesh according to his gift ;
And he gave her freely to them that love him (1 : 1-10),

and as a Rabbi remarked : Man should in this respect imitate the Holy One, blessed be he. As with God it is a gift of free grace, so should man make it a free gift.[8]

Next to the function of teaching came that of prayer. Prayer is, of course, not the invention of the Synagogue. It is, to use the words of an old mystic, as natural an expression of the intimate relations between heaven and earth as courtship between the sexes. Inarticulate whisperings, however, and rapturous effusions at far intervals are sometimes apt to degenerate into mere passing flirtations. The Syna-

gogue, by creating something like a liturgy, appoint-
ing times for prayer, and erecting places of worship,
gave steadiness and duration to these fitful and uncon-
trolled emotions, and raised them to the dignity of a
proper institution.

Of the contents of this early liturgy little more is
known than the pregnant headings of the Benedictions.   They are Fathers (אבות), Strengths (גבורות),
and Holinesses (קדושות), said to have been introduced
by the men of the Great Synagogue, and are thus of
pre-Maccabæan origin.   The first three blessings of
"the original prayers" (sometimes called the Eighteen
Benedictions), still in use in the Synagogue, are known
under the same headings.   The burden of the first
(אבות) is the proclaiming of God as the God of the
Fathers, and "possessing heaven and earth."   It has
a striking parallel in Ben Sira's hymn, where thanks
are given to the Shield of Abraham, the Rock of
Isaac, and the Mighty One of Jacob (51: 12, j, k, l.),
whilst the heading "Fathers" strongly reminds one of
Ben Sira's similar superscription on Chapter 44, "The
Praise of the Fathers of the World" (שבח אבות עולם).

The burden of the third is the praise of God in his
attribute of holiness, and has probably its origin in the
theophany of Isaiah, "Holy, holy, holy is the Lord of
hosts."   It is remarkable that the passage commencing, "Now, therefore, O Lord, impose thine awe upon
all thy work" (ובכן תן פחדך), which is inserted in this
Benediction on the New Year's Day, contains many
phrases and expressions to be found in the thirty-sixth

chapter of Ben Sira. There is thus no objection to
assuming that the contents of the Fathers and the
Holinesses Benedictions of the age of Ben Sira were
almost identical with those recited by the Jews of the
present day. It is more difficult to say what the exact
wording of the Strengths Benediction was. The term
itself, גבורות, seems to have been suggested by Job 26:
14, "But the thunder of his strength (or power), who
can understand?" The Rabbis also speak often of
the גבורות גשמים, the power of God as shown by his
bringing rain. The Strengths Benediction would
thus mean the praise of God in his manifestation
through nature. The text, however, of the Blessing
of the same name in the Jewish Common Prayer-Book
is, "Thou, O Lord, art mighty forever, thou quick-
enest the dead," etc.

This is practically less of a Benediction than the
promulgation of a doctrine that the dead will rise one
day. And here the question presents itself whether
the belief in resurrection was a universally accepted
dogma in the days of Ben Sira. I think this question
must be answered in the negative. It is true that
there is no real evidence that Ben Sira was opposed to
this dogma. For such desponding passages as are
reproduced by Dr. Edersheim and other writers,
tending to show Ben Sira's despair of man's condition
after death, may be mere repetitions of the corresponding verses in Ecclesiastes, Job, and Psalms,
and need not thus express the author's own views.
Yet it must be admitted that there is some truth in

Dr. Edersheim's exclamation: "What becomes of the spirit in Hades is scarcely clear to our writer, as there is no distinct reference to the doctrine of immortality or resurrection in Ben Sira." Dr. Edersheim also complains that Ben Sira is reluctant to enlarge upon the subject of angels, as well as that he is still more chary in his references to Satan. He also suspects that Ben Sira's creed did not include the doctrine of "original sin in the New Testament sense."[9] I am not responsible for the heterodoxies of Ben Sira, and am in no way anxious to convert him to a scheme of salvation of a much later period. But I may say in his defence, that with Ben Sira all those metaphysical hypotheses and theological certainties probably belonged to those "conceits of men and imagination of thoughts leading them astray," against which he warns us with the words:

> Search not the things that are too wonderful for thee,
> And seek not that which is hid from thee.
> What thou art permitted, think thereupon,
> But thou hast no business with the secret things (3 : 21-22).

As Ben Sira lived in an age sadly deficient in all theological enterprise, but great in its admiration of the prophets, we can even imagine him replying to an intrusive inquirer: "Hadst thou the same belief in God's just government of the world as an Isaiah had, thou wouldst speak less about man's condition after death, and more about the rights and duties of life, less about angels and more about men, less of Satan and more of God;" and if

> The life of man is numbered by days,
> The days of Israel are innumerable (37 : 25).

The great principle which he would impress upon mortals would be

> Prosperity and adversity, life and death,
> Poverty and riches come of the Lord (11 : 14).

But as to the mysterious workings of Providence in apportioning his lot to each man, nothing remains but to pray,

> For great is the mercy of God,
> And he revealeth his secret to the meek (3 : 20).

I need hardly say that in the days of Hillel and Shammai, the doctrine of immortality was fully developed, and universally accepted by all the Pharisaic Schools.

The Synagogue found a powerful auxiliary in the home. The Sabbath was then more strictly observed than in later ages. The dietary laws, forming a part of the holiness code, and probably kept originally only by the priests, now helped to hallow every Jewish home which came under the influence of the Synagogue. The "Words of the Scribes," as well as most of the other ordinances and laws whose origin can no longer be traced, probably arose about this time. These tended to give distinction and character to the nation at large. The Synagogue became a Temple on a small scale, and the Jewish home a Synagogue in miniature.

When speaking of the artisan, Ben Sira says:

> But they will maintain the fabric of the world;
> And in the handiwork of their craft is their prayer (38 : 34)[10].

Let us now consider prayer outside of the appointed place of worship. I therefore propose that we quit Temple and Synagogue, and betake ourselves to more secular surroundings, to learn something of the social life of the Jew. I am the more anxious for this shifting of scenes, since there is some notion abroad that one of the evil effects of the introduction of the "Priestly Code" was to convert a Nation into a Church, thus leading to the impression that a religious life, in the sense of the Torah, was incompatible with what we understand by a civilised polity. The glimpses which the market-place and the Jewish home will now afford us will show how erroneous this conception is. Here we find the Jew occupied as farmer and cattle-breeder, or active as carpenter, builder, iron-smith, potter, and in similar trades. Ben Sira, a *savant* of the most approved type, has no particular sympathy with such vocations, thinking that conversation with animals and the noise of the hammer and the anvil are not conducive to wisdom (38: 33 *et seq.*). He admits, however, that "without these cannot a city be inhabited, and that every one is wise in his works" (38: 32). Hence his injunction,

> Hate not appointed service of laborious work,
> For it has been apportioned of God" (7 : 15).

Ben Sira was less tolerant of the commercial classes, of whom he says:

> A merchant shall hardly keep himself from wrong-doing.
> And a huckster shall not be acquitted from sin,
> For if he stumbles not in this, he stumbles in that (26 : 29).[11]

This is quite in harmony with the Rabbinic sentiment, which, though having a higher opinion of the dignity of labour than Ben Sira, declares the hawker and the shop-keeper to be engaged in trades of "bad odour," whilst the latter is said to practise the "handicraft of robbery."[12] These are harsh words, and I can say nothing in mitigation of them, except that they were not actuated by the kindly feelings which the gentleman presiding in his office on the first floor entertains for his dear neighbour behind the counter on the ground floor. It was not a question of wholesale or retail with Ben Sira.

"Offend not" he says, "with a word him who labours truly,
Nor even the hired man who gives his soul" (7 : 20).[13]

His aversion was certainly not social. It was founded on his impression, rightly or wrongly conceived, that

As a nail sticketh fast between the joinings of the stone,
So doth sin stick close between buying and selling (27 : 2).

Of professions we have to record four : the military, the clerical, the scholastic, and the medical. As to the first, we have evidence in contemporary documents that Jews served as soldiers in the Ptolemaic armies. The chivalrous injunction of Ben Sira,

Forget not a companion in the battle,
And forsake him not in thy booty (37 : 6),

also points to the existence of such a class in the age of Ben Sira. But it does not seem that the position of the Tommy Atkins of antiquity was much better than that of his modern brother-in-arms.

"Who will trust" says Ben Sira "a troop of warriors skipping
from city to city?" (36 : 31),

whilst in times of peace he was utterly neglected, so
that Ben Sira exclaims :

> There be two things that grieve my heart,
> And the third that makes me angry :
> A man of war that suffers poverty (26 : 28).

The story of the Absent-minded Beggar all over
again!

The clerical and the scholastic can hardly be
called professions in the sense we attach to the word,
since the former was not a matter of choice or of
special training, but a mere accident of birth, whilst
the latter, as indicated above, did not carry any
pecuniary compensation with it. Ben Sira's invitation to those he wishes to instruct runs thus :

> Turn unto me, O ye fools,
> And lodge in my house of learning.
> I opened my mouth and spake of her,
> Get ye wisdom in your possession without money (51: 23,25).

With regard to the priests, the Rabbis speak of the
twenty-four Gifts, or sources of revenue, of the priesthood.[14] Still, I am inclined to think that it may seriously be doubted whether the common priest, כהן הדיוט,
at least, found himself in much better circumstances
than the general scribe. Of the twenty-four gifts, the
Terumah (heave-offering) was the one on which the
priest mostly depended, since it provided him with the
products of the soil of which bread was made. This
Terumah revenue, however, consisted, as later sources

report, only of a tax of two per cent of the harvest in kind, and was hardly commensurate with the numbers of the priests, who must have constituted a much larger proportion of the population than one in fifty. Moreover, there were various subterfuges making it possible for the people to evade the whole law, of which probably many availed themselves. Nehemiah's surprise expressed in the words, "And I perceived that the portions of the Levites had not been given to them" (13 : 10), must have been experienced by many a Jewish authority during the Second Temple. The daily press of those ages does not record any cases of "conscience-money." But even when the "portions" were punctually delivered, there were so many physical and other causes putting the priest into a state of Levitical impurity, and thus excluding him from every contact with "holy things," that the enjoyment of the Terumah and similar gifts was limited to the short intervals when he and his family and their dependents were "painfully clean." In seasons of "defilement" all that he could do with his Terumah was to use it as fuel. Again, on the gifts due him from the various sacrifices, consisting of meats, oils, and cakes, he could depend only for the time he was in active service in the Temple, and this did not extend over two weeks in the year according to the arrangement of "the twenty-four priestly districts."

There must have been, of course, some offices in the Temple worth having, especially those connected with the superintendence of the finances. But it would seem that such sinecures were kept for the special benefit of "the younger sons and older daughters of the high priests," and were not within the reach of the lower clergy. "Woe unto us," exclaimed an old Rabbi, "because of the House of Ishmael ben Piabi. Woe unto us because of their fist (violence). They themselves are high priests, their sons managers, and their sons-in-law treasurers, whilst their slaves tyrannise over the people with sticks." [15] The common priests without family patronage had thus little hope of advancement. Indeed, their position was sometimes so desperate that some used to hire themselves out as hands on the threshing-floor, with the purpose of engaging the good-will of the owner of the harvest, who could patronise with his gifts any priest he liked. The Rabbis stigmatise such a procedure as a degradation of the priesthood and as a "pollution of the holy things." [16] But we who know so much of the story of the perpetual curate with the large family and the small stipend will be inclined rather to pity than to anger. It must probably have been with an eye to this neglect of the priest and his abject poverty that Ben Sira wrote the following lines:

> Fear the Lord with all thy soul,
> And reverence his priests.
> With all thy strength love him that made thee,
> And forsake not his ministers.
> Honour the Lord and glorify the priest,
> And give him his portion even as it is commanded thee
> (7: 29,31).

More of a profession in our sense of the word was the medical one. Ben Sira devotes a whole chapter to it, and we learn from it that

> The knowledge of the physician shall lift his head,
> He shall stand before the nobles,
> And from the king he shall receive gifts (38 : 3, 2).

He was thus, like the modern physician, a student of some sort, and likewise expected to be compensated for his services. Anatomy, physiology, etc., are not likely to have formed a part of his knowledge, though there is evidence from the second century that some Rabbis tried their hands at dissecting dead bodies.[17] As it would seem, it consisted mainly in knowing the virtues of various herbs, for, as Ben Sira says,

> God bringeth out medicines from the earth;
> And let a prudent man not refuse them. . . . . . .
> By them doth the physician assuage pain (38 : 4, 7).

Ben Sira's pleading,

> Was not water made sweet with wood
> To acquaint every man with his [God's] power? (38 : 5),

seems to have been directed against a sort of Jewish scientists who saw in the physician a man counteracting the designs of God. The Rabbinic remark on Exodus 21 : 19, "that the Law gave permission to the physician to practise his art," [18] points also to the existence of such objections on the part of some "peculiar" Jews. "Nothing is new under the sun," not even folly.

Of course, as a pious Jew, Ben Sira perceived in the physician an instrument of Providence, or, as he expresses it,

> From God a physician getteth wisdom (38 : 2).

Hence his advice to the patient:

> Pray unto the Lord, for he will heal (38 : 9).

Ben Sira likewise assumes of the physician that

> He, too, will supplicate unto God,
> That he will prosper to him the mixture (38 : 14).

But he distinctly warns the people not to neglect the physician. "Honour the physician," Ben Sira says, "before thou hast need of him" (38 : 1), and concludes the chapter with the words :

> He that sinneth against his Maker,
> Will behave himself proudly against a physician (38 : 15).

In consequence of a misreading of the Hebrew by the Greek translator, the versions give

> He that sinneth before his Maker,
> Let him fall into the hands of the physician.

Now, a community which has artisans and traders, hired men and employers, professionals and privileged classes, could hardly be expected to be free from social inequalities and even social injustices. Ben Sira touches in many a place on these social evils of his time. It was on the basis of such passages that a German Social Democrat, Herr Pfarrer Naumann, declared Ben Sira to have been a prototype of Karl Marx and Lassalle. I know the Pfarrer's article only from quotations given by Pastor Wohlenberg in an Essay headed *Jesus Sirach und die sociale Frage*, in the *Neue Kirchliche Zeitschrift*. To judge from these quotations Pfarrer Naumann's main argument is based on the contents of Ben Sira's Wisdom, Chapter 13, in which such lines as the following occur :

> Wild asses are the prey of lions in the wilderness;
> So poor men are pasture for the rich. . . . .

A rich man speaketh and all keep silence;
And what he saith they extol to the clouds.
A poor man speaketh, and they say, who is this?
And if he stumble, they will help to overthrow him (13:
    19-23).

These, and other verses like these, testify to the
existence of a class rapacious, perfidious, and unscru-
pulous.   Still they must not be interpreted as if they
were meant to set up a conflagration to consume the
foundations of an old world, replacing it by a state
composed of communistic societies and socialistic
brotherhoods.   Nothing could be further from the
thoughts of Ben Sira.   The social problem in Israel is
old, and is in no way characteristic of the age of Ben
Sira.   Those interested in the subject will find a fair
account of it, and the way prophets and lawgivers
tried to deal with it, in Professor Nowack's and Professor Buhl's pamphlets on the social problems in
Israel.   For our present purpose it will suffice to
refer to such passages as the one in Isaiah, "Woe
unto them who join house to house and lay field to
field, till there is no place" (5: 8), or the one in
Amos, "Hear this, ye who swallow up the needy,
even to make the poor of the land to fail, saying,
when will the new moon be gone, that we may sell
the corn . . . . that we may buy the poor for silver
and the needy for a pair of shoes?" (8: 5, 6).   Nor
did the suffering of the exile greatly contribute toward
lessening covetousness.   For we find, that one of the
evils with which Nehemiah had to deal was the rapa-

city of the nobles and princes, who kept in bondage
the sons and the daughters of the people, who were
compelled to sell them for the purpose of obtaining
the barest necessaries of life, or to pay the King's
tribute (Nehemiah 5 : 1-3). The only new feature in
Ben Sira is possibly the fact that with him the Hebrew
word עשיר, usually meaning "the rich," "the opu-
lent," becomes a sort of equivalent to our word
"plutocrat," with this difference, that the עשיר employs his powers for his own unrighteous purposes,
and hence is a synonym with רשע, "the wicked."
Says Ben Sira :

> What fellowship shall wolf have with lamb?
> Such is the wicked unto the righteous :
> And so is the rich unto a man that is destitute (13 : 17-18).[19]

And the fact might be easily explained by the
aggravating turn matters took under Hellenistic influence, when priests of aristocratic descent became
tax-farmers, and the wealthy classes in their train,
aping the nobility, probably abandoned themselves to
outlandish and ungodly fashions and luxury, so that
the rich could be easily described as "the children of
the violent among thy people, who do wickedly against
the covenant."

In spite, however, of these passionate outbursts of
indignation, we must not infer that Ben Sira in any
way aspired to the rôle of social reformer. In the first
place, Ben Sira was, as already hinted at, a *savant* and
a man of the world. Unlike the later Rabbis, who
taught that the study of the Torah without a handicraft

must fail in the end, and become the cause of sin, and were even proud of the fact that Hillel, the President of the Sanhedrin, began life as a wood-chopper, Ben Sira believed leisure to be indispensable for the acquisition of wisdom. For it is only "the man devoid of occupation who shall become wise." He will

> Seek out the wisdom of all the ancients ;
> And will be occupied in prophecies.
> He will serve among great men,
> And appear before him that ruleth.
> He will travel through the land of strange nations
> (39 : 3-4).

But serving among the great and mixing with courtiers and travelling require leisure and freedom from what Ben Sira would have called "the sordid cares of existence." He could thus hardly have disowned a class which by means of its wealth enjoyed the privileges so dear to his heart.

In the second place, Ben Sira was a highly conservative gentleman, and entertained little doubt of the dogma of "the sacredness of property." It is true that he had a strong suspicion that large fortunes are not always made in the most desirable way.

> He that pursues after gold shall not be innocent . . .
> For it is a stumbling block to a fool (31 : 5, 7).

Still his doctrine was :

> Good things and evil, life and death,
> Poverty and riches, are from the Lord (11 : 14).

Riches and poverty being thus alike meted out by Heaven, every human effort toward bringing about a radical reform in this respect must prove idle and vain. With many a Jewish philosopher he probably thought that every society has the rich it deserves.

"When the Lord", says Alcharizi, "is wroth against a community, he gives wealth to the wicked and those who shut their hands ; when he loves them, he bestows it on the best and most noble-minded."

The only remedies which Ben Sira offers against the evils bound to come with such a state of society, are charity and liberality on the side of the rich, and modesty and resignation on the side of the poor.   To the former (the rich man) he says :

> He that gives to the poor lendeth to the Lord,
> And who rewardeth but he? (35 : 11—gloss).

Or :

> Be as a father to the orphans,
> And instead of a husband to the widows.
> And God shall call thee son,
> And shall be gracious to thee (4 : 10).

But almsgiving alone is not sufficient, for

> The gift of a fool shall not profit thee.
> He will give little and upbraid much,
> And he will open his mouth like a crier (20 : 14, 15).

In accordance with the Rabbinic sentiment, that charity is rewarded only in proportion to the graciousness which accompanies it,[20] Ben Sira gives the instruction :

> My son, to thy good deeds add no blemish,
> And no grief of words in any way of giving.
> Shall not the dew assuage the scorching heat?
> So is a word better than a gift (18 : 15–16).

The rich man also receives the solemn warning,

that accumulation of wealth by means of oppressing
the poor will be speedily avenged by a righteous God.
For

> He that buildeth his house with other men's money,
> Is like one that gathereth himself stones for the tomb
> of his burial (21 : 8).

Nor will church windows or any other donations
atone for his iniquities, for

> Whoso bringeth an offering of the goods of the poor,
> Doeth as one that killeth the son before his father's
> eyes (34 : 18).

To the latter (the poor) Ben Sira gives the counsel:

> With little or much be well satisfied (29 : 23),

since

> Better is the life of a poor man under shelter of logs,
> Than sumptuous fare in another man's house (29 : 22).

And far from considering poverty a vice,—as Renan
somewhere imputes to Judaism,—Ben Sira perceives
in it, as in all manner of suffering, a discipline:

> For gold is tried in the fire,
> And acceptable men in the furnace of adversity (2 : 5).

Hence, as in other cases of suffering, the only safe-
guards against it are patience and confidence in God,
or, as Ben Sira expresses it,

> Accept whatsoever is brought upon thee;
> And be long-suffering in the changes of thy humiliation.
> Put thy trust in him and he will help thee (2: 4, 6).

I described Ben Sira as "a man of the world."
But no reproach was meant by it. All that this
epithet implies is, that Ben Sira represented a type
of mind which, lacking both ignorance and en-

thusiasm, made him sadly unfit for the rôle of
social reformer. He may perhaps be best described
as a gentleman of the old school. In religion the
doctrines of the Prophets were good enough for him,
and he would, as we have seen, discourage every theological speculation on " things hidden," as imperti-
nent inquisitiveness. In politics the only principle
he would urge was strict honesty and forbearance, for,
as he says,

Sovereignty is transferred from nation to nation
Because of iniquities, pride, and greed of money (10 : 8).

Otherwise, as we can see from his panegyrics, he
revered " the powers that be," and as a good conservative probably believed them to be meek and honest.

Whether Ben Sira would have been quite welcome
in the circles of those known to history by the name
of Chasidim, or Saints, is rather doubtful. They
certainly need not have been ashamed of the man
whose maxim was

Flee from sin as from the face of a serpent (21 : 2).

But if it be true, as some historians maintain, that
the saints of that period were given to an ascetic life,
they could not have been very eager for the company of one who, as we shall see presently, manifested a great predilection for the good things of this
world. If this was the case, I can only be sorry for
them. But their loss is our gain. For it is precisely

this touch of worldliness in Ben Sira which affords us that glimpse of the social life of his time for which there is very little room in the work of a mere saint.

The diary of the somewhat profane Pepys—to give an instance near at hand—is both amusing and instructive, whilst the jottings of the godly Nehemiah Wallington are certainly more edifying, but withal dull and unprofitable reading for the historian.

Ben Sira was not profane, but he had a special weakness for a good dinner, declaring that

> Him that is liberal of his meats the lips shall bless,
> And the testimony of his excellence shall be believed
> (31 : 23).

With our present object in hand we cannot do better than accompany him to this important social function. I call it a function, for a dinner in Jerusalem to which guests were invited was quite a solemn affair, though it never assumed the sad and sacramental character which distinguishes our banquets. The first duty to be performed would be to appoint by lot or election a chairman, or "head of the banquet house."

The election to this office carried with it, as it seems, a certain dignity, of which vain men were not a little proud. For, among the petty conceits of which a man should not, according to the advice of an old Rabbi, boast to his wife, lest she despise him in her heart, is also this, that he should not go home and say unto his wife, "I have been made the ruler of the feast."[21] The injunction of Ben Sira,

> Have they made thee ruler of a feast?
> Be not lifted up (32 : 1),

points to the same fact.

What the particular function of this ruler was is not clearly stated, but, as far as we can gather from Ben Sira and succeeding Rabbinic sources, it consisted in arranging the seats, or rather couches, superintending all the preparations, and doing the honours of the occasion:

> Take thought for them and then lie down,
> Supply their wants and afterwards recline,
> That thou mayest rejoice in their honour (32 : 1, 2).[22]

It is not impossible that he had also to draw up a list of the guests to be invited, since we know from a later source that "the men of a refined mind" in Jerusalem never accepted an invitation, unless they knew beforehand the names of those who were to be their fellow-guests.[23]   The hour for dining seems to coincide, in the Rabbinic age at least, with that of the Romans, namely eleven o'clock in the morning.[24]   The guests were expected to appear some time before, when they were taken to the vestibule, to wait there for their friends, and be treated to refreshments.   In Jerusalem the fashion was to pass round three courses of refreshments, during which time a flag was hoisted on the front of the house, as a signal for the guests to appear.   With the removal of the flag after the third course of refreshments, the "ten minutes of grace" were over, and the assembled guests entered the dining hall.   This was furnished with couches and small tables, in the arrangement of which more heed was paid, I believe, to the rules of precedence than to those of comfort. The Talmud has a regular "order of the table," which is exceedingly interesting,[25] and should be studied in connexion with corresponding matter in Marquardt's *Privatleben der Römer*. Here we must confine ourselves chiefly to Ben Sira.

As to the menu, Ben Sira tells us "the chief thing for life is water and bread" (29:21). This is rather too frugal. More satisfactory is another passage, in which among "the things necessary for life" are given "salt and flour of wheat and honey and milk and the blood of grapes and oil" (39: 26). One would not starve on this, but, as a fact, the Jews were not limited to a vegetarian diet on "good days." The general rule was "no festive dinner without meat." In Jerusalem in particular the butchers were also employed as caterers, and heavily fined if the bill of fare did not answer the conditions under which the banquet was entrusted to them.[26] Nor was quantity a sole condition; for, as Ben Sira shrewdly remarks,

The throat devours every meat,
Yet one meat is more pleasant than another (36: 23),

whilst in another place he tells us:

Not all is good for all,
Not every soul chooses every kind (37 : 28).

Quality and variety apparently are also insisted upon. We even have it on record that a grateful guest was expected to admire the various kinds of wine which were placed before him, and the different sorts of pastry and meats of which he had a choice,[27] and it is to be assumed that the host on his part was expected to do his best to deserve the compliment. A feast thus meant by no means a fast. What Ben Sira would urge would be gentlemanly behaviour and temperance. Here are a few of his injunctions:

> Sittest thou at the table of the great, be not greedy upon it,
> And say not, many are the things upon it.
> Stretch not thine hand whithersoever it [the eye] looketh,
> And thrust not thyself with it into the dish,
> Consider thy neighbour's liking by thine own;
> And be discreet in every point.
> Eat as becometh a man those things which are set before thee;
> And eat not greedily, lest thou be hated.
> Be first to leave off for manners' sake,
> And be not insatiable, lest thou offend.
> And if thou sittest among many,
> Reach not out thy hand before them (31: 12, 14-18).
>
> Be not insatiable for every luxury
> And be not effuse in all dainties.
> For in much luxury resteth sickness;
> By intemperance many perish utterly,
> But he that taketh heed shall add to life (37: 29-31).

Another rule of Ben Sira's is: "At the time of the table multiply not words," [28] which the Talmud paraphrases: "They talk not during meals." It is thus to be supposed that the gaieties did not begin till the actual eating was over. First, however, the toasts had to be given in honour of the host and the more important guests. A good number of these have come down to us from Jewish antiquity. They are mostly of a homiletic nature, but they all have the virtue of brevity.[29]

The obscure lines in Ben Sira addressed to the "ruler of the feast," "for good manners thou shalt receive favour" (32: 2), may perhaps be construed to mean something similar to our vote of thanks to the chairman. More probably, however, the Hebrew text in this place is corrupt, and should read, as partly suggested by the Greek,

That thou mayest receive a *crown* for thy well-ordering (32 ; 2).

Some of the sources seem to hint at a custom, that the man honoured with saying the grace crowned himself with a wreath for this function. The Hebrew formula picturing the saints in the world to come as sitting with wreaths on their heads and feasting on the glory of the Divine Presence, also points to the popularity of this adornment among the Jews. Should the custom just mentioned date back as far as 200 B. C. E., we might perceive in the crown of Ben Sira a preparation for reading the grace after the meal, which also fell within the duties of the ruler of the feast.[30]

When toasts and grace were over, the gaieties began. These consisted in the joys of the cup and in listening to music. The Biblical term משתה, literally, drinking, for feast or banquet, shows the important part wine played on such occasions. Ben Sira and his generation must have had a special fondness for "the blood of the grape," which he defines, as we have seen, as one of "the necessaries of life." Thus Ben Sira exclaims :

> What life is there to him who is without wine?
> It was from the beginning created for joy (31 : 27).

And again he says:

> Joy of heart, gladness, and an ornament
> Is wine in its *time and proper season* (31 : 28).

Indeed, it would seem that Ben Sira was so eager for the full enjoyment of the liquid "that gladdens God and men," that he would advise men to avoid anything which might prove a disturbing element. His words are:

> Rebuke not thy neighbour at a banquet of wine,
> Neither set him at naught in his mirth:
> Speak not unto him a word of reproach,
> And press not upon him by asking him back a debt (31: 31).

But please notice the qualification of time and season, whilst in another place Ben Sira also insists on measure. For the abuse of wine, as for the abuse of food, Ben Sira has only words of condemnation:

> A workman that is a drunkard shall not become rich.
> He that loveth flesh shall inherit poverty (19 : 1),

whilst in another passage he says

> Show not thyself valiant in wine;
> For wine hath destroyed many (31 : 25).
> Drunkenness increaseth the rage of a fool unto his hurt;
> It diminisheth strength and addeth wounds (31 : 30).

Indeed, next to sexual immorality, there is nothing which Ben Sira abhors more than drunkenness. For

> Wine and vice will make a man of understanding fall away
>   (19 : 2)

(namely, from God).

Yet Ben Sira advocated only temperance and moderation, not total abstinence. With his hero, Simon the Just, he might in exceptional cases approve perhaps of a man taking the vows of the Nazarite, who had to refrain from all intoxicating drinks.[31] But he would certainly never have allowed the constitution of an ascetic order to become the rule of the nation at large. As of iron, salt, and other useful and indispensable articles, he says also of wine: .

> All these things for good to the godly,
> So to the sinner they shall be turned into evil (39 : 27).

The wine was accompanied by music. The enjoyment of a concert on festive occasions was not a post-exilic invention. "Woe unto those," we read in Isaiah, "that continue until night till wine inflame them. And the harp and the viol, the tabret and the pipe, and wine are in their feasts" (5 : 12). But whilst the prophet protested, as they were probably then a source of abuse, Ben Sira thoroughly relished such performances, for

> As a signet of carbuncle in a setting of gold,
> So is a concert of music in a banquet of wine.
> As a signet of emerald in a work of gold,
> So is a strain of music with pleasant wine (32 : 5-6).

There is a story in the Talmud of a Rabbi who gave a dinner to his pupils, and who felt rather uncomfortable because of their shyness. Whereupon he said to his servant, "Give wine to the young men, that they may break their silence." [32] We may thus imagine that also in the times of Ben Sira the wine served as a signal for the opening of the conversation.

His remarks in this respect are not uninteresting. There is first the venerable, serene, and sedate elder, but liable to become serious and heavy. To him Ben Sira says:

> Speak, O elder, for it becometh thee.
> And be modestly wise and hinder not song.
> In a place for wine pour not forth talk.
> Wherefore shouldst thou be overwise out of season? (32: 3-4).

These lines recall strongly a saying in later Rabbinic literature to the following effect: "Three things make man popular with his fellow-creatures—an open hand, a free table, and a little gaiety." [33]

There is also the assertive youth attending, perhaps, his first banquet, and rather inclined to monopolise the conversation. To him Ben Sira's counsel is:

> Speak, young man, if thou must,
> With an effort, if he asks thee twice or thrice.
> Compress the word and diminish it exceedingly (32: 7-8).

He also gives him the gentle hint, that it is modesty and blushing which will endear him to his elders for

> Before hail spreadeth lightning,
> And before one that is shamefaced favour (32: 10).

On the other hand, there is the bore of superior airs, who is constantly in fear of committing himself, and tries to impose by his silence. Him Ben Sira would address with the words:

> Refrain not from speech in season,
> And hide not thy wisdom for the sake of fair-seeming (4: 23).

The most unbearable bore is he who never sees a point:

> He that telleth a tale to a fool, speaketh to one in slumber,
> When he hath told his tale, he will say, what is it? (22 : 8).

Yet it must not be thought that Ben Sira was blind to the evils of the tongue. None perhaps warned against them more emphatically than he. To be saved from them man requires special assistance from Heaven, for which Ben Sira prays in the following words :

> Who shall set a watch over my mouth,
> And a seal of shrewdness upon my lips,
> That I fall not suddenly by them, and that my tongue de-
>   stroy me not? (22 : 27).
> O Lord, Father and Master of my life,
> Abandon me not to their counsel :
> Suffer me not to fall by them (23 : 1).

The pitfalls set by the tongue are slandering, lying, perjuring, backbiting, betraying a friend's secret, and the uttering of obscene words. Nay, the very thought of things impure is sinful and defiling. Hence Ben Sira's exclamation :

> Who will set scourges over my thought ;
> And a discipline of wisdom over mine heart?
> That they spare me not for mine ignorances,
> And my heart pass not by their sins (23 : 2).

But even in the speech without sin Ben Sira is constantly recommending caution, discretion, and reticence :

> Lo, thou surround thy vineyard with a hedge,
> And make a door and bar for thy mouth (28 : 24).
> Hast thou heard a word, let it die with thee,
> Take courage, it will not burst thee (19 : 10).

Indeed, the difference between the fool and the wise man is :

The heart of fools is in their mouth ;
But the mouth of wise men is in their heart (21 : 26).

The effusive gentleman would thus have been out of
place at a banquet in Jerusalem.   But

Wine and music rejoice the heart,
But the love of friends is above them both (40 : 20).

"Friendship or death" was an old Jewish proverb,
and no sacrifice was considered too great to obtain
friendship.[34]   "Acquire for thyself a friend or a companion" is the injunction of Joshua ben Perachyah,
who lived before our era, but the comment given on
it by the Rabbis of later generations is : Let a man
buy himself a friend who will eat and drink with him,
who will study with him the written and the oral law,
and to whom he will entrust all his secrets both of a
spiritual and a secular nature.[35]   Ben Sira, however,
the man of the world, and apparently of much experience, which alone, as he maintains, saved him from
" danger even unto death," brought about "by cun-
ning lips and weavers of lies," is less effusive, and
even inclined to suspicion.   His counsel is :

Separate thyself from thy enemies,
And beware of thy friends (6 : 13).

Still he in no way undervalued the blessing of true
friendship, and he tells us,

A faithful friend is balm of life,
He that feareth God shall obtain him (6 : 16),

only he would advise to caution, till the friend is tried
and found not wanting :

> As new wine so is a new friend.
> If it becomes thee, thou shalt drink it with gladness (9 : 10).

What one has mainly to guard against in the acquiring of new friends is the tendency toward selfishness, sacrificing all to its own ends. Hence

> Let thyself beware of a counsellor,
> And know *before* what is his interest (37 : 8).

Very interesting is Ben Sira's counsel as to those from whom we should not take advice :

> Take not counsel with a woman about her rival ;
> Neither with a coward about war ;
> Nor with a merchant about exchange ;
> Nor with a buyer about selling ;
> Nor with an envious man about thankfulness ;
> Nor with an unmerciful man about kindliness ;
> Nor with a sluggard about any kind of work ;
> Nor with a hireling in thy house about finishing his work ;
> Nor with an idle servant about much business (37 : 11 *et seq.*).

Prudence and foresight do not exclude charitableness and kindness toward the bulk of mankind. At least they were compatible enough in the view of Ben Sira, who teaches :

> Forgive thy neighbour the hurt that he has done thee,
> And then thy sins shall be pardoned when thou prayest.
> Man cherishes anger against man,
> And does he seek healing from the Lord ?
> Upon a man like himself he hath no mercy,
> And does he make supplication for his sins ? (28 : 2-3).

The same thought is expressed in Rabbinic literature by the words : He only who is merciful with mankind may expect mercy from Heaven.[36] Such sentiments alone should suffice to discharge Ben Sira from the guilt of selfishness and cynicism brought against him by a certain school.

> But a friend and partner behave as occasion requires,
> And a prudent wife is above them (40 : 23).

The prudent woman or the good woman is the constant theme of Ben Sira's praises, as he never gets tired of enlarging upon the evils of the bad woman or the foolish woman.

The fraternity of bachelors was not popular with the Jews, the Talmud speaking of the wifeless man as deficient in humanity, whilst Ben Sira stigmatises him as a vagabond, wandering up and down.   One of the two types of women a man was thus bound to have.   The latter (the bad woman) was considered a punishment of God, "which shall fall to the lot of the sinner," the former (the good wife) was looked upon as a blessing from Heaven and the reward of "such as fear the Lord."

How far heiresses were fashionable in ancient Jerusalem it is difficult to say.   At present I can recall one case, of Joshua ben Gamala, whose *fiancée*, the millionairess Maratta bath Boëthus, bought for him, from Agrippa II, the commission of high priest.   But it must be owned that he made good use of his opportunities, for it was this Joshua who introduced compulsory education for children from the age of six and upward.[37]   Still, both the Rabbis and Ben Sira con-

demned such marriages as unworthy and degrading.
The words of the latter are :

> There is anger and impudence and great reproach
> If a woman maintains her husband (25 : 22)

The considerations which should weigh with a man in
the choice of a wife are, according to Ben Sira, noble
descent, beauty, modesty, thrift, and faithfulness.   For

> A silent and loving woman is a gift from the Lord,
> And there is nothing so much worth as a well-instructed
>   soul.
> As the sun when it arises in the highest places of the Lord,
> So is the beauty of a good wife in the ordering of a man's
>   house (26 : 14, 16),

whilst her devotion to religion is described as follows :

> Eternal foundations on solid rock,
> And the laws of God in the heart of a saintly woman.[38]

Another consideration with Ben Sira, as with the
later Rabbis, is יחום, or noble pedigree, for

> So thy race which thou lovest shall be magnified,
> Having the confidence of their good descent (26 : 21).

Good descent, however, is not everything, as children given to haughtiness and extravagance "do
stain the nobility of their kindred." To insure "the
goodness of the stock" a sound education is indispensable. In the times of Ben Sira this was still left
entirely to the father. According to the Rabbis the
main duties of a father toward his son consisted in
instructing him in the Torah, bringing him into wedlock, and teaching him a trade, or, to be more accurate, teaching him a handicraft.[39] Ben Sira, in accord-

ance with his low opinion of labour omits the third duty, and says:

> Hast thou sons, instruct them,
> And marry wives to them in their youth (7 : 23).

But instruction was a serious business, and could not, in the view of Ben Sira, be successfully carried out without the aid of cane and rod:

> Bow down his neck in his youth,
> And smite his loins, when he is a little one (30 : 12).
> He that loveth his son causeth him oft to feel the rod (30:1).

This is, of course, in accordance with the sentiment expressed so often in the Book of Proverbs and in other parts of the Old Testament. But this fact in no way relieves the severity of such a passage as

> Play with him and he will grieve thee;
> Laugh not with him, lest thou have sorrow with him
>   (30 : 9, 10).

With Ben Sira, as it would seem, the child is neither an angel nor a devil, but a mere mischievous animal. Hence his simile:

> An unbroken horse becomes stubborn,
> And a son left at large becometh headstrong (30 : 8).

Not less severe was the education of girls, though they are never mentioned in connexion with the infliction of corporal punishment. This decency probably forbade. The more strict was the watch kept over them. Ben Sira's maxim was:

> Hast thou daughters, guard them (7 : 24).

The education of a girl tended mainly, to judge

from various Rabbinic sources, toward making a good
housewife of her; and consisted in enabling her to
attain such accomplishments as weaving, spinning,
cooking, baking, nursing, and arranging the furniture.[40]
These were, indeed, the services a woman had to do
for her husband. Of course, it was a question of
means, and the ability to keep servants might relieve her from some of the more onerous duties.
But work of the lighter kind was insisted on even
with the richest, as the best remedy against whims
and morbidness. The choice of a husband was
entirely in the hands of the parents, and success in
obtaining good matches for one's offspring was a
source of congratulation.

> Give away a daughter, and thou shalt have accomplished
> a great work,
> But join her to a man of understanding (7: 25).

In later Jewish literature daughters are spoken of
as the winged birds taking flight after their husbands
when married.[41] The hope of the family thus reposed
in the male line. The filial duties were many and
arduous, the son being bound to maintain his parents
in their old age and to serve them. But he was also
expected to continue the traditions of the family, becoming heir to its feuds and its alliances. It was a
special comfort when a father

> Left behind him an avenger against his enemies,
> And one to requite kindness to his friends (30: 6).

In fact the immortality of whole chains of progenitors
was invested in the dear boy, for

His father dieth and is as though he has not died,
For he has left behind him one like himself (30: 4).

In the map of life with its diversity of colours mark-
ing the high-roads of our earthly career with their
innumerable by-ways and cross-ways, there is ever
facing us in the distance a little dark spot to which all
roads and ways converge.   The distance is entirely a
relative one, varying with our state of health, our
sweetness of temper, and the disposition of our mind,
morbid or cheerful.   But there it remains ever con-
fronting us, and not to be removed out of sight by
any variety of euphemism, such as "haven of rest,"
"land of peace," or "a better world."   Its real name
is Death.

Our sketch of life in ancient Jerusalem will be
more than incomplete, unless we throw a glance, at
least, at its decline toward the great borderland.

Death, as a rule, is preceded by illness, and we
have already seen the important part assigned to the
physician.   But he was assisted in his duties by
nearly the whole of the community.   Ben Sira's
injunction is:

> Be not slow to visit the sick,
> For through this thou shalt be beloved (7 : 35).

This duty is known in Rabbinic literature under the
term *Bikkur Cholim*, visiting the sick, which, as is
clear from certain injunctions in the Talmud in connexion with this duty,[42] included in the case of need

also nursing and sweeping the room. His friends
also prayed for the patient, and it was a part of their
duty to remind him to make a will and confess
his sins, "for all those who were about to die
had to confess their sins." They had also the belief
that a confession which concluded with a prayer for
forgiveness of sins might bring about his recovery.
This is, as is clear from the whole context, the confession to which the Apostle James refers at the end
of his Epistle. Ben Sira's counsel to the sick man is:

> And from all transgressions cleanse thy heart (38 : 10).

Ben Sira, whatever his shortcomings may have been,
—indeed, he was hardly what we would call a sound
theologian,—was not given to platitudes. He freely
admits that death is a very "bitter remembrance"
to the prosperous man of great possessions and a
capacity for pleasure (31 : 1). Yet it had no terrors
for him, for he regarded it not in the light of a punishment, but in that of a Divine law, which has to be
obeyed and fulfilled with the same submission and
devotion as any law in the Torah, and thus he says:

> Be not afraid of death, thy covenant.
> Remember that those who went before, and they which
>   come after will be with thee.
> This is the portion of all flesh from the Lord,
> And why dost thou refuse the Torah of the Most High?
>   (41 : 3-4).

When death entered, the funeral ceremonies began,
which, at a later period, before the reform of Rabban
Gamaliel, were costly and rather showy. They
became so heavy a tax, that sometimes the near-

est relatives would take to flight, leaving the corpora-
tion to take care of the dead body.   Hence Ben Sira's
injunction :

> According to the custom bury his flesh,
> And hide not thyself when they die (38 : 16).

The mourning lasted seven days, in which friends
and acquaintances were expected to join :

> Be not wanting to them that weep,
> And mourn with them that mourn (7 : 34).

In the time of the Rabbis the mourning in the case
of parents extended over twelve months.   But neither
the Rabbis nor Ben Sira approved of prolonged
mourning for an indefinite period.   The Rabbis perceived in it a presumption on the part of man to be
more merciful than God,[43] whilst Ben Sira thought that
we ought to save our tears for greater calamities :

> Weep for the dead, for light hath failed him;
> And weep for a fool, for understanding hath failed him.
> Weep more softly for the dead, because he hath found
>   rest (22 : 11).

Looking back at this life, we feel that for the most
part we have been moving in a world very much like
ours, guided by the same motives, moved by the same
passions, and on the whole striving after the same
ideals.   The "Sacred Volume" tells us : "Say not
that the days of yore were better than these," for it is
unwisdom to say so.   The lesson to be derived from
Ben Sira is, say not that our days are better than the
days of yore, for it is ignorance to say so.

ON THE STUDY OF THE TALMUD[1]

It is now more than half a century since Renan put the question, "Has Jewish tradition anything to teach us concerning Jesus?" This question must be answered in the negative. As far as the contemporaneous Jewish literature goes, it does not contain a single reference to the founder of Christianity. All the so-called Anti-Christiana collected by mediæval fanatics, and freshened up again by modern ignoramuses, belong to the later centuries, when history and biography had given way to myth and speculation. Almost every Christian sect, every Christian community, created a Christ after its own image or dogma. The Jewish legend—a growth of those later centuries —gave him an aspect of its own, purely apocryphal in its character, neither meant nor ever taken by the Jews as real history.

But if the Rabbis have nothing to tell us about the personality of Jesus, Rabbinic literature has a good deal to teach us about the times in which he lived and laboured. And what is more important is that a thorough study of this literature might, with due discretion, help us to a better understanding of the writings attributed to Jesus and his disciples. To prove this by a few instances will be the aim of my present lecture. It is intended as an invitation to fellow-

students to devote more attention to a branch of literature, from the study of which the Christian divine
might derive as much profit as the Jewish Rabbi.

In justice to by-gone times, it should be pointed
out that this fact had by no means escaped the search-
ing eyes of Christian scholars of previous generations.
They both recognised the importance of the Talmud for
a better knowledge of the two Testaments, and applied
themselves to an honest study of its contents. As
the fruits of these studies, it is sufficient to mention
here the *Porta Mosis* of Pocock, the *De Synedriis* of
Selden, the *Horae Rabbinicae* of Lightfoot. The Cambridge Platonists also deserve honourable mention.
These great and hospitable minds extended the range
of their literary acquaintances also to the Rabbis, and
the *Select Discourses* of John Smith, and the *Discourse
on the Lord's Supper* by Cudworth,[2] show that this
acquaintance was by no means a passing one.

All the names just given belong to England, but
the Continent in no way remained behind. The names
of the Continental students of Rabbinism are duly recorded in Zunz's *Zur Literatur und Geschichte*, and in
other bibliographical works. It is sufficient to mention
the name of Reuchlin, who saved the Talmud from the
torch which a converted Jew was about to apply to it ;
the two Buxtorfs, whose works bearing on Rabbinic
literature fill pages in the catalogues of the British
Museum; and Vitringa, whose books on Rabbinic
topics are considered by the best scholars as classical
pieces of work.

However, these good things are (as already indicated) a matter of the past. The present shows a decided deterioration. Not only has the number of students devoting themselves to Rabbinic literature shrunk to a miserable minimum, but the quality of the work produced by these latter-day students is such as to show a distinct decay, among the very few praiseworthy exceptions being, for instance, the theological works of Dr. C. Taylor. No student who is interested in the constitution of the ancient Synagogue dare neglect Vitringa's *De Synagoga vetere*, which appeared in the year 1696; but he would certainly lose nothing by omitting to read most of the productions of our own century on the same subject.

The causes of this decay are not to be sought for far off. There was first the influence of Schleiermacher, whose interpretation of Christianity formed, as far as its negative side is concerned, one long strained effort to divorce it from Judaism. "I hate historic relations of this sort," he exclaims in one place; and proceeds to say, "every religion is conditioned by itself, and forms an eternal necessity." Schleiermacher's theory of the origin of Christianity was, as is well known, mainly based on the Johannine Gospel, to the disparagement of the Synoptics. The German Marcion had thus every reason to hate history. But as the Talmud still reminded the world of these historical relations, Schleiermacher and his school adopted the course of vulgar *parvenus*, and cut the Rabbis and their literary remains. The second cause of this decay is the suspicion thrown on all Jewish tradition by the higher criticism. Anybody who has ever read any modern Introductions to the Old Testament will remember, that as a rule they open with a reference to the Rabbinic account of the rise of the Canon, followed by a lengthy exposition showing its utter untrustworthiness. To make matters more complete, efforts were made to disqualify the Rabbis from bearing witness even to events which took place when the Synagogue was a fully-established institution, administered by the ancestors of the Rabbis in their capacity as scribes and saints, or Chasidim. I am referring to the controversy as to the existence of the so-called Great Synagogue, commencing, according to tradition, with Ezra the Scribe, and succeeded by a permanent court, consisting of seventy-one members, called Sanhedrin; which court again was, according to tradition, presided over by two members, the one called Nasi, or Prince-President, whilst the other bore the title of Ab-Beth-Din, Father of the Court of Justice, or Vice-President, both of whom were recruited for the most part from Pharisaic circles. Modern criticism, mainly on the strength of certain passages in Josephus and in the New Testament, maintains a negative attitude toward these accounts. The questions involved are too important and too complicated to be entered upon in a casual way. We need notice only the following fact. This is, that the doubts regarding the traditional account of the constitution of the Sanhedrin were first raised in this century

by Krochmal in the "forties," taken up again by
Kuenen in the "sixties," to be followed by Wellhausen in the "eighties." But when reading their
works you will observe that, whilst Krochmal respect-
fully questions tradition, and Kuenen enters into elaborate examination of the documents, Wellhausen sum-
marily dismisses them. Matters have now, indeed,
come to such a pass that the principle has been laid
down, that it is not necessary to have a thorough
knowledge of Rabbinic literature in order to express
an opinion about its merits or demerits. It is probably thought that we may condemn it by mere intuition It is impossible to argue with transcendental
ignorance.

Trusting that none of those present have any reason to hate history, or to believe in the superior virtue
of ignorance, I will now proceed to the subject of my
lecture.

Let me first state the fact that the impression conveyed to the Rabbinic student by the perusal of the
New Testament is in parts like that gained by reading
certain Rabbinic homilies. On the very threshold
of the New Testament he is confronted by a gene-
alogical table,[3] a feature not uncommon in the later
Rabbinic versions of the Old Testament, which are
rather fond of providing Biblical heroes with long pedi-
grees. They are not always accurate, but have as a
rule some edifying purpose in view. The Rabbis even
declare that the Book of Chronicles, with its long
series of names, has no other purpose than that of

being interpreted,[4] that is to say, of enabling us to derive some lesson from them. In the fifth chapter of the Sayings of the Jewish Fathers, dealing mostly with round numbers, we read : "There were ten generations from Noah to Abraham to make known how long-suffering God is."

In the second chapter of Matthew the Rabbinic student meets with many features known to him from the Rabbinic narratives about the birth of Abraham; the story of the Magi in particular impresses him as a homiletical illustration of Num. 24: 17, "There shall come a star out of Jacob," which star the interpretation of the Synagogue referred to the star of the Messiah.[5] This impression grows stronger the more we advance with the reading of the Apostle's writings. Take, for instance, Matt. 3: 9, "Bring forth fruit worthy of repentance." This verse, like so many others in the New Testament in which fruits or harvest are used as metaphors or similes in parables, gains both in intensity and in freshness when studied in connexion with many allegorical interpretations of the Rabbis in which the produce of the field and the vineyard play a similar part. One or two instances will not be uninteresting. Thus, with reference to Song of Songs 2: 2, "As the lily among the thorns, so is my love among the daughters," a famous Rabbi says: There was a king who had a paradise (or garden), which he had laid out with rows of fig-trees, rows of vines, and rows of pomegranates. He put the paradise in the hands of a tenant, and left. In

after days the king came to see what his tenant had
accomplished.   He found the garden neglected, and
full of thorns and thistles.   He then brought wood-
cutters to cut it down.   Suddenly he perceived a lily.
The king plucked it, and smelled it, and his soul returned upon him.   He turned and said, "For the
sake of the lily the garden shall be saved."   The lily
is the Congregation of Israel ; intent on the strength
of its devotion to the Torah, it saved the world from
the destruction to which the generation of the deluge
had condemned it by their wicked deeds.[6]

In another place, however, it is the individual who
is compared to the lily.   Thus, Song of Songs 6 : 2,
"My beloved went down to his garden to gather the
lilies," is applied to the death of the righteous, whose
departure from this world is a gathering of flowers
undertaken by God himself, who is the beloved one.[7]

In connexion with this we may mention another
Rabbinic parable, in which the wheat takes the place
of the lily.   It is given as an illustration of Song of
Songs 7 : 3, and Psalm 2 : 12.   The Scriptural words
in the latter place are נשקו בר, which the Rabbis explain to mean "kiss the wheat," illustrating it by the
following parable : The straw and the chaff were argu-
ing together.   The straw maintained that it was for
its sake that the field was sown and ploughed, whilst
the stem insisted that it was on its account that the
work was undertaken.   Thereupon the wheat said,
"Wait until the harvest comes, and we shall know with
what purpose the field was sown."   When the harvest

came, and the work of threshing began, the chaff was
scattered to the wind, the stem was given to the
flames, whilst the wheat was carefully gathered on the
floor. In a similar way the heathens say, "It is for
our sake that the world was created," whilst Israel
makes the same claim for itself. But wait for the Day
of Judgment, when the chaff will be eliminated, and
the wheat will be kissed. I need hardly remind you
of the parable in Matt. 13.[8]

To return to Chapter 3. I will quote verse 11, in
which the Baptist in his testimony to Jesus says, " I,
indeed, baptised you with water unto repentance, but
he that cometh after me is mightier than I, whose
shoes I am not worthy to bear ; he shall baptise you
with the Holy Ghost and with fire." The baptism, of
course, represents the טבילה, or immersion, of the Bible,
enforced by the Rabbis in the case of proselytes. According to some authorities it was also customary with
people entering on a course of repentance.[9] The expression, "whose shoes I am not worthy to bear," reminds one of the similar Talmudic phrase, running,
"he who will explain to me a certain word, I will
carry his cloth after him to the bath,"[10] that is to say,
he will show submission to his authority by performing
menial work for him. As to the term, " baptism by
the Holy Ghost and fire," the latter has a parallel in
the Talmudic dictum, that the main טבילה, immersion,
as a means of purification, is by fire.[11] The former
term, " baptism by the Holy Ghost," is certainly obscure, and has given a good deal of trouble to the

commentators ; but it must have been readily understood by the Jews, who even spoke of drawing the
Holy Spirit, שואבין רוח הקודש, a term applied only to
liquids.[12]   Note also the following passage from a sermon by R. Akiba: "Blessed are ye Israelites.   Before
whom are ye purified, and who is he who purifies you?
Ye are purified before your Father in Heaven, and it
is he who purifies you," as it is said, "The Lord is
the *Mikweh* of Israel." [13]   The word מקוה is taken in
the sense in which it occurs several times in the Pentateuch, meaning "a gathering of waters," or a ritual
bath, taken after various kinds of uncleanness.   The
Rabbi then derives from the words of Jeremiah (17 :
13) the lesson, that as the *Mikweh* is the means of
purification for defilement (in the sense of the Levitical
legislation), so God is the source of purity for Israel.
It should be borne in mind, that according to the
Rabbinic interpretation, the term טומאה, "defilement,"
applies to all kinds of sins, ritual as well as moral,
especially the latter, whilst the process of purifying
mostly concerns the heart.   " Purify our hearts, that
we serve thee in truth," is the constant prayer of the
Synagogue.

טָהֳרָה, or "purification," is, according to the mystic
R. Phinehas ben Jair, of the second century, one of the
higher rungs on the ladder leading to the attainment
of the holy spirit.[14]   I do not know how far this conception may be connected with the gospel narrative,
according to which the baptism of Jesus (or the
Taharah of Jesus) was followed by the descent of the

holy spirit. If R. Phinehas ben Jair could be taken, as
some maintain, as one of the last representatives of
the Essenes, there would, indeed, be no objection to
see in the synoptic account an illustration of the principle laid down by these mystics. At any rate, it
may serve as a transition to the verses I am about to
quote from Matt. 3 (16, 17), running thus: "And
Jesus, when he was baptised, went up straightway
from the water: and, lo, the heavens were opened
unto him, and he saw the Spirit of God descending
as a dove, and coming upon him: and, lo, a voice out
of the heavens saying, This is my beloved son in
whom I am well pleased." The symbolism of the
Holy Ghost by a dove is a common notion in Rabbinic literature. The dove is considered as the most
chaste among the birds, never forsaking her mate.
The congregation of Israel, which never betrays its
God, is therefore compared to the dove.[15] "Once
upon a time," so runs a Rabbinic legend, which I
give here in substance, "King David went out on a
hawking expedition. Whereupon Satan came and
turned himself into a deer, which David tried to hit,
but could not reach. Constantly pursuing the animal,
David was thus carried from his suite, owing to the
machinations of Satan, into the land of the Philistines,
where he was suddenly confronted by the relatives of
Goliath, who were all thirsting for his blood. Thereupon a dove descended before Abishai, who had remained behind in the king's camp, and began to emit
wailing tones. Abishai at once understood its mean-

ing, saying, 'The congregation of Israel is compared to a dove, as it is said, Wings of a dove covered with silver' (Ps. 68: 14), and thus interpreted the appearance of the dove as a sign that King David, the hope of Israel, was in danger of his life, and he set out to his rescue." [16]

A closer parallel, however, is the following passage attributed to the well-known mystic, Ben Soma, a younger contemporary of the Apostles. The passage runs thus: R. Joshua ben Hananiah was standing upon the terrace of the Temple mountain. Ben Soma saw him, but did not rise up before him (as he ought to have done, seeing that R. Joshua was his master). R. Joshua asked him, "Whence and whither, Ben Soma?" The answer Ben Soma gave him was, "I was looking at (or rather meditating upon) the upper waters (above the firmament) and the under waters (under the firmament). The space between the two waters is not broader than three fingers; as it is said, 'the Spirit of God was brooding upon the face of the waters,' like a dove brooding over her young, partly touching them and partly not touching them." [17]

I need hardly say that we have here to deal with a fragment of a Jewish Gnosis, and I must refer the reader to the works of Joel, Graetz, and Freudenthal, for more information upon this point, but it must be noted that some parallel passages read "eagle" instead of "dove." Deut. 32: 11 lends some countenance to this reading, but the parallels just quoted from the New Testament as well as the famous vision of R.

Jose, in which the daughter-voice is complaining in a tender voice like a dove, saying "Woe unto the father, whose children were expelled from his table," [18] speak for the reading given first.

After the appearance of the Holy Ghost, Jesus is greeted, as we have seen, by a voice from the heavens, saying, "This is my beloved son, in whom I am well pleased." These words represent, as rightly remarked by the commentators, a combined paraphrase of Ps. 2:7 and Isa. 41:1. The voice from heaven, as is well known, corresponds with the Rabbinic "daughter of a voice" (בת קול), or daughter-voice, occupying the third place in the scale of revelation. I cannot enter here into the various aspects and functions of the daughter-voice, about which a good deal has been written, but I should like to note two peculiar features. [19]

The first is, that in many cases the daughter-voice, when employed as a means of revelation, finds its expression, not in a fresh message, but in reproducing some verse or sentence from the Hebrew Bible. Thus it is recorded by the Rabbis that when they (the authorities) intended to include King Solomon in the number of those who forfeited their salvation, the daughter-voice put in the protest of heaven, in the words of Job (34:33), "Shall his recompense be as thou wilt, that thou refusest it?" [20] The great reconciliation, again, of God with the house of David, as represented by the exiled king Jeconiah, when the Babylonian captivity was nearing its end, was announced by the daughter-voice in the words of Jeremiah, "Return, ye backsliding children, and I will heal your backslidings. Behold, we come unto thee; for thou art the Lord our God" (3 : 22).[21] It should be noted, however, that the daughter-voice is not confined in its quotations to the Canonical Scriptures. Sometimes the daughter-voice even quotes sentences from the Apocrypha. This was the case in Jabneh, where the Sanhedrin met after the destruction of the Temple. There a voice from heaven was heard reproducing a verse from the Wisdom of Ben Sira (3 : 22), "Ye have no need of the things that are secret."[22] It is true that Ben Sira has "thou hast no need" (in the singular), but it would seem as if the voice from heaven is not always very exact in its quotations, adapting them in its own way to the message to be announced. Thus, for instance, on the occasion of Saul's disobeying the commandment of God regarding the extermination of the Amalekites, there came the daughter-voice and said unto him, "Be not more righteous than thy Maker," אל תצדק יתר מקונך.[23] We will easily recognise in this warning the words of Ecclesiastes (7 : 16), "Be not righteous overmuch," אל תצדק הרבה, only that הרבה was altered into יתר, required by the prefix of מקונך, which word was apparently added by the voice from heaven.

Another important feature of the daughter-voice is, that in some cases it is audible only to those who are prepared to hear it. "Every day," says the rather mystically inclined R. Joshua ben Levi, "goes forth a voice from Mount Sinai, and makes proclama-

tion and says, 'Woe to the creatures for their contempt of the Torah.'"   As rightly pointed out by the
commentators, this voice is heard only by fine, sensitive natures that are susceptible to Divine messages
even after the discontinuance of prophecy.[24]   In this
case the daughter-voice becomes something quite subjective, and loses a great deal of its authoritative character.   The renegade Elisha ben Abuyah, or, as he is
commonly called, אחר, the "other one," in his despair
of "doing repentance", heard a voice coming straight
from behind the throne of God, saying unto him,
"Come back, ye backsliding children, except thou
'other one,'" and thus he abandoned himself to an
immoral life.[25]   Contrast this story with that of Manasseh, the worst sinner among the kings of Judah.
It is to this effect.   When the captains of the King of
Assyria defeated Manasseh and put him among thorns,
and inflicted upon him the most cruel tortures, he
invoked all the strange gods he was in the habit of
worshipping, but no relief came.   Suddenly he said,
"I remember my father once made me read the following verses (Deut. 4 : 30, 31), 'When thou art in
tribulation, and all these things are come upon thee,
. . . return thou to the Lord thy God.   For the Lord
thy God is a merciful God; he will not forsake thee
nor destroy thee.'"   He then began to address his
prayers to God.   The angels—in a most unangelic
way, I am sorry to say—shut up the gates of heaven
against his prayer, but the Holy One, blessed be he,
said, "If I do not receive him, I shut the gate in the

face of repentance.' And thus he was entreated of
him and heard his supplication.' " [26]   The moral of the
two stories is, that the " other one " trusted to fresh
messages, and went to perdition, while Manasseh fell
back upon the family Bible and was saved.   It is
probable that it was such moral catastrophes as recorded in the case of the "other one" which brought
the voice of heaven into disrepute.   The verdict of
the Rabbis in the second century was, that no attention is to be paid to it when it presumes to decide
against the moral conviction of the majority.   The
Torah is not in heaven. [27]   Its interpretation is left to
the conscience of catholic Israel.

Now it is this conscience of Israel which is not
satisfied with the lesson to be derived from the Scriptures at the first glance, or rather the first hearing,
but insists upon its expansion.   Thus when interpreting Lev. 19: 36, the Rabbis somehow managed to
derive from it the law of " let your speech be yea,
yea ; nay, nay." [28]   Again, when commenting upon
the seventh commandment, they interpreted it in such
a way as to include the prohibition of even an un-
chaste look or immoral thought. [29]   The rules of interpretation by which such maxims were derived from
the Scriptures would perhaps not satisfy the modern
philologian.   They, indeed, belong to the "second
sense " of the Scriptures, the sense which is the heart
and soul of all history and development.   "God hath
spoken once, twice I have heard this" (Ps. 62: 12),
which verse is interpreted by the Rabbis to mean that

Scripture is capable of many interpretations or hear-
ings.[30]   But it is interesting to find that these interpretations of the Scriptures tending to improve upon the
"first sense" are sometimes introduced by the formula:
"I might hear so-and-so, therefore there is a teaching
to say that," etc. שומע אני ... תלמוד לומר.[31]   Put into
modern language the formula means this: The words
of the Scriptures might be at the first glance (or first
hearing) conceived to have this or that meaning, but
if we consider the context or the way in which the
sentences are worded, we must arrive at a different
conclusion.   This parallel may perhaps throw some
light on the expression ἠκούσατε, "you have heard that
it was said . . . but I say unto you," a phrase frequent in the Sermon on the Mount.   After the
declaration made by Jesus of his attachment to the
Torah, it is not likely that he would quote passages
from it showing its inferiority.   The only way to get
over the difficulty is to assume that Jesus used some
such phrase as the one just quoted, שומע אני, "I might
hear," or "one might hear," that is to say, "one
might be mistaken in pressing the literal sense of the
verses in question too closely."   Against such a narrow way of dealing with Scripture he warned his disciples by some formula, as תלמוד לומר, "there is a
teaching to say that the words must not be taken in
such a sense."   But the formula being a strictly Rabbinic idiom, it was not rendered quite accurately by
the Greek translator.   Hence the apparent contradic-
tion between Matt. 3: 17, 20, and the matter follow-

ing upon these verses. I only wish to add that in
Rabbinic literature it is sometimes God himself who
undertakes such rectifications. Thus we read in an
ancient Midrash with reference to Jer. 4: 2, "And
thou shalt swear as the Lord liveth, in truth and in
judgment": "The Holy One, blessed be he, said
unto Israel, 'Think not that you may swear by my
name, even in truth. You may not do so unless you
have obtained that high degree of sanctity by which
Abraham, Joseph, and Job were distinguished, who
were called God-fearing men (יראי אלהים).'" This limi-
tation of swearing, even in truth, is indicated according to the Rabbis in Deut. 20: 10, which verse is interpreted to mean, "If thou fearest thy God, and art
exclusively in his service, thou mayest swear by his
name," not otherwise.[32]

Having mentioned the name of the patriarch, I
may perhaps state the fact that, beside the epithets
"the God-fearing" Abraham, or Abraham "the friend
of God," Abraham also bears in Rabbinic literature
the title of Rock. The wording of the Rabbinical
passage and the terms used in it will not be uninteresting to the student of the New Testament. In
Matt. 16: 18 we read: "And I also say unto thee,
that thou art *Petros*, and upon this *petra* I will build
my church." The Rabbinic passage forms an illustration of Num. 23: 9, "For from the top of the
rocks I see him," and runs thus: There was a king
who desired to build, and to lay foundations he dug
constantly deeper, but found only a swamp. At last

he dug and found a *petra* (this is the very word the Rabbi uses). He said, "On this spot I shall build and lay the foundations." So the Holy One, blessed be he, desired to create the world, but meditating upon the generations of Enoch and the deluge, he said, "How shall I create the world seeing that those wicked men will only provoke me?" But as soon as God perceived that there would rise an Abraham, he said, "Behold, I have found the *petra* upon which to build and to lay foundations." Therefore he called Abraham Rock, as it is said, "Look unto the rock whence ye are hewn. Look unto Abraham, your father" (Isa. 51: 1, 2).[33]

The parallels given so far have been more according to the letter. I will now give one or two parallels according to the spirit.

I have already referred to the attempts made by various authors to describe the life and times of Jesus Christ. The best book of this class is undoubtedly Schürer's *History of the Jewish People in the Age of Jesus Christ*. It is a very learned work, particularly as far as the Greek and Roman documents are concerned. Its treatment of such topics as the geography of Palestine, the topography of Jerusalem, the plan of the Temple, and kindred subjects, is almost perfect. A most excellent feature in it is the completeness of its bibliography, there being hardly any dissertation or article in any of the learned periodicals which is not duly registered by the author. But all these fine things are, to use a quaint Rabbinic phrase, only "after-courses of wisdom." Bibliography in particular is not even an after-course. It partakes more of the nature of the menu served sometimes by very ignorant waiters, possessing neither judgment nor discretion. The general vice attaching to this whole class of works is, that no attempt is made in them to gain acquaintance with the inner life of the Jewish nation at the period about which they write. Take, for instance, the subject of prayer. Considering that pre-Christian Judaism gave to the world the Psalms, and that post-Christian Judaism produced one of the richest liturgies; considering again that among the various prayers which have come down to us through the medium of the Talmud, there is also one that forms a close parallel to the "Lord's Prayer;" considering all this, one might expect that also in the times of Jesus the Jews were able to pray, and in fact did pray. The contents of their prayers might be of the greatest importance for the student, expressing as they probably did the religious sentiments of the age and the ideal aspirations of the nation. But what our theological waiters dish up is a minimum of prayer dressed up in a quantity of rubrics, in such a fashion as to stigmatise their authors as miserable pedants. And no attempt is made to enter into the spirit of even this minimum. No explanation is given, for instance, of the meaning of the terms "the kingdom of heaven," the yoke of which the Rabbi was supposed to receive upon himself, the "Hear, O Israel," etc. The terms "sanctification of the name of God," "Father in heaven," and "renewed world," are also frequent in Jewish literature and in the Jewish prayer-book, but no sufficient attention is given to them. To my knowledge Dalman is the only modern Christian scholar who recognises the importance of these terms, and similar ones, in their bearing upon a clearer understanding of the New Testament, and has at least made an attempt at their analysis in his book, *Die Worte Jesu.*

Another important point, which has never been properly examined, is the unique position which the *Keneseth Israel*, the congregation of Israel, or ideal Israel, occupies in Rabbinic theology. Yet it forms a striking parallel to that held by Jesus in Christian theology. The Keneseth Israel was, like the Spirit of the Messiah, created before the world was called into existence. "She is the beloved of God, in whom he rejoices;" and there is no endearing epithet in the language, such as son, daughter, brother, sister, bride, mother, lamb, or eye, which is not, according to the Rabbis, applied by the Scriptures to express the intimate relation between God and the Keneseth Israel. Not even the title of "god," of which God is otherwise so jealous, is denied to Israel, as it is written, "I have said, Ye are gods." Nay, God even says to Moses, "Exalt Israel as much as thou canst, for it is as if thou wert exalting me;" whilst he who denies Israel or rises against Israel denies God. In fact, it is only through the witness of Israel that God is God, and he would cease to be so were Israel to disappear, as it is written, "Ye are my witnesses, . . . and I am

God." [34]   But there is no fear of such a calamity.
Israel is as eternal as the universe, and forms the
rock on which the world was built.   As a rock tower-
ing up in the sea, so the Keneseth Israel stands out in
history, defying all tempests and temptations; for
"many waters cannot quench the love" between God
and the Keneseth Israel.[35]   She is, indeed, approached
by Satan and the nations of the world with the sedu-
cing words, "What is thy beloved more than another?
Beautiful and lovely thou art, if thou wilt mingle
among us.   Why dost thou permit thyself to go
through fire for his sake, to be crucified for his
name?   Come unto us, where all the dignities in our
power await thee."   But Israel resists all temptations; they point to their connexion with God
throughout their history, to his love unto them, shown
by conferring upon them the gift of holiness, which
even a Balaam envied, and to the promise held out to
them of the Messianic times, when suffering will cease
and Israel will revel in the glory of God." [36]   These
few quotations suffice to show what an interesting
chapter might be added to our knowledge of comparative theology.

Again, our knowledge of the spiritual history of
the Jews during the first centuries of our era might be
enriched by a chapter on miracles.   Starting from the
principle that miracles can be explained only by more
miracles, an attempt was made some years ago by a
student to draw up a list of the wonder-workings of
the Rabbis recorded in the Talmud and the Midra-

shim.   He applied himself to the reading of these
works, but his reading was only cursory.   The list
therefore is not complete.   Still it yielded a harvest
of not less than two hundred and fifty miracles.
They cover all classes of supernatural workings
recorded in the Bible, but occur with much greater
frequency.

A repetition of these miracles would be tiresome.
I will content myself with reproducing a story from
Tractate Chagigah, which will illustrate to you how
much even the individual Jew shared in the glories
conferred upon the Keneseth Israel.   I am speaking,
of course, of that individual who is described by the
Rabbis as one " who labours in the Torah for its own
sake, who is called a lover of God and a lover of
humanity.   Unto him kingdom and authority are
given.   Unto him the secrets of the Torah are revealed."   The term "authority," by the way, is
given with the word ממשלה, suggested probably by
Ben Sira 45 : 17, וימשילהו בחוק ומשפט, "and he made
him have authority over statute and judgment;"
whilst Matt. 7 : 29, "and he taught them as one having authority," was probably suggested by Ben Sira
3 : 10, ומושל בה ילמדנה, "and he who has authority
over it shall teach it."   As a man of such authority
we may consider R. Johanan ben Zakkai, the hero of
the story I am about to relate.   He was the younger
member of the " Eighty Club " of the school of Hillel,
and thus a contemporary of the Apostles, though he
survived them.   He was an eye-witness of the terrible

catastrophe of the destruction of the Temple by the
Romans, an event which he prophesied forty years
before it took place.   He is best known by the school
he established in Jabneh, whither the Sanhedrin, and
with them the Divine Presence presiding over this
assembly, emigrated after the fall of Jerusalem.   There
(in Jabneh) he died about 108 c. e.

It is related that Rabbi Johanan ben Zakkai was
riding upon his ass on the road, while his pupil, R.
Eleazar ben Arach, was walking behind him.   Said R.
Eleazar to him, "Master, teach me a chapter about
the matter relating to the chariot," that is, the vision
in the first chapter of Ezekiel.   The master declined,
preferring to hear the pupil.   R. Eleazar said again,
"Wilt thou permit me to repeat in thy presence one
thing which thou hast taught me?" to which he gave
his assent.   R. Johanan then dismounted from his
ass, and wrapped himself in his gown, and seated himself upon a stone under an olive-tree.   He said it was
disrespectful that he should be riding on his beast,
whilst his pupil was lecturing on such awful mysteries,
and the *Shechinah* (the Divine Presence) and the
Malache ha-Shareth (the angels-in-waiting) were accompanying them.   Immediately R. Eleazar began his
exposition.   And there came down fire from heaven
and encircled them and the whole field.   And the
angels assembled and came to hearken, as the sons of
men assemble and come to look on at the festivities
of bride and bridegroom.   And the terebinth-trees in
the field opened their mouths and uttered a song,

" Praise the Lord from the earth, ye dragons and all deeps. . . . Fruitful trees and all cedars, . . . praise ye the Lord." And an angel answered from the fire and said, " This is the matter of the chariot." When he had finished, R. Johanan ben Zakkai stood up and kissed him on his head, saying, " Praised be the God of Abraham, Isaac, and Jacob, who has given our father Abraham a wise son, who knows how to discourse on the glory of our Father in heaven." So much for the story. I need hardly recall to your mind the parallels in the Book of Enoch and in the New Testament.[37]

My lecture is at an end, not so the subject it treats. To accomplish the latter in a properly critical and scientific manner the aid of fellow-workers is necessary. I have often heard the wish expressed that a history of the rise of Christianity might be written by a Jew who could bring Rabbinic learning to bear upon the subject. I do not think that the time is as yet ripe for such an experiment. The best thing to be done at present is, that Christians devote themselves to the study of Rabbinic literature. The history which would be written after such study would certainly be more scientific and more critical, though perhaps less edifying.

THE MEMOIRS OF A JEWESS OF THE SEVENTEENTH CENTURY[1]

Professor Doctor Kaufmann has, by his edition of the *Memoiren der Glückel von Hameln*, earned the thanks of all Jewish students as well as of the Jewish public at large. It is hardly necessary to say that these Memoirs are well edited. "With the great nothing is small." And everyone who has the good fortune to be acquainted with Dr. Kaufmann's works, knows that whatever he did—whether he wrote on the history of the attributes of God in Jewish philosophy, or pointed out the greatness of George Eliot to his countrymen, or described for us the importance of the Anglo-Jewish ritual, or edited the registers of some obscure Jewish community—he did it well, in a thorough, scientific, and scholarly manner. And so these Memoirs, too, are provided with an excellent introduction, in which he not only gives an account of the manuscript from which his edition was prepared, but brings to bear upon his subject all the cognate contemporary literature both in print and in manuscript, whilst the footnotes giving explanations of many strange words and odd observations in the text prove greatly helpful to the reader.

But it must not be inferred from this that the Memoirs belong to Dr. Kaufmann's minor work. Only to those to whom Jewish literature is a mere exhibition of so many Books of the Dead—to be relegated to their dusty shelves after a brief study of the title-page—will the contents of these Memoirs appear trifling and unimportant. Those, however, to whom literature means life, with all its varying phases of folly and wisdom, of grief and joy, happiness and misery, will find in these Memoirs a source of infinite delight and instruction, revealing the history of a life extending over nearly three-quarters of a century. But what is more important is that these revelations come from the heart of a woman. Jewish literature on the whole is not rich in " Lives," but an autobiography written by a woman is an almost unique phenomenon in it.

Frau Glückel Hameln, the author of these Memoirs, was the daughter of Löb Pinkerle, the Parnas or president of the Jewish community in Hamburg. He was a man of great influence among his Jewish fellow-citizens, and is described by his daughter as the means of procuring for his brethren the permission to re-settle in that city after their temporary expulsion from it about this period. Glückel, who was born in 1647, was a child of three years when this expulsion took place.

By this date the reader will at once be prepared not to expect from her a description or a diary in the modern sense of the word. In the seventeenth century people were not yet inclined to undergo the process of self-vivisection, constantly registering their moods and humours and parading them before the world.

Self-torture was not yet considered bliss, and to go down on one's knees and pray to God for a handsome lord was not looked upon as a special act of intellectual spirituality. Matrimonial arrangements were quietly left to the parents. Our Glückel, in particular, with the many vicissitudes and cares which life brought to her, had hardly time for introspection. She was a simple-minded woman, a mere "mother in Israel" and as foolish as all mothers, hence doomed to many a disappointment with her children ; idolising her husband and in consequence almost broken-hearted after his death, and so proud of her own and her husband's family, which she probably overrated, that her own individuality was sunk in theirs. All the more do we hear from her about her connexions and relatives, who were mostly prominent members of the Jewish congregations scattered over a great part of Germany. Her Memoirs thus gain a particular interest, giving us as they do an insight into the social life of the important Jewish communities of Hamburg, Metz, and Altona, such as no other source affords.

Her first recollections date from Altona, to which place (only about a mile from Hamburg) her family removed after the expulsion already mentioned. Altona, in which they found a Jewish community consisting of about twenty-five families, formed at that time a part of the dominions of the "righteous and pious King Frederick III of Denmark." [2] The Jews were, it would seem, permitted to carry on business in their old home during the daytime, after procuring from the Mayor of Hamburg a special passport, for which they had to pay a tax of a ducat, and which had to be renewed every month. If the Jew was so fortunate as to have acquaintances among the politicians, the month was extended to eight weeks. But neither taxes nor the authority of the chief magistrate could protect them against the insolence of the Hamburg mob, so " that every woman thanked the Lord when she saw her husband in peace " back in Altona as the evening approached.[3]

Her family was the first to return to Hamburg. But Glückel had little confidence in the Senate, who were instigated by the clergy not to suffer the Jews to take possession of their old places of worship. As we know from another account, the Lutheran ministers advised the Senate not to grant this privilege to the Jews unless they agreed to the appointment of a " Christian Rabbi " to preach the Gospel in their synagogues. " It lasted a long while," Glückel says, " till we crept back (that is, returned slowly) to our synagogues. May the Lord, in the abundance of his mercy and lovingkindness, have compassion with us and send us our righteous Messiah, when we shall serve him in the integrity of our hearts and shall offer our prayers in the holy Temple in the holy city of Jerusalem. Amen." [4]

With Glückel these words were not a mere phrase. She had cause enough to be eagerly expectant of a redeemer. She was a child of three or four when the Cossack leader, Bogdan Chmielnicki, let loose his

savage hordes against the defenceless Jews of Poland.
Tens of thousands were massacred, many more perished by famine and exposure to cold and all sorts of
disease.   Some, however, managed to escape "the
sword of the hero of holy Orthodox Russia," and
fled to Germany.   Of these many found their way
to Hamburg and Altona, which were overcrowded
with the refugees.   Old Löb Pinkerle, as the Parnas
of the Jewish community, had a hard time of it in
providing these unfortunates with subsistence and
employment.   "It was after this event," Glückel
writes, "that the Wilna Jews ran away from Poland.
Many came to Hamburg.   They were afflicted with
a contagious disease, but we had then no hospital in
Hamburg . . . . and my father, of blessed memory,
accommodated ten of them in the upper floor of the
house."   Her grandmother, who, in spite of all the
remonstrances of her children, insisted on visiting
them four times a day and took care that they should
be wanting in nothing, caught the malady and died
after a few days.   Glückel also caught the contagion.
This was the first severe illness through which she
passed.[5]

The office of Parnas was thus in those troubled
times not very pleasant.   But even this doubtful privilege—of converting his house into a hospital and
endangering the lives of its inmates—poor Pinkerle
was not allowed to enjoy in peace.   As Glückel tells
us, his high dignity was contested by certain malicious
people, who, playing the part of informers to the

Danish Government, tried by these slanderous means
to replace him in the office of Parnas. Pinkerle and
his colleagues had to repair at once to Copenhagen ;
but the court was convinced of their innocence, and
matters were soon settled to the satisfaction of the old
Parnas.[6]

All this occurred before our Glückel reached the
age of twelve, with which year her childhood was
brought to an end. Through the age of girlhood—
the age of lofty dreams and low realities—she never
passed. For her twelfth birthday finds her engaged
to Chayim Hameln, and at fourteen she is married
to him.[7]

The town to which Glückel was transplanted
through her marriage was Hameln, an out-of-the-
way place in the northwest of Germany, better
known to legend than to history. She tells us of the
annoyance caused to her mother by the impossibility
to procure respectable coaches for the journey. They
had to make their way from Hanover to Hameln with
all the wedding train on mean peasant-carts. Her
father-in-law, Joseph Hameln, comforts them with the
fact, that many years back, when he set out to marry,
no vehicles at all were to be found, and, though the
son of the Parnas of all Hessen, he had to make his
entry on foot into Stadthagen, where his dear Freud-
chen lived, whilst his companion Fisch carried the
dowry on his shoulders.[8]

Glückel dwells with evident delight on everything
relating to her new home. The first who won her

heart was, as it would seem, her father-in-law, the amiable and venerable Joseph Hameln, who, together with his wife, gave her much "calmness of spirit." "Who can describe," she exclaims, "their charity and piety, and with what kindness and consideration they treated me; far better than I deserved." She is not quite insensible to the dulness and dreariness of Hameln, which was a petty village in comparison with her native place, only two Jewish families living there. But she quite forgets Hamburg when she thinks of her saintly and energetic father-in-law. He got up every morning at three o'clock, dressed himself in his synagogue suit (*Schulrock*), and read aloud his prayer or other religious book. Her room adjoined his, and the opportunity of observing him and listening to him when he prays or studies fully compensates her for all the delights of the Hanseatic city. And what pious and noble children his were! What a sage her brother-in-law, Reb Abraham! He spoke little, but every word that escaped his mouth "was sheer *Chochma*" (wisdom). As a youth he was sent to Poland, which was then a great centre of Talmudical learning, and he "was full of Torah as a pomegranate is full of seed." Her other brother-in-law, Reb Shmuel, also went to Poland for the purpose of studying. The two brothers there made excellent matches, especially the latter (Shmuel), who married a woman of "a very noble family," the daughter of the great Reb Shulem, the Chief Rabbi of Lemberg.[9]

The Chmielnicki persecution, already referred to,

brought both brothers back to Germany with their
families, and they had to commence life over again.
Shmuel was soon elected Chief Rabbi of Hildesheim, where he lived and died as a saint. Another
of her numerous brothers-in-law was Reb Löb
Bon, a fine character, who, though not a student,
was still "a beautiful knower of books" (*i. e.*, fairly
read in lighter Hebrew literature), who was for a long
time Parnas in the Cologne province. And what a
noble and modest woman her sister-in-law Esther—a
great sufferer, one who bore her affliction with
patience and submission to God! [10]

The most important of the Hamelns—to Glückel
at least—was her husband, Chayim Hameln, the
eighth son of Joseph Hameln. Though she probably never saw him before her wedding, she very soon
finds that the "great, dear God" has "brought them
together and guided them well." She hardly ever
mentions him without the endearing epithet of "the
crown of my head." He is her saint, who, though
in very delicate health and working himself half dead
to earn a living for his family, never omits to go
through his fixed readings in the Torah and to fast on
Mondays and Thursdays. She knew few Rabbis,
Glückel maintains, who read their prayers with so
much devotion (*Kawono*) as her husband did, and he
would not interrupt them even at the risk of losing
great opportunities. To her he is "the consummation of a good Jew," patient and forgiving, modest to
a fault, never putting up as a candidate for any honor-

ary office in the community and exceedingly honest in money transactions.[11] Glückel is not a little proud of the fact that such a saint and good Jew held her in high esteem and kept her "like the apple of his eye," [12] and never consulted anybody but her, though she was so young.[13]

The newly-married couple found Hameln, as it seems, too small a place for their commercial enterprises, and moved soon to Hamburg, where they settled as dealers in jewelry. There they lived in a fair state of prosperity for thirty-eight years, Chayim travelling far and wide, carrying his trade to Leipzig, Frankfort, and Amsterdam, and Glückel attending to her household and nursing the children. Anxious for his health, she prevailed upon him to take a partner, and she sits up the whole night drawing up the contracts. I am sorry to say that the partnership did not prove a success, and she gets a mild scolding for all her kindness.[14] The occasional losses of money, death of relatives, illness of children (who came in rapid succession to the number of twelve), belong to the regular programme of life, and the Hamelns had their share of sorrow as any other mortals. "The Almighty is just," Glückel comforts herself. "We sinful creatures know not what is good. What we look upon as the greatest evil, turns out to be the best fortune which has ever befallen us." [15]

The affairs of the Jewish community, of which the younger Hamelns are now prominent members, are also conducted wisely and soberly by the sage

Parnasim, the congregation incurring no new debts, so that there is very little reason for excitement.[16] The spiritual life is, as everywhere, concentrated in the synagogue. The *Chalphanim* (money-brokers), who apparently constituted a large part of the Hamburg congregation, Glückel tells us, go, after the day's work is over, to the synagogue, where they read Minchah. Thence they proceed to their various *Chebrahs* (a sort of religious club), to study Torah there.[17]

The only great public event during Glückel's residence in her native place worth recording, was the rise of the Pseudo-Messiah Sabbatai Zebi. The Messianic fever which spread from the East was soon caught by almost the whole of European Jewry, and raged most violently in Hamburg.

"About this time" (1665 ?), Glückel reports, "people began to talk of Sabbatai Zebi. Woe unto us, for we have sinned. . . When I think of the 'repentance done' by young and old I despair of describing it. . . And what joy when there arrived letters from Smyrna! Most of these were addressed to the Sephardim. To their synagogue the Germans, too, betook themselves to hear the letters read. The Sephardic youth attending the meetings appeared in their best dress, and wore the colours (green) of Sabbatai Zebi. Many sold their houses and farms, and thus prepared for early emigration. My father-in-law left his house and furniture in Hameln and moved to Hildesheim (to join the Jewish community there in the new exodus), and even sent us to Hamburg two

boxes full of good things as provisions for the way "
(to Palestine). . . All proved an illusion after nearly
three years of excitement. "O my God and Lord,
still thy people Israel despair not, but trust to thy
mercy that thou wilt redeem them whenever it will
be thy holy pleasure to do so. . . I am certain that
thou wouldst long before have had mercy with us,
were we but to fulfil the commandment, 'Thou shalt
love thy neighbour as thyself.' " [18]

The marriage of their daughter Zipporah with
Kossman Gomperz, the son of Elia Gomperz, of
Emmerich, was the great event in the Hameln family.
For Elia was the most prominent Jew in the Prus-
sian provinces, and was held in much esteem by the
Court of the great Elector Frederick William, of
Brandenburg, who employed him in various political
missions to the Dutch Republic. In fact, people were
not willing to believe that the match would ever come
off, considering that Gomperz was a regular German
Kazin (Prince in Israel), whilst the Hamelns had no
claim to such distinction. The wedding, which took
place in Cleves, where they went with a suite of
twenty people, accompanied, as it seems, by a band of
musicians, was the triumph of Glückel's life. The
house in which the guests were lodged resembled a
regular palace, magnificently furnished, and they were
constantly receiving visits from the local aristocracy,
who came to see the bride. "And," fond and foolish
a mother as Glückel was, she adds, "for a truth, my
daughter looked so beautiful that nothing ever seen

could be compared with her." At the ceremony itself, there were present, besides so many people of noble birth, Frederick III, the future king of Prussia, and Prince Maurice of Nassau, holding all the time the hand of her dear Mordecai, a boy of five years, who, attired in his best frock, was declared to be "the prettiest child in the world." There came also to the wedding many influential members of the Jewish-Sephardic community (in Amsterdam). "One among them was named Mocatti, who traded in diamonds. They were all so much occupied in preparing a proper reception for those high personages that they even forgot to write the *Kethubah*, so that the officiating Rabbi had to read it from a book."[19] The festivities concluded with the appearance of masks, who performed the death dance. Mrs. Lily Grove, in her charming and learned book, "Dancing," says that it is still customary in some parts of Germany to perform it at weddings. "The name sounds gruesome, but it is a merry sport, in which kissing is not forgotten."

The Memoirs, besides their bearing upon the social history of our ancestors in ages gone by, of which illustrations have been given above, have also a certain theological interest, which must not be left unnoticed. The interest will perhaps be the greater since we live in a time in which ignorance has almost succeeded in making the world believe that it was only with the introducing of the holy rite of confirmation that Jewish women were brought under the influence of the synagogue.

The reader hardly expects to meet with a Jewish St. Theresa. Glückel was not a *réligieuse*. Piety was not her profession. "I do not consider myself *fromm*" (pious), she says, "I am actually a sinful woman exempt from very few transgressions. O that I might be worthy to supplicate (for mercy) and to be really repentant." The call she received—which, let us hope, was not less Divine than that ever heard by any Abbess in the Middle Ages, or any lady settlement worker about to devote her life to the cause of Humanity in modern times—was to be a mother, and as such she was soon absorbed by her household duties, nursing her darlings, and assisting her husband in various ways. After his death (1689), the whole burden of the family fell on her; she had both to carry on his business and to attend to the bringing up of her eight orphans. She had thus little time left for performing real or apparent devotions. Nor do we think that she could lay any claim to a " superior education." Her Memoirs are written in Hebrew letters, but the language is the current Jüdisch-Deutsch of the time. Her father, she tells us, had his children instructed both in things heavenly and things worldly.[20] By the latter she probably understood some knowledge of French and playing on the " Klaffenzimmer " (Clavier), in which art her half-sister was highly accomplished.[21] We may also assume that she knew sufficient Hebrew to read her daily prayers and to understand various familiar phrases and terms, which became almost a part of the language of the Judengasse. But we doubt whether she was ever able to

read a Hebrew book with ease. At least we know
that when she wished to make herself acquainted with
the contents of R. Abraham Hurwitz's Ethical Will,
she had to have it read to her in an *extempore* German
translation.[22] The store from which she drew her
spiritual nourishment was, apart from the Bible, that
edifying literature written in Jüdisch-Deutsch so
admirably described in an essay by the late Dr. P. F.
Frankl on the *Erbauungslectüre unserer Altvorderen.*[23]
But such books could be and were probably read by
all who were educated at the Cheder in their youth,
as Glückel had been.[24] Her views about God and the
world offer thus nothing exceptional, but just on that
account they are the more interesting to us as representing the general way of thinking by Jewish women
of that age.

She opens her Memoirs with the words: " What-
soever the Holy One, blessed be he, created, he
created but for his glory. The world is built up by
mercy. We know that God, praised be he and
praised be his name, does not require us . . . . but
created everything out of sheer lovingkindness and
mercy." [25] This is followed by a long theodicy explaining and justifying the ways of Providence. Her rea-
soning is just as little cogent as that of all other
theodicies. The real point is that, she herself being
convinced of the soundness of her argument, hers
was a just God, and she had not to face the taunt
hurled against those who, carrying the doctrine of
necessity to its utmost consequences, were told that

they ought to add to their creed : " I believe in God
because he is unjust."

The conception of God's mercy and love pervades
all of Glückel's thoughts. She expresses herself in
the following way : " The great good God is merciful.
We are his children. His mercy upon us surpasses
that of a father (of flesh and blood). For this latter
may sometimes lose patience with his wicked son and
disown him at last; but we poor children are constantly sinning against God. Still the great, good
Heavenly Father, in spite of the impurity attaching to
us through our transgressions, tells us that we have
only to repent of our sins, and he will again receive
us as his children. Hence, my heartily beloved
children, despair not. . . . . The Lord *is* merciful
and gracious, long-suffering, to righteous and to
sinners alike." [26]　Even suffering and pain are only an
effluence of God's goodness. The sinful creatures are
mischievous children in whose education the great
gracious God takes a pleasure, so that we may be
worthy children and servants of our Father and
Lord.[27] "I implore you," she says to her children,
"to accept everything that God sends (suffering
and pain) in a humble and submissive spirit, and never
cease to pray to him. We sinful creatures know not
what is really good for us." [28]　We ought to rejoice in
suffering and thank God for it. And on a certain
occasion of great grief and loss which she could not
help feeling deeply, she reproached herself with the
words : " I know that this complaining and mourning

is a weakness of mine. It would be much better for me to praise and thank the great and gracious God for all his mercy toward such an unworthy woman as I am. How many better and worthier people are there who have not the means of defraying even a single meal." [29] On another similar sad occasion she says: "And for all this I thank and praise thee, my Creator, who, even in thy chastisement, showest to me, an unworthy, sinful woman, more grace and mercy than I deserve, and teachest me through these troubles patience and humility. . . . I do pray thee, Almighty good God, for thy grace, which will give me the strength to serve thee, so that I may not appear in a state of impurity before thee." [30]

The appearance before God takes place after death when man has " to give account and reckoning before the King of kings, the Holy One, blessed be he." This belief in immortality, which permeates all her thoughts, forms a part of Glückel's theodicy; for it is in the next world that man has to pay his real debts or has to expect his real reward, wherefore he should submit to suffering in meekness and joy as a means of salvation. [31] The terror of sin consists partly in this, that in some mystical way it takes possession of man's soul, so that not even death can relieve him, and it accompanies him to the next world. [32] In brief, the soul is given in trust to man only for a certain time, returning unto him who has given it to us. [33] And when the " crown of her head " was so roughly removed by the premature death of her husband, her comfort

was that he was transplanted to a better and eternal
world.   "It is for us," she continues, "to pray that our
end should be in accordance with his will and pleasure, and that it should please the Most High to bring
us to the *Gan Eden*." [34]   The world is a stormy sea
full of dangerous temptations, in which man is easily
drowned.   But the Torah is the life-belt which the
great, gracious God has thrown out in these bottom-
less depths that man may get hold of it and be saved.
This is the meaning of the words in the Scripture,
" Therefore choose life." [35]

This was the belief of Jewish men and Jewish
women for thousands of years, and we would hardly
dwell on it but for the fact that a certain class of
amateur theologians, who supply our periodical literature with divinity and morality, show a strong bias
to make the doctrine of immortality an exclusive
monopoly of Christianity.   Whatever may have been
the attitude of ancient Judaism towards this doctrine,
there can be little doubt that belief in reward and
punishment after death has been an essential dogma
of the Synagogue for more than two thousand years.
" The way to eternal life or salvation is given in the
holy beloved Torah."

The term Heavenly Father is with Glückel, as with
many Jewish moralists, a favourite expression.   And,
she argues, if we are commanded in the Torah to
honour our parents, how much more careful must we
be to honour our Father in heaven, and not do anything that might call forth the anger of the great,

kindly God.[36] " The readiness of our ancestor Abraham to sacrifice his only son Isaac at the command of
God—and I, as a mother, know that parents suffer
more at seeing their children in affliction than when
they are themselves in pain—should alone suffice as
an example how to serve God, and to give up for
his sake all worldly considerations and joys." [37]

Another main point is, Thou shalt love thy
neighbour as thyself, which, she says, "is so little
observed in our generation." "We know," she
says, "that it is the Most High who said it, and if we
were truly pious from the bottom of our hearts and
not so bad as we are, I am certain that God would
have mercy with us, if we would only keep the said
law." [38] It is interesting to notice how like a child
Glückel speaks of the law and its commandments.
When reading of the crime of certain of her co-religion-
ists, who tried to hide it afterwards, she says, " But it is
written in our *Ten Words*, 'Thou shalt not steal,' and
therefore the Omnipresent, blessed be he, did not help
them." [39] But with wives and mothers the first lessons
in altruism are given in the family circle, and charity
begins with them at home; "for the great Heavenly
Father and only God has established in his wisdom "
that we first love our children, then our near relatives;
otherwise the world could not exist.[40] There is,
indeed, a certain practical vein running through the
whole of these Memoirs, showing that she well knew
how to take care of herself. But even in her harsh
moments, which are usually when she thinks that

the offspring of Chayim and Glückel Hameln are not so well treated by the world as they deserve, she is always under the control of religion, and reproaches herself for her complaints. "Great, Only God, I implore thee from the depth of my heart to forgive me, because it is possible that I have wronged him (the enemy of her son). Perhaps he acted as he did (with the best intentions) for God's sake." [41] On another similar occasion she prays that the Name, blessed be he, should forgive those who enticed a relative of hers to live in Hameln, which was the cause of great misfortune and misery to him. Lastly, we give here her injunctions to her children for whose benefit these Memoirs were composed, and whom she entreats to be indulgent with her as she was in great distress when she wrote them. "Serve God," she says, "my dear children, with all your hearts, without hypocrisy and falsehood. . . . Say your prayers with devotion and awe. . . . and do not interrupt them by talk, which you must consider as a great sin. . . . But have a fixed time for the study of the Torah every day. Attend diligently to your business, for the providing a livelihood for one's wife and children is a great religious work (*Mitzwah*). In particular, be honest in your money dealings, both with Jews and non-Jews, so that the name of Heaven be not profaned through you. If you have in hand money or wares of other people, then be more anxious about them than if they were your own ; so that you, God forbid, wrong nobody. The first question put to man in the next world is, whether he was faithful in his money transactions." [42] " I give thanks and praise to God," she says somewhere, "who enabled me to leave Hamburg without owing a farthing to Jew or Christian." [43]

Glückel survived her husband for nearly thirty-five years. It is a gloomy, hard life which she leads, full of care, anxiety, and trouble. She travels far and wide to the great fairs, which expose her to the most unbearable heat in summer and bitterest cold in winter, and spends the days in her warehouse.[44] As it would seem, her plans were, after settling her children in life, "to give up the vanities of the world, and, as every pious and good Jewess ought to do, emigrate to Palestine to serve there the Lord with all her soul and all her might." [45] But this was not to be. For her children, aware of her intentions, are naturally anxious to retain her near them ; and it is at their urging that, after having refused many proposals, she allows herself to be persuaded to enter wedlock for a second time with Cerf Levy of Metz, where her daughter Esther Schwab lived. The wedding with Cerf Levy, the Parnas of the Jewish community and the greatest banker in Lorraine, took place in Metz in 1700 ; and with it begins a new series of misery and distress in Glückel's life. For Levy, after two years (1702), fails in his business, the firm is ruined, and Glückel, who is so proud of her good name in the commercial world, has the mortification to see her husband unable to fulfil his obligations toward his creditors. The little fortune she brought to him was also lost, and they had to live on a grant from his children. Levy dies a broken-hearted man in 1712. Glückel, who always dreaded the thought of becoming a burden to her children, lived for three years longer in great isolation and privation, till at last (1715) starvation compelled her to yield to the entreaties of her good daughter Esther, who was the support and the consolation of her old age. Glückel despairs of doing justice to Esther's virtues. She is modest, saving, and an excellent housekeeper, and her mother-in-law, Frau Jachet-Agathe Schwab, bears witness to the superiority of Esther to herself in the great art of preparing nice dishes. She is very regular in her attendance at the synagogue, never absenting herself from any Divine service. Her house is open wide to the poor, and her table is always adorned by the presence of her Rabbi (a sort of domestic chaplain) and that of an alumnus of the Talmudical College.[46] She and her husband, who is now Parnas of the community, are popular with poor and rich, all enjoying their hospitality. As to Glückel herself, they are exceedingly kind to her, "showing her all the honours in the world" and treating her with great consideration and regard. "May Heaven reward them" for all their goodness.[47]

Glückel, who continued her Memoirs to 1719, died on the 19th of September, 1724. She departed from this world "with a good name." The Memoirs were copied out by her grandson, Moses Hameln, Chief Rabbi of Baiersdorf. After a hundred and seventy-two years of dead silence Glückel speaks to us again. And her words are well worth listening to.

SAINTS AND SAINTLINESS[1]

Some two years ago, in a conversation with a lady of the Jewish persuasion, of high culture and wide reading, she made the remark to me that, as far as she knows, Judaism is the only one among the great religions which has never produced a saint, and that there is, indeed, no room in it for that element of saintliness which, in other creeds, forms the goal the true believer endeavors to reach. The conclusion which she drew from this alleged fact was, that good enough as Judaism may prove for the daily wear and tear of life, men and women of finer texture of soul than the common run of humanity must look to other religions for higher aspirations than to that which had come down to her from her ancestors.

Strange as such an assertion must appear to the student of Hebrew literature, I was not altogether surprised at her statements, considering the religious environment in which she had been brought up. Carlyle said of Voltaire that " he dearly loved truth, but of the triumphant kind." My lady-friend loved Judaism fairly in her own patronising way, but her Judaism was of the sane and plausible kind. It made no demand on faith. It was devoid of dogma, and shunned everything in the nature of a doctrine. Its great virtue consisted in its elasticity, in being adaptable to the latest result of the latest reconstruction of the Bible, and in being compatible with any system of philosophy ever advanced,—provided, of course, that the system in question was still a subject of languid conversation in fashionable drawing-rooms. Above all, Judaism was with her a sober religion, hostile to all excesses of mysticism and enthusiasm, all prudence and common sense, but little of wisdom and less of soul and emotion. But enthusiasm and mysticism are the very soil upon which saintliness thrives best. It is, therefore, not to be wondered at if Saints and Saintliness were excluded from Judaism as conceived by her and her teachers.

It is not my intention to enter into a controversy as to such a conception of Judaism. Starting afresh in the world as we did, to a certain extent, at the end of the eighteenth century, it was only natural that with the zeal of new converts we should be eager to assimilate all sorts of ideas; and whilst we have learned a good deal of Latin, a good deal of Greek, a good deal of history, and also acquired some methodical habits in our scientific work,—for all of which benefits we ought to feel truly grateful,—we have been at the same time too much accessible to all kinds of rationalistic platitudes, and to a sort of free-thinking and materialistic dogmatism long ago obsolete among the great majority of thinkers. It is ample time that we become free men, and begin to use our powers of discretion. We ought to remember that we live now in the twentieth century, not at the end of the eighteenth. True, the twentieth century is still in its infancy, and has hardly had time to develop a line of thought of its own. But as it is the heir of the past, we know that among the ideals bequeathed to it by the last decades of the nineteenth century which it cherishes most, are the following: That in religion catholicity is good, sectarianism is bad; that great religions can live only on ideas and ideals, not on mere organisation; that plausibility is more often a sign of mediocrity than a test of truth; that soberness is good, but that inspiration and enthusiasm are better, and that every religion wanting in the necessary sprinkling of Saints and Saintliness is doomed in the end to degenerate into commonplace virtues in action, and Philistinism in thought, certain to disappear at the first contact with higher life and higher thought.

It will readily be perceived that under these altered conditions of thought there must be much in the scheme of salvation drawn up some seventy or eighty years ago that is badly in need of revision. And this revision does take place, in spite of all the frenzied attacks upon romanticism, mysticism, and Orientalism. The only section of humanity never afflicted with this last vice were, as far as I know, the Red Indians. They were good Western gentlemen *sans reproche*, without a taint of Orientalism and all its terrible consequences. However, I do not wish to argue this point just now. Here we shall confine ourselves to the subject of Saints and Saintliness in Judaism, an aspect of Judaism almost entirely neglected by our "theologians."

The best Hebrew equivalent for the term saint is the adjective חסיד, commonly used in the sense of pious, devout, reverend, godly; but the noun חסד is found together with חן and רחמים, thus implying the qualities of grace, graciousness, gracefulness, and kindness. Thus we read of Esther, "And the King loved Esther above all the women, and she obtained חן and חסד in his sight" (Esther 2 : 17); that is to say, she found grace and kindness in his sight. Of the virtuous woman it is said, "She opens her mouth with wisdom, and in her tongue is תורת חסד, the law of kindness (or graciousness)" (Prov. 31 : 26). When God reminds Israel of the honeymoon at the outset of her spiritual career, when she was wedded to the Torah, he says, " I remember thee the grace (חסד) of thy youth," etc. (Jer. 2 : 2). When an ancient Rabbi wanted to be polite to a newly-married couple, he would compliment the bride with the words, נאה וחסודה (beautiful and graceful).[2] Applied to matters spiritual, the best equivalent for חסידים or חסידות would be "beautiful souls."

Closely connected with the terms Chasiduth and Chasid are the terms Kedushah (holiness) and Kadosh (holy). The two ideas are so naturally allied with each other that they are interchangeably used in Rabbinic texts. But it must be remarked that the term Kedushah does not entirely cover the English word holiness, the mystical and higher aspect of it being better represented by the term Chasiduth (saintliness). Whilst I shall thus consider myself at

liberty to utilise freely such Biblical and Rabbinic matter as gives evidence of the existence and nature of
Kedushah in Judaism, I shall, on the other hand, try
to sift the material in such a way as to give prominence to the element of Chasiduth, and all that this
term implies.

The notion of Chasiduth, or saintliness, is variously
described by different Jewish writers. The only
point about which they fairly agree is the feature of
individualism that distinguishes the Chasid, or saint,
from other religionists.[3] The golden mean, so much
praised by philosophers and teachers of ethics, has
no existence for him, and he is rather inclined to excesses. Nor can he be measured by the standard of
the Law, for it is one of the characteristics of the
saint that he never waits for a distinctive commandment. The various precepts of the Bible are for him
so many memoranda, or head-lines, each leading to
new trains of thought and suggestive of any number
of inferences. But inferences are subject to different
interpretations.[4] Hence the fact that each writer
emphasises the special feature in the saint with which
he was most in sympathy by reason of his own bent
of mind or particular religious passion. The saint
thus belonging to the subjective species, our theme
would be best treated by a series of monographs, or
lives of the various saints. But those could hardly
be brought within the compass of an essay. It will
therefore be best for our purpose to combine the
various features characteristic of the saint into a gen-

eral sketch, though such a mode of treatment will necessarily bring more into prominence the thing saintliness, than the person practising it.

In speaking of saints it should be premised that I am not referring to organisations or societies bearing this name. The references in Jewish literature to such organisations are few and of a doubtful nature, and will certainly not stand the test of any scientific criticism. Besides, one does not become a saint by reason of a corporate act, or by subscribing to a certain set of rules, though a man may be a saint despite his being a member of a society or community composed of professional saints. Saintliness is essentially a subjective quality. An ancient Rabbi put the matter well when he said, "As often as Israel perceived the Holy One, blessed be he, they became saints." [5] Put in a modern equivalent, we should say that saintliness is the effect of a personal religious experience when man enters into close communion with the Divine. Some New England mystic describes such communion as the mingling of the individual soul with the universal soul. This is just as obscure as any other term the new or the old world may choose to describe old ideas. When the Rabbis spoke of perceiving God, they probably thought of Psalm 17 : 15, "I will behold thy face in righteousness; I will be satisfied when I awake with thine image." [6] Some versions paraphrase the second half of the just quoted verse : "I will be satisfied by gazing on thy likeness," an expression denoting the highest fellowship with God, almost, as it were, a fellowship of the senses.

As to the way in which these blissful moments of close communion with the Divine might be made lasting and effective, the Rabbis give us a hint when they say that Israel, when they became saints, sang a song.[7] The same thought may also perhaps be divined in the words of another Rabbi, who maintained that saintliness consists in man's zealous compliance with the prescriptions in Berachoth, the Talmudic tractate dealing mostly with matter appertaining to benediction and prayer.[8] Under song and prayer we have to understand all those manifestations of the soul in which the individual attempts to reciprocate his revelation of the Divine. As was pointed out in another place[9] with regard to the Bible, its unique character consists in furnishing us with both the revelation of God to man, as given in the Pentateuch and in the Prophets, and the revelation of man to God, as contained in the Psalms and in other portions of the Scriptures of a liturgical nature.[10] Hence the value the saint attached to prayer. He longs for the moments when he can pour out his soul before his God in adoration and supplication. The hours of the day appointed for the three prayers, evening, morning, and noon, are for him, a Jewish saint expresses it, the very heart of the day.[11] Apparently, however, the saint is not satisfied with these appointed times. He is so full of expectation of the time of prayer, that he devotes a whole hour of preparation to put himself in the proper frame of mind for it, and he is so reluctant to sever himself from such blissful moments that he lingers for a whole hour after the prayer, in "after-meditation." It was in this way that the ancient saints spent nine hours of the day in meditation and supplication.[12] The ancient Rabbis had a special formula of thanksgiving for the privilege of prayer, and the saints availed themselves of this privilege to its full extent.[13] Besides the obligatory prayers, the Jewish saint had his own individual prayers, some of which have come down to us. The burden of these is mostly an appeal to God's mercy for help, that he may find him worthy to do his will. "May it be thy will," runs one of these prayers, "that we be single-hearted in the fear of thy name; that thou remove us from all thou hatest; that thou bring us near to all thou lovest, and that thou deal with us graciously for thy name's sake."[14] Another Rabbi prayed, "It is revealed before thee, God, that we have not the power to resist the evil inclination. May it be thy will to remove it from us, so that we may accomplish thy will with a perfect heart."[15] In such prayer God and man meet, for, as an old Agadist expressed it, in a rather hyperbolic way, "From the beginning of the world, the Holy One, blessed be he, established a tent for himself in Jerusalem, in which, if one may say so, he prayed, 'May it be my will that my children accomplish my will.'"[16]

Midnight, with its awe-inspiring silence and the feeling of utter isolation which comes upon man, was considered by the saints as another favourable moment

for prayer.   In allusion to Psalm 119 : 62, the Rabbis
report that above the couch of David there hung a
harp.[17]   "The midnight breeze, as it rippled over the
strings, made such music that the poet-king was con-
strained to rise from his bed, and, till the dawn flushed
the Eastern skies, he wedded words to the strains."
The music was not silenced with the disappearance of
the harp of David.   It kept awake many a Jewish
saint even during the Middle Ages.   Of one of these
saints the record is that he used to rise up in the
depths of the night and pray :   "My God, thou hast
brought upon me starvation and penury.   Into the
depths of darkness thou hast driven me, and thy
might and strength hast thou taught me.   But even
if they burn me in fire, only the more will I love thee
and rejoice in thee, for so said the Prophet, 'And
thou shalt love thy God with all thy heart.'"[18]   In the
later Middle Ages, a whole liturgy was developed,
known under the name of תיקון הצות, or "The Order
of Prayers for Midnight."   It is composed of a collection of Psalms and Biblical verses, mostly of a mourn-
ful nature, expressing Israel's grief over the destruction of the Holy Temple and the suffering of God's
children in the dispersion.   It is accompanied by a
number of soul-stirring hymns, composed by the poets
of the Synagogue.   They are mostly of a deep, spiritual nature, of matchless beauty, infinitely superior to
any we have acquired lately in our modern hymn
books.[19]   It is one of the great tragedies of modern
Judaism that it knows itself so little.   A people that

has produced the Psalmists, a R. Judah Halevi, a R. Israel Nagara, and other hymnologists and liturgists counted by hundreds, has no need to pass round the hat to all possible denominations begging for a prayer or a hymn. It contains further a confession of sins which are the cause of deferring the manifestation of the glory of God and the establishing of the kingdom of heaven on earth. Perhaps I may remark that confession of sin is an especial feature of the Jewish liturgy, which the Jew is eager to repeat as often as the opportunity offers itself. The Occidental man, in his self-complacency, thinks this a mark of Oriental cringing, unworthy of a citizen who believes himself good, and is prosperous. Perhaps the reader will be more reconciled to this feature in our liturgy if I quote the following from a letter of Lincoln to Thurlow Weed. It probably refers to a passage in his second inaugural, in which, if I am not mistaken, he makes the whole nation a participant in the sin of slavery. He writes : "I believe it is not immediately popular. Men are not flattered by being shown that there has been a difference of purpose between them and the Almighty. To deny it, however, in this case, is to deny that there is a God governing the world. It is a truth which I thought needed to be told, and, as whatever of humiliation there is in it falls most directly on myself, I thought others might afford for me to tell it." [20] When the Jewish saint said, " We have sinned, we have betrayed," and so on, he meant chiefly himself, and others might at least afford for him to tell it.

The Sabbath, with its opportunities for rest and devotion, is described as the harvest of the week,[21] the advent of which is impatiently awaited by the saint. It is a gift of the Lord, and the saint shows his gratitude by the preparations he makes to accept it. Indeed, he would avoid anything which in some circuitous way might lead to the breaking of the Sabbath, even in such cases where breaking it would be permitted by the Law. Queen Sabbath is met by him on her way with song and praise, and greeted royally; and when she has arrived, he experiences that sense of the plus-soul, or over-soul,[22] which imparts to his devotion and his rest a foretaste of the bliss to come. Other nations, it is pointed out, have also days of rest, but they stand in the same relation to the Jewish Sabbath as a copy to the original— wanting in life and soul.[23] The Sabbath is mystically described as the mate of Israel.[24] Hence, with the saint, every profane or secular thought would be considered as a breach of connubial duty. And when, against his will, his thoughts were directed to money transactions, or improvement in his estate, the saint would decline to profit by them.[25] But, as a rule, his very thoughts rest on that day. Even in the prayers nothing concerning mundane affairs is allowed to come in.[26] It is all joy and no contrition. It is entirely the day of the Lord.

The same may be applied to the festivals, which the saint observes with similar strictness; for they are so many occasions of enjoying fellowship with the

Divine. The Penitential Days, extending from the first to the tenth of the month of Tishri, with the opportunity they afford for reconciliation with God, are the subject of his special solicitude. A well-known saint expressed himself, that all the year he does nothing but listen impatiently to catch the sound of the hammer, knocking at the doors in the early hours of the morning, calling the faithful to the synagogue, when the Penitential Days are about to arrive.[27]

The saint is further described as a regent,[28] having absolute control over all his organs. Of these the mouth is one of the most important. The maxim of Judaism, as conceived by the great moralists, is that the things which enter the mouth as well as those which proceed from the mouth may be unclean. Accordingly the Jewish saint would constantly watch both the imports and the exports of his mouth. With regard to the former it is hardly necessary to say that the saint would refrain from all those various forbidden foods which the Bible describes as " unclean, an abomination," and fetid. These have, according to the general Jewish opinion, the effect of polluting the soul, and there is no difference upon this point between the teachings of the Pentateuch and those of the Prophets, unless we choose to interpret these latter in the spirit of Paul and Marcion, and their modern successors. The saint, with his abhorrence of anything impure, would avoid the least contact with them. True, the saint is an individualist, but an extensive menu and the indulgence of other appetites forbidden

by the Scriptures, are no mark of a strong personality. We Occidentals are greatly proud and jealous
of our right of private judgment. But the first condition for private judgment is that the judge should
not be bribed by considerations of comfort and con-
venience. The great majority of Jewish saints had
no difficulty in reconciling themselves to any observance or ceremony. Speech about the Divine
has to be in metaphors, and action corresponding
to such speech can be only in signs and symbols.
Those mystically inclined perceived in them the
reflex of things unseen, assuming proportions in
the regions above never dreamt of by the vulgar.
Certainly, there were a few, especially among the
mystics, who had antinominian tendencies, but they
never stopped at the ritual part. They equally
resented the moral restraint imposed upon them by
the Torah. They all became notorious profligates,
and terminated in apostasy.

The individualism of the saint found expression in the following principle : "Sanctify thyself
even in that which is permitted to thee." [29] As
Nachmanides points out, the Torah has forbidden
us certain kinds of food, but allowed the eating
of meat and the drinking of wine, but even within
these limits can the man of impure appetite become a drunkard and a glutton. From doing this,
man is warded off by the general commandment of
holiness, which keeps him aloof from all animal de-
sires.[30] R. Joseph Caro had his menu regulated by

his angel, or the spirit of the Mishnah, created by his devotion to that part of the oral law, who, again and again, impresses upon him the fact that every morsel of food and drop of drink not absolutely necessary to support life is a sacrifice to the strange god. Even the luxury of drinking too much water is considered by him a concession to the Evil One.[31]

On the whole, the saint would be rather inclined to asceticism. His inference from such commandments as, for instance, that regarding the Nazarite who had to abstain from wine, or that concerning the refraining from food altogether on the Day of Atonement, would be, that restraint and discipline in every respect are pleasing to his Father in Heaven. The statement is often made that Judaism is not an ascetic religion, and, indeed, there are passages in Jewish literature which might be cited in corroboration of this view. But the saint, by reason of his aspirations to superior holiness, will never insist on privileges and concessions. His models will be the heroic Elijah, with his rough mantle of camel's hair, his dwelling in the cherit, and sleeping under a desert-broom, and preparing himself for a revelation on Mount Horeb by a fast of forty days; or the Psalmist, who says, "My knees are weak from fasting, and my flesh faileth of fatness"; or the laymen of the Second Temple, called "Men of the Station," representing the Third Estate in the Holy Temple, where they fasted four days a week, and spent their time in meditation and prayer.[32] And thus we find any number of saints in

Jewish history, as notorious for their asceticism with all its extravagances as those of any other religion. Long lists might be drawn up of Jewish saints who fasted, as the phrase is, from the beginning of the week to the end, except the Sabbath ; or, at least, Monday and Thursday of every week. Others again, confined themselves to vegetable food and plain water; whilst others inflicted upon themselves all sorts of torture, taking snow baths in winter and exposing themselves to the heat in summer.[33] The remarkable thing about these saints is, that many among them warned their disciples against asceticism. Of the Gaon of Wilna, the story is, that when he remonstrated with his disciple R. Zalman against wasting himself by frequent fasts and keeping vigils through the night, he answered him, "But I understand the master himself lived such an ascetic life in his younger days." "Yes," answered the Rabbi, "I did; but I regret it deeply now." The rejoinder of Rabbi Zalman was, "I also wish to have something to regret." [34] The reader will probably have noticed that even the modern man, notwithstanding all his admiration for flesh and muscle, speaks of a fine ascetic face, which he usually identifies with spirituality and inner worth. Even the community at large, which could not afford to spend itself in fasts and vigils, never doubted that self-denial is better than self-indulgence. They were all strongly impressed with the truth that the man insisting upon his three square meals a day, and everything else in

correspondence, is less accessible to discipline and
self-sacrifice than the man who follows the rule of the
sages: "A morsel of bread with salt thou must eat,
and water by measure thou must drink, thou must
sleep upon the ground, and live a life of trouble the
while thou toilest in the Torah." [35]   The toiler in
the Torah is hardly conscious of the trouble.   The
story is of a famous Jewish saint who indulged in
the luxury of fasting the first six days in the week;
when asked how he accomplished this feat, he answered that he never meant to fast: he simply forgot
to eat.

Even more stringent was the watch which the
saint would keep over the things which proceed from
the mouth.   "Be careful not to utter an untruth,"
says an old Jewish saint, even in the way of a joke, or
in the way of over-emphasis, "for," an old Jewish
moralist tells us, "against the most weighty sins we are
warned in the Bible with only one prohibitive command,
whilst the law forbidding the speaking of untruth is
ever so many times repeated in the Scriptures." [36]   Indeed, truth is one of the specialties of the Jewish saint.
"The soul," the moralist remarks, "is extracted from
the place of the holy spirit, hewn out from a place all
purity.   She is created of the superior splendour, the
throne of glory.   In the Holy of Holies, there is
no falsehood; all is truth; as it is said: 'God—
truth.'. . . He who will meditate over these things, that
his soul is extracted from the very source of truth,
will do truth; never allow a lie an inlet into the place

of the holiness of truth." [37]   "Truth," again the ancient Rabbis said, "is the seal of the Holy One, blessed be he," and everything proceeding from the saint, either in thought, or in word, or in deed, would bear this impress.   He speaks the truth in his very heart. Untruth has no existence for him, and he would, under no consideration, agree to any concession or compromise in this direction.   Thus, one of the saints prescribes, "Guard thyself against anger, flattery, and falsehood.   If untruth has become a matter of habit with thee, make it a rule to tell people, 'I lied,' and thus thou wilt accustom thyself that no falsehood escape thy mouth." [38]   "The Messiah will come," a Jewish saint said, "only when the world will have realised that to speak an untruth is as heinous a crime as adultery." [39]   The same saint was wont to say to his disciples, "Rather allow your soul to expire than that an untruth should proceed from your mouth," and considered this prohibitive commandment among the precepts of the Torah for which man is bound to undergo martyrdom. [40]   It is of this saint, or a pupil of his, that the story is recorded that the Russian Government, suspecting the Jews of his town of smuggling, consented to withdraw the charge if he declared his brethren innocent.   Having no alternative but either to bring misfortune on his brethren or to tell an untruth, he prayed to God to save him from this dilemma by sending death upon him.   And, lo, a miracle happened!   When the officials came to fetch him before the law court, they found him dead.

The last paragraph brings us to that part in the programme of the saint which the Talmud calls "laws regulating the relations between man and man," and which we would classify under the general heading of conduct. "He who is desirous of being a saint," one Rabbi remarked, "let him fulfil the precepts of that part of the law which deals with 'damages.'"[41] In observing these, he avoids everything that might result in an injury to his fellow-man. We need not enlarge here upon matters of commonplace integrity, "which it is no honour to have, but simply a disgrace to want." Lying, backbiting, slandering, and the acquisition of wealth by dishonest means come under the prohibitive laws, the transgression of which has, according to the Rabbis, a defiling effect, and they are put into the same category as murder and idolatry.[42] It is thus no special mark of saintliness to avoid these deadly sins. But the saint would go further: he would speak the truth in his very heart. He would, for instance, consider himself bound to a money transaction even when the promise made never assumed the shape of a committal by word of mouth, having been only a determination of the heart.[43] As to avoiding injury, he would do this at the very risk of his life, though not bound to do so by the letter of the law. Thus, when the Roman Government once besieged the town of Lydda, and insisted upon the extradition of a certain Ula bar Koseheb, threatening the defenders with the destruction of the place and the massacre of its inhabitants in the case of further resistance, R. Joshua ben Levi exerted his influence with Ula, that he would voluntarily deliver himself to the Romans, so that the place might be saved. Thereupon, the Prophet Elijah, who often had communion with R. Joshua ben Levi, stopped his visits. After a great deal of penance, which the Rabbi imposed upon himself, Elijah came back and said, "Am I expected to reveal myself to informers?" Whereupon the Rabbi asked, " Have I not acted in accordance with the strict letter of the law?" "But," retorted Elijah, "this is not the law of the saints." [44]

By injury is also understood anything which might cause one's fellow-man the feeling of nausea or disgust. As it would seem, these were cases which the court could not well reach. They fell under the class of secret things, but the rabbis applied to them the verse in Ecclesiastes (12 : 14), " God shall bring every work into judgment with every secret thing." But we have on record that there were saints who made it a specialty to go about cleaning such public places as by the carelessness of passers-by might have proved offensive to the public.[45]

Altogether, there is no room in the soul of the saint for those ugly qualities which, in one way or another, are bound to impair the proper relations between man and his fellow-man. These are, according to one authority, "pride, anger, petulance, despair, hatred, jealousy, dissipation, covetousness, desire for power, and self-assertion." They all belong to the ugly qualities of man, making man's communion with

God impossible, and hence are incompatible with saintliness." [46] "Pride," or vanity, it is pointed out, "is at the root of all evils," man setting up himself as an idol, worshipping his own self, and thus bound to come into collision with both God and fellow-man.[47] Hence, the prayer at the conclusion of the Eighteen Benedictions : "O my God! Guard my tongue from evil and my lips from speaking guile ; and to such as curse me let my soul be dumb, yea, let my soul be unto all as the dust." [48] Man's love of self is, however, too deeply rooted to be overcome by these reminders, few and too far between. We therefore read of a saint who was overheard constantly whispering the prayer : "May the Merciful save me from pride." "The man who has a taint of pride or insolence, though he be righteous and upright in all other respects, is worth nothing. Indeed, a man may fulfil ever so many laws and fast six days in the week, and be nevertheless a disciple of the wicked Balaam," who though a prophet was of a haughty spirit and a swelled soul, and thus destined to perdition.[49] The same saint was in the habit of saying, "The devil will make man all possible concessions, if he can only succeed in impressing upon him the fact of his prominence and his greatness. He will show him what a great scholar he is, what a pious man he is, what a great orator he is, what a clear fine hand he writes, what a fine figure he makes when dancing, and so on." [50] Should a man happen to be devoid of all accomplishments, and a fool in the bargain, he

will compliment him on his sagacity and wisdom.
Should he be lacking in all sympathy with religion,
especially of the practical and living kind, he will con-
gratulate him on his deep spirituality. Infatuated
with his own importance, man before long will be in
opposition to man and God, who keep his due from
him. The best remedy against this ugly quality is
love. Hence the warning of the saint: 'He who
hates an Israelite, hates Abraham, Isaac, and Jacob,
the grandsires of Israel.'" Again, he who hates man,
hates the Holy One, blessed be he, who created man.
We are all children unto the Lord our God, all souls
rooting in him.[51] The injunction of the saint is, therefore, "Let man love all creatures, including Gentiles,
and let him envy none." [52] This, by the way, is the
distinct precept of the Jewish saint of the sixteenth
century. It is not known to me that any Christian
saint of the same period made the love of the Jew a
condition of saintliness. This is a love which leaves
no room for self. Man will not succeed in attaining
to this love until he has acquired the virtues of humility and meekness. There is hardly any Jewish moralist who does not enlarge upon the significance of
humility, and the references to it would easily fill a
volume. One of the most emphatic is, "Be exceedingly lowly of spirit, since the hope of man is but the
worm." [53]

Man must be so thoroughly convinced of his own
unworthiness, that he is even bidden to love those
who rebuke him and hate those who praise him.[54]

Nay, he should feel under torture when he hears his
own praise, as it is sure to be undeserved.[55]   In addition to this, there is with the saint the conception
of the superiority of his fellow-man, which proves
another stimulus toward the cultivation of meekness
and humbleness.   When man quits the world, he
is asked, according to an ancient Midrash, "Hast
thou been busy in the study of the Torah, and in
works of lovingkindness?   Hast thou declared thy
Maker as King morning and evening?   Hast thou
acknowledged thy fellow-man as king over thee
in meekness of spirit?" [56]   Man should accordingly
perceive in his fellow-man not only an equal whose
rights he is bound to respect, but a superior whom he
is obliged to revere and love.   In every person, it is
pointed out by these saints, precious and noble elements are latent, not to be found with anybody else.
In fact, every human being is a servant of God *in
posse*.   One of these saints declined to be considered
as one of the righteous of his generation, saying he
had no right to this distinction so long as he felt
that he loved his children better than the rest of mankind.[57]   Whenever the saint heard of a birth in the
community, he used to break out in wild joy, wel-
coming the new-born child as a future volunteer in
the service of God, taking his or her place in the rank
and file of militant Judaism.   Hence, the prayer of
certain of these saints : "May it be thy will that we
shall not sin either against thee or against thy creatures;"[58] whilst another saint used to add to his morn-

ing prayer, the short prayer, "O God, establish in my
heart faith, humility, and meekness," and his favourite
saying was, "As a man is anxious for his very life, so
should he be anxious to be permeated by the thought
that he is less important than anybody else." [59]   He
used especially to be very severe with his family when
they dared be unkind to his domestics.   Another of
the saints expresses it, "Let each man be considered
in thy eyes as better than thou, even the servant in
thy house." [60]   Of one of these godly men legend reports that he was in the habit of addressing all the
people with whom he came in contact as "saints," or
"righteous ones," and, indeed, believing them to be
so.   One day, the story is, when walking in the street,
he saw two cabmen fighting over the right of way,
giving force to their arguments with the whips which
they applied to each other.   The godly man was
embarrassed, and he prayed, "Lord of the universe, it
is my duty to separate them, but who dares interfere
between two saints?"

Another consequence of this love is that men
should never break out in anger against any one.
This is a precept to be found in all the moralist literature of the different ages, but R. Joseph Caro, even
the author of the *Shulchan Aruch*, in the special manual
for his own guidance adds, that anger should be
avoided even in the cause of religion, where zeal
for the glory of God might give some justification for
it.[61]   Indeed, we should love all, including those who
have gone astray, this being the only means of bring-

ing them back into the fold. When a certain pious man came to the saint, asking his advice as to what he should do with his son who had left the faith of his ancestors, the answer was, "Love him. The influence of thy love will be his salvation." And so it came to pass. Of another saint, the story is that he used to make special journeys to places settled by converts to the dominant religion. To these converts he made a gift of his share of the bliss awaiting the pious in the world to come, at the same time eliciting the promise that they would read every day the verse, שמע ישראל, "Hear, O Israel, the Lord our God, the Lord is One." This proved a link between them and the faith they had left, to which, in time, many of them returned.[62] Indeed, prayer must be universal. He who prays shall not direct his attention to himself. Any prayer in which the whole of Israel is not included, is no prayer. Nay, one must pray even for the wicked among the Gentiles.[63] Of course, there were other saints who were distinguished more by their zeal than by their powers of persuasion. They were good haters, and Elijah was their model, but it may be said in their favour, that so far as Judaism is concerned their motives were pure; their zeal was never dictated by consideration of self or by ambition. Sometimes I am inclined to think that the haters and the lovers were both right.

In matters of philanthropy, the saint would be inclined to extravagance. "It is a strange though

true thing," some philosopher has remarked, "that
virtue itself has need of limits." At a certain epoch
in history, when mendicancy was made a special sign
of holiness, the Rabbis drew the limit when they said,
"He who wishes to be lavish in his philanthropic
work, let him not spend more than twenty per cent of
his income." [64] The saint transgresses this limit,
taking as his norm, "What is mine is thine, and what
is thine is thine." [65] He would also remove any barrier
or obstacle preventing the poor from reaching him
personally, whilst he would, at the same time, save
no effort to make others do their duty to the poor.[66]
And this duty practically means to make the poor
equal partners in one's property. Thus, in the sacred
letter of R. Shneor (Senior) Zalman, a well-known
saint of Russia, he writes to his adherents to the
following effect :

"My beloved ones, my brethren and my friends :—I have no
doubt about the distress of the time. The means of getting a
livelihood have become very small, and certain acquaintances
of mine, whom I knew to have been in prosperous circumstances, are now compelled to borrow in order to maintain their
families. May the Lord have mercy upon them. Nevertheless,
they do not act properly when they shut their hands and refuse
to supply the poor with their needs. If we have no mercy with
them, who will ? It is true that the law teaches that man's own
life comes first, but this is to be applied only to things on which
life depends, as, for instance, when men are in a desert, and there
is sufficient water to quench the thirst of only one person, and
save him from death. In this case we say that the owner has
first right upon it. But if it is a question of bread and clothes
and wood on one side, and dinners with fish and meat and fruit
on the other side, the latter have to be given up as things super-

fluous.   First the poor must be provided with the necessaries
of life.   This is the real meaning of the law, but it is indeed
not worthy of a man to insist upon the law in such cases.   He
ought not to think of his life.   We are all in need of the mercy
of heaven, and those who have no mercy on earth, be their
reason what it may, can never hope for God's mercy.'' [67]

He then proceeds, in a long, mystical discourse, to
show how this grace of heaven can be encouraged to
flow into the proper channels, as the term is, only by
manifestations of grace on earth, heaven and earth
acting in harmony to reveal the great attribute of love.

The literature and stories bearing on charity and
the saint's share in it are too extensive to be entered
upon here, even in a casual way.   The greatest sacrifice is told of a certain Rabbi who used to save the
whole of the year enough money to enable him to
buy an *Ethrog* for the Feast of Tabernacles (Lev. 23:
40).   When he was in possession of six rubles
he made a special journey from his village to Brody,
to buy the *Ethrog*.   But on the way he met a poor
man who made a livelihood by means of his horse-cart,
on which he carried water for the neighbourhood.   Unfortunately, the horse died on the way.   Thereupon
the Rabbi gave him his six rubles to buy another
beast, saying, " What is the difference ?   To buy an
Ethrog is a command of God, and to help this poor
man is also a command of God."   Naturally, a miracle happened afterwards.   The Rabbi was presented
by some rich man with a fine *Ethrog* for the feast.[68]
I will only remark that charity belongs, according to
the mystics, to the commandments that work a certain

re-birth in man, or rather give a new soul to those
who make strenuous efforts to fulfil them.[69]

It will, perhaps, be interesting to hear, that these
saints were by no means so unpractical as their mystical discourses would lead us to imagine. The successor of this R. Shneor Zalman, Rabbi Beer, in an
epistle written in a time of great distress and persecution, writes to his followers not to engage so much
in commerce.

" The best for you," he says, " is to learn proper
trades, in factories, under the superintendence of practical men." He also gives them counsel to take up
agricultural pursuits, buy land either from the great
landlords, or from the Government, and employ for
the first two or three years non-Jews who will teach
them this new vocation. " Did we not," he says, " in
Palestine derive all our livelihood from our labour in
field and in vineyard? It is only in this way," he
says, " that we can hope to find favour with the Government. Who knows what will be our end? They
may, God forbid, expel us to some far-away country." [70]

Sympathy and tenderness are by the saint not confined to the human species. They extend also to
dumb creation. Thus we read in the " Little Book of
Saints," " Refrain thy kindness and thy mercy from
nothing which the Holy One, blessed be he, created
in this world. Never beat nor inflict pain on any animal, beast, bird, or insect; nor throw stones at a dog
or a cat; nor kill flies or wasps." [71]   Indeed, man will

be punished who will make his animal carry larger burdens than it is able to bear. In connexion with this, we read the story of a man who was cruel to his dog. The dog, however, sought refuge under the robes of a sage. When the man approached the dog with the purpose of beating him, the sage protested with the words, "Since this dog sought my protection, you shall not touch it," and applied to him the verse in Genesis (19: 8), "Only unto these do nothing, for they came under the shadow of my roof." [72] Another story illustrating the same trait in the saint is the following: R. Isaac Loria was once the guest of a good and upright man. Before he left, the saint said to his host, "How can I compensate you for your kind hospitality?" The master of the house then answered that his only grief was that God had not given him the blessing of children. Whereupon Loria, who knew everything going on in heaven and earth, said to him, "The cause of your misfortune is, that you were not kind to animals." After making inquiries it turned out that the man had poultry in his yard, with a cistern in it. In this cistern there was a ladder by means of which the water at the bottom could be reached by the young chickens as yet unable to use their wings. Once his wife inadvertently had the ladder removed, which fact was the cause of great suffering to the animals. The man replaced the ladder, and the children came in due time. [73]

The relations between the sexes are regulated by the law. Judaism, as we know, not only did not encourage, but distinctly objected to celibacy. Only one or two instances are recorded of Jewish saints who remained single all their lives. But, on the other hand, if marriage was not made a sacrament in the Roman Catholic sense, it was a thing holy. Maimonides, with that fine tact so characteristic of him, grouped the marriage laws under the general heading of "Kedushah" (Holiness); whilst Nachmanides wrote a whole treatise called the "Sacred Letter," dealing exclusively with the most intimate moments in the lives of the sexes, and showing how even such functions as were declared by other religions as distinctly animalic, can with the saint be elevated into moments of worship and religious exaltation. It is, in fact, a vindication of the flesh from a religious point of view. All the more strongly did the Jewish saint insist upon making these relations pure and chaste, stigmatising even an impure thought as being as bad as an impure action, if not worse. It was only by reason of the purification of these relations and their thorough sanctification, that the whole vocabulary of love could afterwards, in moments of rapture and ecstasy, be used by the saints in their prayers and hymns, to symbolise the relation between the human and the Divine, and the longing of man for the moment of total absorption in the Deity. The Song of Songs became the great allegory, picturing the connexion between God and Israel. The act of revelation is described as the wedding between heaven and earth. The death of the righteous, when the soul returns unto God, is described as a kiss ; whilst each individual mystic considered his particular action of losing himself in the Divine as a new matrimonial act.

I have referred once or twice to saints who were visited by angels, who had peculiar visions, and who even wrought miracles. Writing for a modern public, I consider it due to these true saints that the reader should not suspect them of untruth, because of failure to reconcile these happenings with his own experiences. Things absolutely impossible to us may have been, and, indeed, were, an actual reality with them. Ruskin, in his lecture, "Pleasures of Faith," given in a not less sceptical age than ours, thus said to his hearers:

"You have all been taught by Lord Macaulay and his school that because you have carpets instead of rushes for your feet ; and feather-beds instead of fern for your backs ; and kickshaws instead of beef for your eating ; and drains instead of holy wells for your drinking ;—that, therefore, you are the cream of creation, and every one of you a seven-headed Solomon. Stay in those pleasant circumstances and convictions, if you please ; but don't accuse your roughly-bred and fed fathers of telling lies about the aspect the earth and sky bore to *them*,—till you have trodden the earth as they, barefoot, and seen the heavens as they, face to face."

I grudge no one his Persian rugs or his mineral-waters. I have even personally a sneaking desire for such things, and do prefer the electric light to the tallow-candle with which I was brought up. But one has a right to resent the superior smile which one meets when speaking of those times and those men. I find that the terms saints, mystics, and Cabbalists, are used as terms of reproach nowadays. This attitude is quite inconceivable to me. Has the German nation ever disowned its Master Ekkehart, or its Boehme? Has the French nation ever looked with contempt on the School of the Jansenists, or is it not even more proud of Pascal's *Pensées* than of his scientific discoveries? If one will attempt to live like these saints, he will have the same experiences. Let him try only to spend nine hours a day in prayer, and the rest in the study of the Law, and in the relief of suffering; to fast six days out of seven, and break the fast on bread and water; to give to sleep three hours out of twenty-four, and these on a stone instead of a feather-bed. Let him make martyrdom the dwelling-point of his thoughts for a time, and the death of a martyr the goal of his ambitions and achievements. Let him make this experiment for half a year only, and see whether the experiences which he will have to relate will not be the same as those of a Loria, a Caro, and other saints.

The saint must not be judged by the common standard of humanity. Consciousness of sin and the assurance of grace are the two great motive powers in the working of religion. Without them, religion sinks to the level of a mere cult, or a kind of ethico-æsthetico-spiritual sport in which there is no room for devotion and submission; but what is with the common religionist a mere dogma, is with the saint an awful reality, dominating all

his actions and pervading all his being. Under these
two realities—the reality of sin and the reality of
grace—the saint is constantly labouring. " My sin is
ever before me," is the cry of the Psalmist, and it is
echoed by every Jewish saint. Hence the tendency
toward self-accusation so manifest in many a composition by the Jewish saints. Sometimes it is the sin
of his fellow-man for which he holds himself fully
responsible. We possess formulas of confessions written and read by Jewish saints, in which they arraign
themselves for the most heinous offences, and which
it would take a dozen lifetimes to commit. This is
rightly explained on the ground that the sense of
solidarity and responsibility was so keen with the
Jewish saint that he saw nothing incongruous in pleading guilty to the sum total of iniquities committed by his
contemporaries.[74] But, with the Psalmist, he is equally
certain of the assurance expressed in the passage, "I
have set God before me continually : for with him at
my right hand I cannot be moved. Therefore my
heart is glad and my glory exults, my flesh also
dwells in safety." [75] One of our higher critics thinks
that these verses may, without effort, be called Christian. I am proud to call them Jewish. The notion
of the permanency of the Divine Presence is the great
safeguard against sin. The exhortation to feel shame
before the Holy One, blessed be he, who is present
everywhere and witnesses man's deeds, is a favourite
appeal with all the Jewish moralists. The saint, however, is so strongly overawed by the shame before

God, that he said : "A sinful thought should bring a
blush to man's face, and make him experience the
same sensation of confusion and shame, as he would
at the sudden appearance of an intimate friend at the
moment when he is about to engage in some dis-
graceful action." Thus the saint "cannot be moved,"
but when a slip happens, there is the Divine grace
surviving sin, which latter is only an outcome of
human frailty. The very realisation on the part of
man of his loss through his departure from God has
brought him back to God; or, as a Jewish liturgical
poet expressed it, "And where shall I flee, if not from
thee to thee?" Hence the despondency bordering
on despair which you will find in the composition of
many a saint, but which suddenly passes into exaltation and joy. For, indeed, for him the world is God-
full, though disfigured by sin and misery; but, even
in the depths of this misery and sin, the saint divines
those "inshinings of the pure rays of holy celestial
light," which, in God's own time, will lift and purify
fallen creation. The Devil himself is an angel of
God, though a fallen angel, and he has to be prayed
for, whilst the hope is expressed that Hell itself will,
with the disappearance of sin, be converted into a
Paradise.[76]

The period of struggle in the life of the saint, and
the stage of serenity and peace following upon it, are
described by one of the saints in the following words :

"And when the soul has realised God's omnipotence and
his greatness, she prostrates herself in dread before his great-

ness and glory, and remains in this state till she receives his assurance, when her fear and anxiety cease. Then she drinks of the cup of love to God. She has no other occupation than his service, no other thought than of him, no other intent than the accomplishment of his will, and no other utterance than his praise." [77]

But even during his struggle the fear of the saint is not of punishment, for suffering is looked upon by him as another token of God's love, indeed, as a gift of heaven; nor is his hope connected with reward, which he would consider unworthy and mercenary. Death has no terrors for him. "When I am afar from thee," prayed an ancient Jewish saint, "my death is in my life; when I cleave to thee, my life is in my death." [78] What he dreads is separation from God, what he longs for is fellowship with God.

Some mystics defined the saint, or the Chasid, as one who acts Chasid-like with his Maker, which may be interpreted to mean that not only does he not insist upon the letter of the Law, but all his worship is an act of grace without any hope of reward or fear of punishment. [79]

One of the saints expressed this thought in the following rather bold words :

"I have no wish for thy Paradise, nor any desire for the bliss in the world to come. I want thee and thee alone." [80]

FOUR EPISTLES TO THE JEWS OF ENGLAND [1]

JEWS AND ANGLO-SAXONS

I beg to submit to your readers the following passage taken from "The Letters of Robert Louis Stevenson":

What a strange idea to think me a Jew-hater! Isaiah and David and Heine are good enough for me, and I leave more unsaid. . . . The ascendant hand is what I feel most strongly; I am bound in and with my forbears; were he one of mine I should not be struck at all by Mr. Moss, of Bevis Marks, I should still see behind him Moses of the Mount and the Tables, and the shining face. We are nobly born; fortunate those who know it; blessed those who remember.

I quote Stevenson as an author familiar to your readers. The same sentiment, however, is expressed, if less forcibly, by hundreds of Jewish writers in ancient and modern times, all of which goes to show that the now fashionable cry (among the Little-Israelites), of our being Anglo-Saxons or Englishmen of the Jewish persuasion, is but a sickly platitude.

Those familiar with Judaica know that the cry was raised in Germany some generations ago, many Rabbis and many more laymen shouting it with the whole power of their lungs: "We are *Germanen* of the Mosaic persuasion!" The theory is now exploded in Germany, and our repeating such platitudes after the terrible experience of the last decades can only be explained on the principle of Martineau, who remarks somewhere that in matters intellectual the English are sometimes apt to act as the younger brothers of the Germans, putting on the trousers which their elder brothers left off wearing years ago.

The doctrine professed now by those who are not carried away by the new-fangled "yellow" theology is, there is no Judaism without Jews, and there are no Jews without Judaism. We can thus only be Jews of the Jewish persuasion. "Blessed those who remember!"

JEWS AS MISSIONARIES

I offer for the consideration of your readers another quotation. It is taken from a correspondence, still in manuscript, between two scholars of my acquaintance: "Can you imagine the ancient chosen people of God going about begging for a nationality—clamoring everywhere, 'We are you!'—joining the Boxers of every nation on earth, and using the last crumbs of the sacred language in which God-Shalom addressed his children to invoke his blessing upon the 'Mitrailleuse,' the 'Krupp gun,' 'Dum-dum' and 'Long-tom,' and other anti-Messianic contrivances?"

The terrible irony of the situation becomes apparent when we remember that while millions of Aryans lay eager claim to the name and heritage of Israel, Israel, ashamed of its Semitic origin, seeks to disavow itself and to ape the Occident in all things except its admiration for Israel. It has become for it almost a sacred duty to occidentalise its religion. It

forgets all the while that, however richly endowed the
European genius may be, religion is not one of its
gifts.   Not a single European god has survived the
awakening of mankind from savagery and barbarism.
Nor has Europe produced a single great religious
founder.   St. Francis of Assisi, the hero of modern
sentimentalism, remains, despite all decoration in the
latest French style, a crude imitation of the Semitic
original.

But perhaps the saddest feature amid so much that
is farcical is that we still profess to have a mission to
the world.   The idea of this mission is certainly an
old one.   A community forming a Kingdom of Priests
must have the whole world for its parish.   But is the
constant endeavour to level down the intellectual and
spiritual standard to that of our surroundings compatible with the missionary ideal?   Missionaries are
only *with* the people, but not *of* the people.   They
share their griefs, but hold aloof from their orgies.
They convert the world, but do not allow the world
to convert them.   They neither court popularity nor
pander to prejudice.   They must destroy the idol before they can proclaim the God.   Abraham, the first
missionary, the "Friend of God," had to stand alone
contra mundum, and in this his real greatness is said
to have consisted.   Such passive virtues as we may
possess are somewhat too common to be very imposing, while our success in the various callings of life
is of too material a nature to be used as a spiritual
weapon.   In the realms of pure thought we remain in

spite of all our boasting only second-rate, not possessing a single man who might be called a leader of
thought.   It is more than passing strange that under
the screw of the Inquisition and the *Cherem* we could
produce a Spinoza, while to-day, with all our prosperity, we cannot show even a commentator on
Spinoza.   But the world will never be conquered by
mediocrities.   If, then, our endless talk about a religious mission is not to degenerate into mere cant, a
religious atmosphere will have to be created quite
different to that in which we have lived hitherto.
This atmosphere will, in the first place, have to be
thoroughly and intensely Jewish.   The centre of
gravity of all our thought and sympathies will have
to be placed, irrespective of country, among Jews.
Whatever our political destiny may be, our religious
destiny can never be worked out by the West in isolation.   The religious energies of all our brethren of
the West and of the East, in closest communion, will
be required for its consummation.   We have got the
men, we have got the money, and a good deal of system, too, but they have the simple faith, they have the
knowledge of Jewish lore, and they have the will and
the strength, inured as they are to suffering, to live
and to die for their conception of Judaism.   They
permit no "free love" in religion.   Universality means
with them what it meant with the prophets and their
Jewish successors—that the whole world should become Jews, not that Judaism should fade out into the
world.   We have the method and they have the mad-

ness; only if we combine can the victory be ours. A closer communion of sympathies will probably be facilitated by our devoting some more time to the Hebrew language, which is still the depository of all that is sacred to the Eastern Jew. From this literature we shall obtain the revelation of his standard of religious fervour and real spirituality, the height of which remains unsuspected and undreamt of by the Occidentals.

Above all, religious enthusiasm and zeal, if they are to be effective, will have to be brought to the boiling point. It is only that zeal which will consume all worldliness, which will suffer no rival, and which will not falter in its devotion because of any dread of one-sidedness that can be of any use to the missionary. Now Judaism has often been accused of being deficient in enthusiasm, the great mysterious power of spiritual propagation. It was always inconceivable to me how such an accusation could be brought against a people which has produced the Psalms, or, in a later period, the great allegorical commentaries on the Song of Songs. But in view of the constant boast of our common sense, and the pains we take to avoid anything which might be suspected of eccentricity or even idealism, our morbid craving for the applause of the majority, and our eager desire to lose ourselves in the majority, our deification of the balance-sheet and the cold, stiff, business-like spirit in which our institutions are conducted, we cannot deny all justification for these attacks. I shall probably be told that we are acting thus as practical Englishmen. But where are then our John Wesleys, our Newmans, or even our Liddons? Surely, they, too, were eminently English!

SPIRITUAL RELIGION VERSUS SPIRITUAL MEN

I had occasion in my last letter to use the word "spirituality." The term is obscure, and it has caused a good deal of confusion. A few explanatory remarks, therefore, may perhaps prove instructive to your readers.

Some, indeed, identify the term with "morality." There is some truth in this, inasmuch as nothing immoral can possibly be spiritual. But, unfortunately, people are too eager to be guided by the principle of Becky Sharp, according to which your chances of heaven increase with the number of the ciphers in your banking account, and they are thus inclined to think spirituality the exclusive privilege of wealth. Some witty Bishop is recorded to have said of his worldly brethren of the dissenting camp, "that their second horse stops at the church door of its own accord." Our smart carriages do not stop at the synagogue or at any place of worship, but they are too often the symptoms of a spirituality betokened by a strong antipathy to the religion of the humbler classes, and an insatiable appetite for new prayers—chiefly written for the benefit of the poor.

Others, again, believe spirituality to be opposed to the Law, and especially the ceremonial part of it.

Their religious superiority can, therefore, only be shown by the rejection of both. For instance, if you refrain from food and drink on the Kippur, walk to the Synagogue, and spend the day there reading your ancient liturgy, and listen to an exposition by your preacher of the lesson from the Scriptures, then you are a worshipper of the common type, a slave labouring under the yoke of the letter. But if you ride up to the Temple after an ordinary breakfast, pass an hour or two there listening to an oratorio and in following a sermon on the merits of the last novel of Hall Caine, or on the more subtle subject of the intellectual relations between Master David Grieve and the Reverend Robert Elsmere, and employ the rest of the day in looking after your affairs and taking your other two meals, as a rational being should, then you have acted as a spiritual Jew, and have worshipped your God in spirit and in truth. This may seem a caricature, but signs are not wanting that matters are drifting that way.

Now, I do not intend to give a new definition of "spirituality." It is as indefinable as the spirit itself, and its meaning can be as little conveyed in words as a soul can be painted. But I may be permitted to reproduce here the substance of a conversation between a foreign gentleman and myself bearing upon our subject, which conversation, though rambling in part and largely coloured by prejudice and partiality, is not without the merit of freshness. I must only premise that my benighted foreigner hailed from a

certain town in Russia where he lived as a mere lay-
man, occupied with his trade; which circumstance,
however, did not prevent him from being an excellent Talmudist and well-versed in other branches of
Jewish literature.

Our acquaintance is of comparatively recent date,
and was made in a German watering place. Our conversations were long and many, on all possible subjects, English Jews and English Judaism among
them. And then there happened a strange thing.
Whilst he spoke with the utmost deference of our
great philanthropists and the enduring merit of their .
labours on behalf of Israel, he fairly staggered at our
claims to the religious leadership of Judaism. On
my representing to him that there was probably no
Jewish community in the world in which the subject
of religion occupies the mind of the people so much
as in ours, and this, too, as I added with some emphasis, *spiritual* religion, he answered, "That is exactly
where we differ. You incessantly prate about a
spiritual *religion*, whilst we insist upon spiritual *men*."

When I asked for further explanation, he replied
vehemently: "It is your Western arrogance with your
pretensions to perfection—your theologians, indeed,
have never forgiven Judaism for insisting upon man's
shortcomings—which prevents you from tracing the
evil to its real sources. It flatters your vanity to think
yourselves demi-gods, or even gods only hyphenated
with man. When you find your idols wallowing in
the mire of their appetite, like any other animal, you

proceed to blame religion for its lack of spirituality, as
not being sublime enough for your darling gods.
But did the Psalmist, whom even you consent to
patronise in your moments of condescension, plead
for new commandments, or did he pray for a new
heart and a new spirit to perceive the wonders of the
old ones? We, of the East, have a less elevated
opinion of ourselves. You reproach us with being
servile and cringing, which means, in fact, that we are
not blind to our inferiority. Instead of blaming religion, we reproach ourselves. It is *not* that which
comes from the Torah which defiles. It is the things
which proceed out of the *man*, his mental attitude
during the performance of the Divine commandment,
his purpose in fulfilling it, which may leave a defiling
effect even on things heavenly and pure. 'Two men
may be eating the Paschal lamb,' say the ancient
Rabbis, 'the one devours it like a mere glutton, with
the intention of satisfying his appetite, and is a
stumbling sinner; the other eats it with the purpose of
showing obedience to his Maker, and is a walker in
righteousness.' Even more incisive are the Jewish
mystics who declare that 'Torah (or religion) performed without love and awe never takes its flight
into the regions above.' Man has thus to furnish the
Law with wings of love and awe to make it return
to God who gave it, and it is his fault if, instead of
this, he becomes a dead weight to the Law, dragging
it down to the earth and to things earthly against its
real nature. But your much-glorified man is, unfortu-

nately, an unreliable beast. 'Wherever a man is, there shall be a lie,' was a favourite saying of a great writer. This may be an exaggeration, but he is certainly a creature of mixed motives, full of cross-references, which mostly point to his own dear self."

My friend continued: "Now, having recognised how greatly the proper performance of a Mitzwah is dependent on the nature of the performer, and that it is man who becomes a burden to the Law, not the Law a burden to man, we left religion undisturbed, and set to work upon man. Our remedy for all evil is the principle, *l'shmah*, or *l'shmo*, which insists that the commandments of the Torah should be carried out with the sole purpose of pleasing God, thus raising the standard of the performer to that of the performance, in the same proportion as he is able to divest himself of worldly interests and selfish motives. Hence the radical difference between your ideal of a great man and ours. When you speak of your leaders, you praise them as 'men of affairs,' 'great organisers,' 'finished orators,' 'suave diplomatists,' 'statesmen,' and similar expressions, all of which have a certain ring of worldliness and worldly success about them, suggesting the acting of a part, and the acting it well. When *we* get enthusiastic about our Rabbis or Zaddikim, we describe them as 'sacred unto God,' 'holy and pure,' 'contrite of spirit' (*zerbrochener Jüd*), or as 'men hiding themselves in the stuff' (1 Sam. 10: 22), and by similar phrases conveying the idea of an ascetic life, a shrinking from publicity,—religious delicacy."

I interposed that asceticism was a monastic ideal, and that there is no room for it in Judaism.

"Oh!" he exclaimed angrily, "this is again one of your platitudes. *Who* is Judaism? You and I, or is it the prophet Elijah, Rabbi Zadok, R. Simon ben Yochai, Bachye, and the Gaon of Wilna?"

"To be sure," he added, "you are the people of *muscular* Judaism. Of course, you are only parroting the silly phrase prevalent some half-century ago when it was suddenly discovered that outdoor sports and good feeding and brutality of the martial kind were an integral part of primitive Christianity. You at once took up the phrase, and are now thoroughly convinced that nothing is so conducive to holiness as underdone beef and stout, bare knees and championship contests at football. It is only your ignorance of Jewish life and Jewish thought that makes you so susceptible to every fashionable craze of the moment, and ready to claim it as the Jewish ideal."

In this way he went on pouring out torrents of abuse and speech, which I dare not repeat, but I will record here his concluding remark, which was to the following effect: "One of your philosophers," he said, "maintained that the world cannot be too often reminded that there once lived such a person as Socrates, and you cannot too often remember that Baal Shem, R. Elijah Wilna, Krochmal, the last real great reformers of Judaism, not mere æsthetes, were Russian or Polish Jews. As for spirituality in particular, I will only direct your attention to a book, *Nephesh*

ha-Chayim, written by one of the pupils of R. Elijah
Wilna with the express purpose of checking the mystical tendencies represented by the Chasidim, and I
challenge you to show me, in your Anglo-Judæan
publications, a single page equalling it in spirituality
and in depth of religious feeling."

I am now reading the book, and I am compelled
to confess that our "alien" was right.

Despising a Glorious Inheritance

Some time ago, when discussing University topics
with a colleague, my friend made the remark that Jews
and women are in proportion to their lesser numbers
more strongly represented in the various branches of
natural science—to the neglect of all other subjects—
than any other section of the nation. With that in-
veterate habit of ours to interpret all facts in a way
flattering to our vanity, I at once jumped to the conclusion that there must be some mysterious mental
affinity between "Johanna Bull" and "Young Israel,"
making them take up the same intellectual pursuits in
life. My friend shook his head, and said: "The reason is simple enough, neither Jews nor women have
any traditions of real learning." To be a member of
a community in whose ears it is always dinned that it
represents "the people of the Book," and to be suddenly told that one is a mere *parvenu* in the world of
thought, is bad enough ; but what makes it worse is
the unfortunate circumstance that the taunt is not
entirely devoid of truth.

I am only a teacher, not an educationalist, and University statistics do not fall within the range of my studies; there may thus be some flaw in the figures which were at the disposal of my friend. But his remark was perfectly justified, if it was based on the very insignificant part we take in the study of Semitics, more particularly in that of the Hebrew language. In this respect we resemble much more the Japanese and the Hindus whose traditions are pagan, or the African races who have no traditions, than the dwellers of these islands with whom the original language of the Old Testament is an object of deep love and reverential study. Now and then a Jewish undergraduate takes advantage of his confirmation days, and freshening up his *Parashah* and his prayer-book, he manages to carry off a Hebrew exhibition or sizarship. On rare, very rare, occasions it even happens that a Jewish undergraduate takes up Semitics as a subject for honours. But there the matter ends. Unlike the Anglo-Saxon of Christian persuasion, the Anglo-Saxon of Jewish persuasion never becomes a Semitic student or even a "Hebrew scholar," devoting to the study of the sacred language all his time and energies. All classes of the nation are engaged in this labour of love—sons of Cabinet Ministers, sons of generals, sons of high ecclesiastics, sons of great financiers, making theology and the study of the Hebrew language—sometimes the study of the Hebrew language without the theology—the sole occupation of their lives, toiling in it enthusiastically until their dying

day, and enriching it with their contributions. We are
the only cool-headed people who remain perfectly indifferent in the presence of all this enthusiasm. The
consequence is that with one glorious exception we
are as little represented in that gigantic literature
which centres round the Bible—commentaries, arch-
æological researches, studies in Cuneiform and Egyptology, grammatical treatises, histories of Israel, and
other helps to the "Book"—as the semi-civilised races
mentioned above. Like politics in America, theology
and all that is connected with it has become with us a
close profession of no mortal interest to those who are
not in it, which a gentleman may tolerate and even
contribute toward maintaining, but in which he must
never engage personally.

The situation becomes serious when we have to
witness that even those classes that are supposed to
constitute the close profession of theology are gradually drifting away from the study of the Torah, becoming strangers to any deeper knowledge of Jewish
literature. I am referring to the Jewish clergy, who,
labouring under a cruel system which reduces man to a
mere plaything of politico-economic forces, are rapidly
losing touch with the venerable Rabbi of Jewish tradition, whose chief office was to teach and to *learn* Torah.
With us the duty of learning (or study of the Torah)
seems to be of least moment in the life of the minister.
As long as he is *in statu pupillari*, most of his energies
are directed toward acquiring the amount of secular
learning necessary for the obtaining of a University de-

gree, whilst in his capacity as full Reverend he is expected to divide his time between the offices of cantor,
prayer, preacher, book-keeper, debt-collector, al-
moner, and social agitator.   No leisure is left to him to
enable him to increase his scanty stock of Hebrew
knowledge acquired in his undergraduate days.   Occasionally rumour spreads anent some minister, that he
neglects his duty to his congregation through his
being secretly addicted to Jewish learning.   But such
rumours often turn out to be sheer malice, and form in
the worst case only the exception to the rule.   Of
course, as in so many other respects, we are also in
this only imitating the Establishment, in which, by a
peculiar history of its own, the man of business or the
great organiser has of late years gained the ascendency over the man of thought and learning.

Now, there is even in the Church a party which
resents this ascendency, rightly feeling that souls cannot be "organised" and that the qualities which go
toward the making of a "man of God" are not exactly those required of a successful manager of a
company.   But this distrust of the man of affairs must
grow deeper in a community professing a religion that,
unlike Christianity, which to a certain extent began
life with defying learning and throwing down the
gauntlet to scholars, entered upon its career (of Rabbinic Judaism) with the declaration, "On three things
the world is based: on the study of the Torah, on
worship, and on lovingkindness."   Such a religion
cannot well convert itself suddenly into a large charity

agency, without doing serious injury to one of its most important life-springs. Nor must it be forgotten that the Church is not quite dependent for its necessary modicum of learning upon the bishops' bench or on the rest of the active clergy. For this ample provision is made in our great universities where Queen Theology is still holding her own, and where there is hardly any branch of divinity for which a chair was not created and endowed in such a way as to make its occupation desirable. But there is naturally little room in our *alma mater* for that special sort of learning of which the Synagogue is in need (of post-Biblical literature), whilst we can hardly hope that the laity will devote itself to a subject holding out little hope of success in the world and public recognition. We can, therefore, only rely upon our Rabbis, who were always considered the depositaries of the Torah, to remain faithful to their trust; and unless we choose to degenerate into a mere ranting sect, we shall have to give up looking upon our ministers as a sort of superior clerks in whom the business-like capacity is more in demand than any other virtues they may possess.

But if there was ever a time when a revival of Hebrew learning meant the very existence of Judaism, it is this. It must be clear to everybody, I think, who does not allow himself to be deceived by the few political distinctions which have fallen to our share within the last fifty years, that the new century does not open under very favourable auspices for Judaism.

Everything seems to be out of gear. Our Scriptures are the constant object of attack, our history is questioned, and its morality is declared to be of an inferior sort, our brethren are either directly persecuted, or allowed to exist only on sufferance everywhere with the exception of England and Italy. The number of conversions is constantly increasing, assuming in the less enlightened countries such frightful proportions as are known to history only in the days of Ferdinand the Catholic ; whilst even in the more civilised parts of the world, where we enjoy full equality with our fellow-citizens, some of our greatest families, forming in the days of yore the pride and the hope of Israel, are perpetually crumbling away through conscious and unconscious amalgamation. It is no exaggeration to say that every letter patent conferring nobility upon a Jew contains an indirect invitation to leave the Pale and join the majority of his new compeers. Worst of all is the attitude of the younger generation, who, if not directly hostile, are by dint of mere ignorance sadly indifferent to everything Jewish, and thus incapable of taking the place of their parents in the Synagogue. Notwithstanding our self-congratulating speeches at the annual distributions of religious prizes, it is a fact that ignorance is on the increase among our better situated classes. Very few are capable of reading their prayers, and less are able to understand what they read ; whilst the number of those who know anything of Israel's past and share in its hopes for Israel's future, forms almost a negligible quan-

tity. Those who have some dim recollection of the
religious exercises practised in the houses of their
fathers, still entertain some warm regard for Jewish
life and Jewish ways of thinking; but religious warmth,
like heat in general, is apt to evaporate with the increasing distance of the conductors, and the children
or the grandchildren of these sympathetic lookers-on
are bound to end in that cold critical attitude toward
Judaism terminating in the drifting away from it altogether.

The outlook is thus dark enough; dark enough,
indeed, to be followed by some great revival or renaissance, or as the Rabbis put it : " The redemption of
Israel is preceded, like the dawn, by intense darkness,
as it is said : When I sit in darkness, the Lord shall
be a light unto me." Now the Renaissance is usually
described as the moment in history in which man discovered himself. In a similar way the Jew will also
have to re-discover himself. This discovery, which
should be undertaken with a view to strengthening
the Jewish consciousness, can be made only by means
of Jewish literature, which retains all that is immortal
in the nation. There it will be found that we have no
need to borrow commentaries on our Scriptures from
the Christians, nor constantly to use foreign fertilisers
in our sermons. Jewish soil is rich enough for all
purposes, and those who, instead of using their dictionary of quotations and other aids to pious composition, will courageously dig in the perennial mines
of Jewish thought, will find that there is no need to

go begging for an "over-soul" from Emerson, or for crumbs of a tame pantheism from Wordsworth, or for a somewhat brusque immortality from Tennyson, or even for a Kingdom of God with something like a converted political economy from Ruskin. I yield to no man in respect for these writers, but unless we are prepared to see the Synagogue lose its Jewish complexion, the Jewish pulpit must be reserved for the teaching of the Bible with such illustrative matter as is to be found in the Mechilta, Siphre, Pesikta, and in the writings of Ibn Gabirol, Jehudah Halevi, Maimonides, Nachmanides, Luzzatto, the Gaon, the Baal Shem, and other Jewish classics.

Above all, however, it is, as already indicated, of supreme importance that we re-possess ourselves of our Scriptures. The Torah is, as the Rabbis express it, "the bride of the congregation of Jacob," but to acquire a knowledge of it through the medium of Christian commentaries means to love by proxy, and never to gain the spiritual nearness which made it so easy for our ancestors to die and even to live for it. I am not unmindful of the profit which the Biblical student may derive from the works of such men as Ewald, Dillmann, Kuenen, and many others of the same schools. But it must not be forgotten that there is such a thing as a Christian bias, prevalent even in works of the Higher Criticism, and to ignore Rashi, Ibn Ezra, and Kimchi, in favor of Stade and Duhm, means to move from the "Judengasse" into the Christian Ghetto. With Christian commentators, whether

orthodox or liberal, the Old Testament is only a pre-
amble to the New Testament, all the prophecies and
hope of salvation culminating in Jesus. Post-Biblical
Judaism is almost entirely neglected by them, in spite
of the light it may shed on many Biblical points,
insisting as they do that Jewish history terminated
about the year 30 of our era. With the Jew the Old
Testament is final, though its aspects may vary with
the interpretation given to it by an ever-changing history and differing phases of thought, whilst it is Israel,
"the servant of God," in whom all the promises and
hopes of the Prophets centre. It is in this spirit that
a Jewish commentary should be written to the *whole*
of the Bible (including the Apocrypha) for the great
majority of the Jewish public, with whom the Scriptures should again become an object both of study
and of edification. This should be the next task to
which our clergy should devote themselves in the near
future. But a quite different standard of learning will
have to be created to enable them to undertake such
a task. Our ministry will surely rejoice in the opportunity of being translated from the noisy platform,
with its temptation of loathsome and vulgar self-adver-
tisement, to the quiet study, and the community, if it
is as much alive to the duties of the West End as it is
to its responsibilities to the East End, will have to relieve the minister from many an uncongenial and unprofitable duty, which not only makes learning among
us impossible, but deters many a noble and independent thinker from entering the sacred profession to
which he could add only lustre.

SAFED IN THE SIXTEENTH CENTURY

A CITY OF LEGISTS AND MYSTICS

Safed is a small city in Upper Galilee situated on a hill in a mountainous country, and forming part of the Holy Land assigned in the Scriptures to the tribe of Naphtali. Of the various cities of Palestine boasting of a large Jewish population it is relatively the most modern. Neither the Bible nor the Talmud has any definite reference to it, whilst the mention of a locality Zephed, by Kalir, is obscure, and can serve little for purposes of identification.[1]

Yet this was the spot of which R. Joseph Caro wrote in the sixteenth century : "After nearly fifteen hundred years of living in the exile and persecution, he (God) remembered unto his people his covenant with their fathers, and brought them back from their captivity, one of a city and two of a family, from the corners of the earth to the land of glory, and they settled in the city of Safed, the desire of all lands."[2]

The impulse under which the "one of a city and two of a family" acted when they preferred the "land of glory" to the great commercial centres of Europe was a religious one.

Samuel Usque, the famous author of the "*Consolacam as tribulacoes de Ysrael*" ("The Consolation and the Tribulations of Israel"), has the following passage in praise of the country in which most of his fellow-sufferers from the Pyrenean peninsula found an asylum : "Great Turkey, . . . there the gates of freedom and equal opportunity for the unhindered practice of Jewish worship are ever open to Israel ; they are never closed against thee. There thou canst renew thy inward life, change thy condition, strip off thy habits, cast away erroneous teachings, recover thy ancient truths, and abandon the practices which, by the violence of the nations among which thou wast a pilgrim, thou wast forced to imitate. In this land thou receivest boundless grace from the Lord, since therein he granteth thee unlimited freedom to begin thy repentance." [3]

The inducement thus held out to the exiled from Spain and Portugal was not only that they would in the new country be allowed to serve their God, without let or hindrance, but also that an opportunity would be granted them of a total regeneration and renewal of heart.

The sense of sin apparently weighing so heavily on Usque may be detected also in other writers, as, for instance, Joseph Jabez, who depicted the spiritual condition of the Jews in Spain in the darkest colours, and describes the men who witnessed the expulsion as an "evil generation, increasing rebellions and transgressions without number." He declared that it was mainly the Spanish Jewesses who remained faithful, and who themselves suffered, and made their husbands suffer, martyrdom for the Sanctification of the Name. [4]

Another instance is found in the chronicler Abraham ben Solomon, of Torrutiel in Spain, who says, "Our iniquities had increased over our heads, and our trespasses had grown up unto the heavens, seeing the evils and the sin and the terrible pride so rampant among the Jews in the kingdom of Spain." Jabez and Abraham ben Solomon belonged to the anti-rationalistic party of the Spanish Jews, and may have exaggerated the evils of the situation in their accusations, but their feelings were very likely shared, to some extent, by all other exiles.[5] Nathan Nata of Hanover, the well-known author of the *Yeven Mezulah*, concludes his account of the terrible suffering of the Jews during the Chmielnicki persecution with the words: "What shall we speak, or how shall we call ourselves? The Lord has found out our sins. Does God execute judgment without justice?"[6] The sufferers of Spain doubtless viewed their misfortunes from the same standpoint. And since these evils must have been in some way proportionate to the greatness of the catastrophe which had overtaken them, those of deeper religious sensitiveness must certainly have felt the need of a new life and a regeneration.

It is to this need that we have to attribute the fact that large numbers of the exiles were impelled to emigrate to the Holy Land, the country which, from the times of the prophets down to Judah Halevi in the twelfth century, and from the time of Judah Halevi down to the disciples of Elijah Wilna and Israel Baal Shem in the eighteenth and nineteenth centuries, was always considered a country of great "spiritual opportunities."

As a Spanish Jew of the thirteenth century who took a vow to emigrate to the Holy Land expressed it, "There (in Jerusalem, or near it) is the place for ful-filling the commandments and receiving upon oneself the Kingdom of Heaven. Our worship there is accept-able, for there is the House of our God and the Gate of Heaven." [7]

Indeed, it may be stated without fear of contradic-tion, that there never was a time in which the Holy Land was not an object of attraction and deep longing for the pious Jew, even though he was not always able to gratify his longing in this respect. As we know now, there were for centuries after the destruction of the Holy Temple, every year during the Feast of Taber-nacles, large meetings on the Mount of Olives con-stituted of pilgrims from Palestine itself, Babylon, Egypt, and perhaps also from Europe. [8]

These meetings were probably brought to an end in the eleventh century through the troubles of the Cru-sades; but the second decade of the thirteenth century witnessed the famous pilgrimage of three hundred Rabbis from France, England, and Spain to the Holy Land.[9] In the fourteenth century the well-known traveller Pharchi explored the Holy Land, and reported about different settlements in various localities.[10] Emigration to Palestine assumed, however, larger dimensions in the fifteenth and sixteenth centuries, caused by the general distress of the Jews in almost all parts of Christendom. The majority of the refugees escaped to Turkey, but a considerable minority, composed, as already indicated, of the more spiritual-minded among them, directed their steps to the Holy Land.

As hinted before, Safed has no Biblical nor even Talmudic record. Its first appearance in Jewish history dates from about the beginning of the thirteenth century, when the traveller Samuel ben Shimshon reports the existence of a community there of more than fifty members. Somewhat later it is mentioned in connexion with a document relating to the Maimonides controversy, which bears also the signatures of R. Moses ben Judah and his colleagues, the Rabbis of Safed. [11] R. Hananel Ibn Askara and R. Shem Tob Ibn Gaon, of Spain, migrated to Safed in the same century;[12] whilst R. Isaac ben Joseph Chelo, of Laresa in Spain, and Pharchi, mentioned above, visited Safed in the fourteenth century and speak of a large Jewish community dwelling there.[13] Joseph Mantabia, who visited Safed in 1481, speaks of it as a "fine" community, numbering about three hundred families, including those living in the neighbouring villages. [14]

It is, however, not until the last decade of the fifteenth century that Safed begins to be especially noted for the importance of its Jewish population. The man who was the most significant factor in the development of this Jewish settlement, which excelled Jerusalem not only in the size of its Jewish population but also in the number of great men it harboured, was R. Joseph Saragossi. Saragossi, hailing perhaps originally from Spain, was an exile from Sicily, and, after a residence in Beyrout and Sidon, finally settled in Safed, where he most likely established a school. He was of humble disposition, making peace between man and man, including non-Jews, and he probably did his best to blend the various elements of the new settlement, consisting of natives, of exiles from Spain, and of immigrants from the Barbary States, into one great community. [15]

The preference given to Safed, a non-Scriptural town, over Jerusalem, the historical metropolis of Palestine and the holiest city of the Holy Land, may be accounted for by the unfavourable conditions prevailing in Jerusalem at that time. As evidenced by certain contemporary documents, the administration of the Jewish community in Jerusalem was influenced by a rather ungenerous spirit, imposing heavy taxes on new arrivals, and making residence there a great hardship. The Mohammedan population seems also to have been hostile to the Jews, rapacious, and extortionate. [16] Safed, on the other hand, never having had before this time an important Jewish population, the community there had no occasion to make regulations calculated to exploit the foreigner, whilst the non-Jewish population seems to have been more kindly disposed toward the Jews, sparing them the heavy taxation which was the rule in Jerusalem. R. Obadiah of Bertinoro, who had no opportunity to visit the north, writes, in his famous letter dated 1489, that, according to report, the Jews of Safed and of other places in Galilee lived in peace and in quiet, not being exposed to persecution on the part of the Mohammedans. He writes, "They are mostly poor, spending their time in villages, going about peddling in houses and on farms, asking for food." [17]

Another reason which may have been decisive in favour of attracting immigrants to Safed was the simple life led by the inhabitants of that city. The old saying, "Love work and hate lordship" (in modern parlance, snobbery), was followed by them to the letter. An anonymous traveller who passed through Safed in the year 1496 writes of the learned Rabbi Pharez Colobi, the head of the community, that he kept a shop where articles of food were sold, by which he made a living. [18] Shlomel of Moravia, the author of one of the legendary biographies of Loria, writing from Safed in the year 1607, says of its citizens that there were to be found among them "great scholars, saints, and men of action, full of Divine wisdom, so that they were worthy of the gift of the Holy Spirit," but what he seemed to admire most was the simplicity and the humility of spirit which they possessed. "None among them," he writes, "is ashamed to go to the well and draw water and carry home the pitcher on his shoulders, or go to the market to buy bread, oil, and vegetables. All the work in the house is done by themselves," without servants. Shlomel's statement may be illustrated by the following story: Once, R. Abraham Galanti, the leading disciple of Cordovero and the author of many works, was carrying a sack of flour on his shoulders from the market. But there came the famous scholar R. Solomon Sagis (?) and snatched away the sack from the shoulders of Galanti, and pronounced an oath, that no man should be permitted to carry this sack of flour to its destination except himself, who was so much younger and stronger. On another occasion, Galanti was carrying a cask of water on his shoulders from a village near Safed when the Saint R. Misod met him and said, "Master, give me a drink, as I am very thirsty." Whereupon Galanti offered him the cask. R. Misod then snatched away the burden and carried it to Galanti's home in Safed. [19]

Thus material as well as spiritual considerations combined to make Safed the chosen city for the time being. The rapid growth of Safed may easily be seen by the fact that whilst, according to one account, Safed counted three synagogues in 1522, and could point perhaps to only one Talmudic college established by Saragossi, it could a few years later boast of being the centre of learning in Palestine, and, in 1603, according to Shlomel's letter of that year, it contained not less than eighteen Talmudic colleges and twenty-one synagogues, besides a large school for the children of the poor, with twenty teachers and four hundred pupils, maintained by wealthy Jews in Constantinople, who also provided the latter with clothes. The Jews in Turkey were particularly interested in maintaining the Safed schools, and special messengers were sent from this community to collect moneys. We even find mention of a single bequest for the Yeshiboth of Safed amounting to 100,000 *lebanim*. [20]

The history of the world, some maintain, is but the record of its great men. This is especially true of the history of Safed in the sixteenth century, which is essentially spiiitual in its character, made and developed by men living lives purified by suffering, and hallowed by constant struggle after purification and holiness. The two figures standing out most prominently among these are R. Joseph Caro, the leading legist of the time, and his contemporary, R. Isaac Loria, the generally recognised head of the mystical school of Safed. It will, therefore, be advisable to group our remarks around these two heroes. From their eminence we shall be able to obtain a general view of the lives of the other mighty men in Israel engaged in the same general religious activities and pursuing the same spiritual ends, contributing their share to the fame which Safed has achieved in Jewish history.

R. Joseph Caro was born in the Pyrenean peninsula (probably Spain) in the year 1488, whence he emigrated as a boy of four, in the year 1492, with his father Ephraim, who was also his first teacher. After many wanderings and great suffering, they reached Nicopolis, in European Turkey, in which city the son Joseph remained until the year 1522.[21] He was advised there by his Maggid, a kind of Mentor-Angel (of whom more presently), to leave this place, whose inhabitants seem to have been rather close-fisted in their relations to the poor, and lacking in devotion to the Torah, and to move to Adrianople, in European Turkey, one of the various gathering points of the Spanish exiles.[22] There he remained for some years, serving in the capacity of the head of the Yeshibah, or Talmudic College. It was in this town that he began the composition of his work *Beth Joseph*, which occupied him for the next thirty years of his life (1522-1552).

The *Beth Joseph* is a gigantic work comprising four big folio volumes, the first edition of which appeared 1550-1559. It forms a sort of commentary to R. Jacob ben Asher's "Digest of the Law," *Arba Turim*, tracing each law to its original sources for nearly fifteen hundred years, pursuing it through its various stages of different interpreters and codifiers, giving in disputed cases the arguments on both sides, and bringing it down to his own time. It is hardly necessary to point to the tremendous learning and unsurpassed acquaintance with the Law in all its branches and ramifications displayed in the *Beth Joseph*. But what distinguishes it above other work of its kind is not only its comprehensiveness, covering as it does all the contents of the Oral Law which had not become obsolete by the destruction of the Holy Temple, but also the methodical treatment in which he was a master, and which enabled him to bring system and order into this chaos of argument, accumulated in every department of the Law, in its passage through the discussions of the schools for many centuries. Caro was by this work soon recognised as the greatest legist of his time, and was appealed to in matters of law even by his contemporaries, as the first Halachic authority.

Next to this in importance is his work *Shulchan Aruch*, which he finished in the year 1555. It forms only a sort of manual intended by Caro to serve chiefly as a repertory for his great book. The *Shulchan Aruch* soon proved to be the most popular code with students, both on account of its practical qualities and its close correspondence with the greater work of Caro, in which the origin of each law could be easily traced. It passed through several editions, and it is still consulted with profit by Rabbis engaged in giving ritual decisions according to the Law of Moses and the Talmud, even at this day representing the great bulk of the Jews— eleven millions and nine hundred thousand out of twelve millions. The *Shulchan Aruch* is disfigured by a few paragraphs expressing views incompatible with our present notions of tolerance. But there the discretion of the Rabbi comes in. By tacit consent these are considered obsolete by all Jewish students. Every Jewish scholar well knows that the fugitive from the tyranny of the pious royal couple, Ferdinand and Isabella of Spain, was not the person to make an effort to suppress intolerant matter. To meet intolerance with equal intolerance was considered a sort of self-defence. Nay, the student is even convinced that Caro himself would have hesitated to put such laws into practice. He would rather have followed the rule laid down by himself for himself, which was never to be betrayed into anger, even in matters of religion.

The other works of Caro published during his life or after his death add little to the greatness of Caro as a scholar, except, perhaps, certain portions of his *Keseph Mishneh*, forming a commentary to Maimonides' *Mishneh Torah*, and in his *Kelale ha-Talmud*, on the methodology of the Talmud, as well as certain Responsa embodied in various collections, in which Caro's passion for system and order and lucid and logical thinking is displayed even more clearly than in the works before named.

There is still one work to be considered, which brings us closer to Caro's personality, and that is the *Maggid Mesharim*, which appeared some thirty years after the death of its author.[23]   The *Maggid Mesharim* is a long dream, lasting for nearly half a century. For, remarkable enough, the great legist and logical thinker was at the same time a dreamer of dreamers. Caro was passionately fond of the Mishnah, to which he is supposed to have written a commentary, lost to us, and its contents became so identified with his own self, that they shaped themselves into a species of Genius taking the form of a living reality personified in the Mentor-Angel above mentioned.   This Mentor-Angel addresses him with such expressions as, "I am the Mishnah that speaketh through thy mouth; I am the soul of the Mishnah; I and the Mishnah and thou are united into one soul."[24]

As a rule, this *I-Mishnah* appeared to him in the depths of the night, after Caro had studied for some time one or more chapters of the Mishnah.   Then the voice of his beloved, as Caro expressed himself, would begin to sound in his mouth, "singing of itself."[25]   The voice was also audible to by-standers, as is clear from the famous letter of Alkabez, of whom I shall speak later, who was once fortunate enough to observe his friend Caro in such a fit of ecstasy, and who has left us a full account of the message delivered by the Mentor-Angel on that occasion. [26]   From a description given by Caro himself of his prospects of being worthy one day to hold communion with the prophet Elijah, and the manner in which this communion will take place, we may also conclude that the listeners recognised in the strange sounds of the Mentor-Angel Caro's own voice, though to Caro himself these sounds appeared something alien, *not* himself.   His other organs seem to have been at complete rest, which fact produced the impression in Caro that he served only as a sort of musical instrument to the sweet melody of the Mishnah.   On the other hand, his mental faculties remained fairly unimpaired, as he retained complete recollection of all the Mentor-Angel revealed to him.

This recollection he wrote down in the *Maggid Mesharim*, which thus forms a mystical diary, recording the spiritual experience of a long lifetime.   The fact that the book containing these recollections fills only a small volume proves nothing against this theory, as we possess it in a very defective state, whilst we also know that he did not always commit to writing the contents of his visions, for which neglect he is reproved by the Mentor-Angel.[27]

It must, however, not be thought that it is the explanation of obscure passages of the Mishnah that are revealed to Caro in his Mishnah visions.   In the whole of the *Maggid Mesharim* there are only a few

lines of a legal nature. Caro was sober enough not
to allow his mystical proclivities to have a marked
influence upon his judgment in matters of law. What
occupied his thoughts in these moments of rapture was
chiefly the mysteries of the Torah, as well as matters
of conduct, falling under the heading of "superior
holiness." I say "chiefly," for the "I," or Self, occasionally asserts itself and introduces matter which
is rather of a private nature, as, for instance, his matrimonial affairs. From these we learn that he became
a widower twice. His third wife, who brought him a
large dowry, was the daughter of R. Zechariah Zech-
sel.[28] Caro also refers in a somewhat unkindly manner
to certain great personalities. These reflections, which
might have better been left unexpressed, were jotted
down probably in moments of depression and resentment, for which we may not judge him too severely.[29]
In the great majority of cases, however, Caro's Self
was under the strict control of the Mishnah, or his ideal
Mentor-Angel.

The Mentor-Angel is very exacting in his demands.
"I am the mother that chastises her children," the
Mishnah says to him, "be strong and cleave unto me."[30]
This chastisement consisted partly in imposing upon
Caro a number of regulations of an ascetic nature.
He is bidden to fast on various occasions, and even on
ordinary days his menu is prescribed for him, reduced
to a minimum. He must not fully satisfy his desire
for food and drink, not even in the first meal after a
day of fasting.[31] Of course, he must not indulge in

much wine, but he is at the same time rebuked by his Mentor-Angel for having allowed himself to be filled with water. [32]   He is likewise warned against too much sleep, and when he married one of his daughters and, according to custom, spent much time at the banquet, so that he went to bed late and got up just one hour after the breaking of dawn, he was reproved for his slothful behaviour, and the Mentor-Angel tells him that it would only serve him right were he to abandon him, seeing that he separated his heart from the Torah for so long a time. [33]   On another occasion, when Caro went to market to buy meat and poultry for Sabbath and failed in his errand, the Mentor-Angel declared himself responsible for this failure, proceeding to say that he wanted to show Caro that meat and wine are the habitation of the Evil One, that the Sabbath can be honoured without such luxuries, and concluding his admonition with the words, "Think about nothing but the Law of the Lord; thou art strictly observed in all thy actions, hence, be careful." [34]

Other instructions worth mentioning here are these: Be exceedingly lowly in spirit.—Never be betrayed into anger, not even in matters relating to Heaven.— Be chaste in thy behaviour.—Have always thy sins before thine eyes, and mourn over them.—Never speak an idle word.—Give a mild answer to every man.—Never indulge in laughter and in scoffing.— When thou readest the *Shema*, let thy thoughts be so single-minded that they become the seat of the Divine Presence. [35]

He is also reminded by the Mentor-Angel of the necessity of reading devotional books; among these the abridged version of Bachye's "Duties of the Heart" is especially recommended.[36] He is further bidden by the Mentor-Angel to devote himself more diligently to the study of the Cabbala, which Caro seems to have neglected for a long time. "If thou wilt have appointed times for the acquisition of the knowledge of the Cabbala, I will open thy heart so that thou shalt receive the most hidden secrets unrevealed to man for many years."[37]

The Mentor-Angel, however, was not always severe. His motherly ways are not limited to chastisement. Thus he once began his address, "Behold, I kiss thee the kiss of love; behold, I embrace thee."[38] Nor does he confine himself to rebukes and strictures. He also holds out hopes and promises. These give us a fair insight into Caro's aspirations as a scholar and a saint. They may, perhaps, be summed up in the following three points.

The first aspiration was that the books with which Caro happened to be occupied, especially the *Beth Joseph*, should be free from error, and after publication accepted as standard works all over the Dispersion, whilst he himself should be recognised as an authority of the first rank.[39] There is a human touch in the fact, that notwithstanding this anxiety Caro regards it as a joyful message when his Mentor-Angel tells him that he will be blessed with a son who, besides being one of the greatest mystics of the

time, will also write strictures on his father's works.[40]
Caro was especially anxious for the privilege of
spreading Torah in Israel, and had the repeated
promise from his Mentor-Angel that he would be
worthy of presiding over the greatest gathering of
disciples in Israel, and that he would also receive
sufficient material support for his college to enable
his disciples to devote themselves entirely to the study
of the Torah.[41]

As a mystic, all things on earth are to Caro only
a reflex of some original in heaven, and thus in his
capacity as the master of the greatest Torah-school
here below, he is brought into communion with its
prototype in the regions above. It is from there
that his Mentor-Angel often brings him greetings in
the typical expression, "Peace from the College of
Heaven." [42] Sometimes the greeting begins with the
words, "Behold the Holy One, blessed be he, and all
the sons of the (heavenly) college, send unto thee
peace, and are opening unto thee the gates of light." [43]
Occasionally these greetings drift off into a string of
solemn promises of the bliss and reward awaiting
Caro in the world to come, where he will associate
with all the heavenly hosts and the souls of the
departed saints and scholars whose interpreter he was
in this world.[44] It is interesting to see how the Mentor-Angel, with pedagogical insight, uses these very
promises for a moral lesson. For instance, in one
place where he gives him a full description of the
glorious reception with which he will meet in the

circle of the righteous, headed by the Divine Presence, and the fêtes which will be given in his honour, he winds up with the words : "Beloved, the Holy One and all the members of the Heavenly Academy send me to make thee acquainted with this secret, in order that thou mayest see thyself in this high degree, and thus thou wilt never come into the power of sin, not even by an evil thought. Should temptation become overpowering, rebuke it and say, ' Shall a man like me, whose future is meant for such glories, allow himself to sin, be it even only by an evil thought ? ' " [45] This is indeed one of the Mentor-Angel's pedagogical tactics, to impress Caro with his great importance, and at the same time show what duties such importance involves. By the very breath of his mouth when occupied with the uttering of the Mishnah, Caro creates whole hosts of angels, surrounding him as a suite surrounds a king. Every word of his, every thought, creates worlds ; but so does it destroy worlds if it is of an unworthy and idle nature.[46]

The second aspiration of Caro was that he might be worthy to settle in the Holy Land.[47] This is a thought which probably occupied his mind for many years before he settled in Safed. The promise to help him realise that wish turns up again and again in the addresses of the Mentor-Angel. Solomon Alkabez, in the letter referred to above, reports how the Mentor-Angel said, " Lose no moment to go up to the Holy Land, for not all times are favourable. Regard not your stuff (i. e., household things) . . . I will maintain thee." It would seem that material considerations, at least for a time, prevented Caro from accomplishing the wish of his heart, for we find in another place, in which the Angel promises him that within a year he will be in Palestine, he says to him : " There is no need for thee to trouble thy mind; thou hast wanted nothing these last forty years, and thou wilt never know want. Thy income is prepared for thee. Thou hast seen this very moment that the Holy One, blessed be he, gave thee as much profit in two thousand Zuz as in five thousand."[48] When Caro tarries too long on his way, through war and other causes, the Mentor-Angel tells him that he may stay in certain cities, such as Salonica and others, for some time, but he must never settle anywhere until he reaches the Holy Land. Of course, with this aspiration is also connected his hope that he will be worthy of becoming the head of the Yeshibah and an elder of the Holy Land.[49]

His third aspiration was that he should die the death of a martyr at the stake. This is a wish which Caro cherished when he was still in Nicopolis, and which mingled with his dreams throughout his entire life.[50] Caro assures us that in visions without number he received the promise that he would be worthy to be burned for the sanctification of the Holy Name,[51] so that every taint of sin which may have cleaved unto him in his passage through this world would be removed, and his soul cleansed, and thus reach the degree of the holy and pure ones. Here again the Mentor-Angel employs this dearest wish of Caro's heart for his pedagogical purposes, as when he tells him : "Behold, I have singled thee out to be a burnt-offering, to be consumed in fire for the sake of the sanctification of the Name, but thou knowest that in the burnt-offering no blemish may be found, not even in thought. Hence, take care that all thy thoughts are absorbed by the Torah." [52] On the whole, the promises of the Mentor-Angel were fairly kept, except this. Turkey was perhaps at no time the country in which the crown of martyrdom could be easily gained. For this, one had to go to the lands of Christendom, where love was preached and murder acted. Caro showed no particular desire to return to Europe. In this connexion it is rather interesting to note that Caro was not quite free from anxiety, for he found it worth his while to write down the following apparently good message of his Mentor-Angel : During the afternoon prayer, when the reader was chanting the portion from the scroll of the Law, I was told, "Know, my beloved and dear Joseph, that the Sultan will win the battle in which he is now engaged against the King of Edom." [53]

The *Maggid Mesharim* occasionally contains references to different personages mentioned in Caro's other works. But whilst in these latter they are cited with their proper titles, as "Rabbi," "Master," or "the great Rabbi," in the *Maggid Mesharim*, as befitting a production of an angelic being, this official stiffness disappears. Titles are, for the most part, dropped, and they are introduced with such endearing epithets as "my chosen Moses" (Maimonides), "my saintly Asher" (Rosh), "my God-fearing Jonah" (Rabbenu Jonah), "my dear Jacob" (Jacob ben Asher, the author of the *Turim*), "my modest Jeruham" (author of a well-known code of the Rabbinic Law). But the name which occurs most frequently is that of "my chosen Solomon." [54] This name is at most times used for Solomon Molko, but it is not impossible that in one or two places it refers to Solomon Alkabez, two beautiful souls who seem to have been the especial favourites of Caro.[55]

We must digress for a moment from Caro himself to consider the career of these two worthies. Solomon Molko deserves a monograph to himself. He would best form the subject of a great historical novel. If our novelists were somewhat less of realists, and would stop their eternal harping on the problem of mixed marriages, which is certainly no problem to those who begin to consider it in the light of a problem, and if they further possessed something of the sympathetic intuition of a Disraeli and the artistic insight into the past of a Sir Walter Scott or Charles Reade, they would find Molko the hero of one of the greatest historical romances ever written. For our purpose of presenting the friend of Caro a few data must suffice.[56]

Solomon Molko was born in Portugal about the year 1501, as a crypto-Jew, or Marrano, where he

received the name Diogo Pires. He was endowed
with all the graces of Nature calculated to make his
personality both pleasing and impressive. He enjoyed
an excellent education, and at an early age he was able
to speak and write Latin, the learned language of the
time. Like so many other Marranos, he received, in
secret, instruction in Hebrew subjects, such as the
Bible and the Talmud, and even the Cabbala, in which
branches of study he acquired great proficiency. His
various accomplishments secured for him rapid advancement in official circles. He was very young when he
was appointed secretary at one of the high courts of
justice in Lisbon. He was also a great favourite at
the Court. But neither the duties of his office nor
the diversions of Court life were sufficient to fill the
vacuum he felt under the false life he led. His thoughts
and his heart were with Judaism, over whose destiny
and his part in it he constantly brooded. This brooding
soon resulted in all sorts of visions and wild dreams,
which visited him day and night. At the first impulse,
supposed to have been given him by the famous
adventurer David Reubeni, who was then travelling
in Europe in the questionable capacity of an ambassador
of the lost Ten Tribes, he was initiated into the
covenant of Abraham, and became a Jew. This
occurred about the year 1523. He then entered upon
a course of ascetic practices, fasting for many days
without interruption, depriving himself of sleep, and
spending his time in prayer and meditation, which was
naturally followed by more visions of an apocalyptic

nature. The visions were manifested to him, as in the case of Caro, by a Maggid, who communed with him from heaven in dreams. In obedience to the command of this heavenly messenger, he left Portugal for Turkey, which was a safer place for men of Molko's cast of mind. There, as it would seem, he spent the next five or six years. The appearance of this enthusiastic, handsome young mystic made a deep impression upon the Jewish communities visited by him. Molko probably visited also Jerusalem and Safed in Palestine. There is no positive evidence for this fact, but it is hardly possible that he should have failed to explore the places which he saw with his spiritual eye in his mystic moments. Legend reports also that even after his death he would pay visits to his *fiancée* in Safed on every Friday evening, reading in her presence the Sanctification-Benediction over the cup of wine (*Kiddush*) with which the Sabbath is initiated. This would doubtless suggest that he had once been at this place.[57] The end of the year 1529 finds him at Ancona in Italy where he preached on the advent of the Messiah. His sermons seem to have made a great sensation, and were listened to by large crowds, both Jews and Christians, including some high dignitaries of the church. Some time after this he repaired to Rome, in which city he had again all sorts of visions and dreams. He soon gained access to the Pope, Clement VII, who felt rather attracted toward him, and together with certain cardinals, not less favourable to Molko than the Holy Father himself, protected him against the dangers threatening him from the Roman police as a renegade from the Christian faith. He predicted to the Pope the flood which was soon to come upon Rome, and went to Venice for a time. He returned to Rome and had several more conferences with the Pope and other high personages, all the time preaching publicly repentance as a preparation for the approaching advent of the Messiah, in which he was to play a conspicuous part, either as the forerunner of the Messiah or as the Messiah ben Joseph. But all the patronage he had did not protect him from the intrigues of his deadly enemy, the Jewish physician Jacob Mantino, who is not to be held entirely guiltless of his falling into the hands of the Emperor, Charles V. The latter, in turn, handed him over to the Inquisition. The end was that Molko was burned as a heretic in Mantua, in 1532. When approaching the stake, he was offered pardon in the name of the Emperor, if he would recant. Molko replied that he longed for the death of a martyr, to become "a burnt-offering of sweet savour unto the Lord; if he had anything to repent of, it was that he had been a Christian in his youth."

Caro's acquaintance with Molko must have been formed either in Adrianople or in Salonica, both of which cities were visited by the latter during his travels. The acquaintance grew into a strong attachment, at least on the part of Caro, who thought himself indebted to Molko for certain spiritual influences which he had on his life. Thus said the Mentor-Angel to Caro, "God brought thee together

with my chosen Solomon to see whether thou wilt
know him, and it was a merit (or rather, good fortune)
that thou didst learn to know him and also didst learn
from him to fear me." [58]　　It is, however, an exaggeration to think that it was Molko who converted Caro
to his belief in the Cabbala, or that it was the martyr-
death of Molko that incited in Caro the desire to end
his life in a similar manner.　Cabbala was in the air ;
the greatest men of Israel were committed to it, and
it required no special agencies to make Caro one of its
adherents.　The fact is, that Molko was lovable, and
Caro loved him.　That the tragic death of Molko made
a deep impression upon Caro, and mingled with his
dreams and visions, only proves that the legalistic
studies which formed the main occupation of Caro's
life, do not incapacitate a man for the qualities of
admiration and love.　As to the longing of Caro for the
death of a martyr, we have seen that he had the privilege
of calls from the Mentor-Angel while he was still a
resident of Nicopolis, and it was there that he received
the promise of martyrdom for the first time from his
heavenly messenger.　This occurred about 1522, long
before Caro even knew of the existence of such a
person as Molko.　It is to be noted that martyrdom
in case of necessity is a regular command, forming one
of the six hundred and thirteen laws.　According to
some authorities, the supreme act of martyrdom, like
the fulfilment of any other command of the Law, should
be preceded by a benediction, namely, "Blessed art
thou, O Lord our God, King of the world, who hast

sanctified us with thy commandments, and hast bidden us to hallow thy Name among the many." Now, if we consider how anxious a legist of Caro's frame of mind must have been to fulfil a commandment,— the characteristic of the legalistic saints of every generation, —no further explanation is needed for Caro's longing for martyrdom. It was simply his desire to fulfil a commandment of the Torah. As one of the saints expresses it : If the Heavenly Court were to decree hell punishment against him, he would jump into the pit-with all his might and without a moment's delay, embracing with joy the opportunity to fulfil a Divine command.[59]

Much less is known of the life of the second Solomon — Solomon Halevi Alkabez. There are no records enabling us to determine the place where he was born, nor the dates of his birth and death. We know, however, that he flourished about the first half of the sixteenth century, that he was the disciple of Joseph Taytasak, Rabbi of Salonica, and that later he became the master and brother-in-law of the famous Cabbalist Moses Cordovero. His acquaintance with Caro probably dates from the third decade of that century, he having met him in Salonica or Adrianople. Alkabez was a scholar and a poet. Of his books it suffices to mention here the *Manoth ha-Levi* (Gifts of the Levite), a homiletical commentary on the Book of Esther, in which he showed his wide acquaintance with Rabbinic literature, having had, as it seems, access to manuscripts which he very judiciously used in the said work. The story is that the title of the book was suggested by the fact that it formed a present to his *fiancée* on the occasion of the Purim festival. His father-in-law and the girl, the tradition is, were more pleased with this gift than with costly jewelry, which young men were then in the habit of sending to their sweethearts on the day of Purim. But he is best known by his poem, *Lechah Dodi*, " Come, my Beloved, etc.," with which he and his friends used to receive Queen Sabbath. The Sabbath was to him a living reality to be welcomed after a six days' absence with that expectant joy and impatient love with which the groom meets his bride. It is perhaps one of the finest pieces of religious poetry in existence, and has been translated by Herder and by Heine into German. Catholic Israel, whose love for Bride Sabbath and whose hope for final redemption it echoed so well, soon honoured Alkabez' poem with a prominent place in almost all its rituals; and the *Lechah Dodi* is now sung all over the world on Sabbath eve, when Queen Sabbath holds her *levée* in the tents of Jacob.[60]

To return to Caro and Safed : When Caro arrived in Palestine, which could not well have been earlier than after the middle of the year 1536, Safed was already grown to the size of one thousand Jewish families. The additions to the community were mostly made up of Spanish and Portuguese exiles, who were soon in a position to build a second synagogue for the purpose of accommodating their newly-

arrived countrymen. [61] Their numbers were so
increased that they considered themselves strong
enough to attempt to force their special usages
with regard to the regulating of dowries upon other
sections of the community. The Spanish language,
the vernacular of the Sephardim, became soon the
teaching medium in the schools, suppressing all other
languages.[62] They quickly won, both by their numbers
and by the distinction of their leaders, such an exceptional position that we find men of importance and
standing among the native Jewish population vain
enough to call themselves Sephardim, the name common to Jews hailing from Spain and Portugal.[63] There
is reason to believe that at this time also a German
Jewish community was established in Safed, perhaps
presided over by the father-in-law of Caro. We have
furthermore references to a Portuguese synagogue, an
Italian synagogue, and a Greek synagogue, dating from
about the same time.[64] The constitution of these
communities seems to have been strictly autonomous,
each community having its own synagogue, its own
preacher, and its own Yeshibah. They were even, to
a certain extent, jealous of every outside interference,
and it was expected that each new arrival would join
the congregation composed of his own fellow-country-
men.[65] On the other hand, there is evidence that they
had a *Beth ha-Wa'ad* (meeting house), forming a sort
of general board consisting of the Rabbis of the
various synagogues, to which occasionally Rabbis
attached to no congregation in particular were invited.

This board probably dealt only with matters of grave importance and of general interest.[66]

The means of gaining a livelihood were various. The natives, or, as they were called, the Moriscos, were probably still engaged in peddling, as their ancestors had been.[67] There is also evidence that they cultivated the ground in the neighbouring villages, producing wheat, barley, beans, cotton, oil, wine, and figs. Those, again, who possessed some capital, which was probably the case with many of the Spanish immigrants, were engaged in trading, exporting grain, wine, and oil to Damascus and other places, and importing from there articles for which there was a demand in Safed.[68] There also grew up in Safed a large trade in the weaving of wool and in the manufacturing of clothes; these trades were entirely in the hands of the Jews.[69] Indeed, R. Levi ben Chabib, of whom I shall speak presently, sarcastically asks whether it was because of the large quantity of clothes manufactured there that Safed arrogated to itself the leadership of Judaism.[70] Wealthy Jews in Constantinople and in Damascus would, as it seems, send ships laden with wool to Safed for the purpose of encouraging the wool industry there and giving employment to those engaged in it. About the year 1600, such a ship, containing wool to the value of nearly 100,000 *Keseph* and 10,000 *Keseph* in cash for the desperate poor, was wrecked on its voyage, which caused distress in Safed.[71] There was also in Safed a great demand for such artisans as weavers, smiths, tailors, tanners, wood-workers, and builders.

There was probably also some demand for men connected with the printing trade, which was established
in Safed about the year 1653 by two German Jews.
The first book printed there was the commentary of
R. Moses Alsheich to Daniel, and was followed by
several other works. " The print of these books is
excellent, and testifies to the good taste and the
prosperity of the Safed community at that time. "[72]
The only profession for which there was not any room
in Safed was that of teacher, since the community
was, we are told, sufficiently provided with schools
and instructors. Nor was there any place for servants,
as everybody, as we have seen, attended to his own
domestic work.[73] The prosperity was so great
that they were envied for it by their brethren abroad.
Thus a Roman Jew writes in 1543, " The good
message has come from the land of Desire (Palestine)
that the Lord remembered his people and his land
and the Children of Israel, granting to them wealth
and honour in most trades."[74]

However, men did not settle in Palestine for the
purpose of developing the natural resources of the
country. What led them there was, as indicated
above, the spiritual wealth which the Holy Land alone
could afford. In such wealth, Safed, at this period,
was particularly rich. I have already mentioned the
letter of Shlomel, with its reference to the population
of Safed and the various Talmudical colleges maintained there.[75] Though Shlomel writes at the
beginning of the seventeenth century, there is nothing

to indicate that the last decades of the sixteenth century witnessed a particular increase of immigration out of proportion to that of the preceding decades. Indeed, we shall see later on that in his time the glory of Safed was already on the wane. We have the right to assume that the number of Rabbis of the sixteenth century was at least not smaller than that of the seventeenth. Shlomel's statistics are, of course, like all statistics, not very reliable; indeed, the number three hundred occurs too frequently in the letters relating to Safed. It has also to be pointed out that the term "Rabbi" with Shlomel does not exactly mean the officiating minister, but simply a man who, both on account of his learning and his saintly life,—two indispensable qualifications for a Rabbi in olden times,—might easily perform the functions of a Rabbi. Still, there can be little doubt that no place in Jewish history since the destruction of the Holy Temple could point to so brilliant a gathering of men, so great in their respective branches, so diversified in the objects of their study, and so united by the dominant thought of religion, as were attracted to Safed during the greater part of the sixteenth century.

The fame of the "saints and men of action" must have spread "outside of the land" early in the sixteenth century, and it was probably the desire for their society which determined Caro in his choice of Safed. For such was the promise given him by the Mentor-Angel : " I will give thee places to walk among these that stand by" (Zech. 3 : 7), "making thee worthy to go up to the land of Israel and join there my beloved Solomon and the Associates to learn and to teach."[76]

The most prominent among these was doubtless R. Jacob Berab. [77] Berab, who was an emigrant from Castile, Spain, and held the office of Rabbi in various Jewish communities, settled in Safed about the year 1535, where he soon became the recognised head of the Jewish community, which consisted at that time of at least seven congregations. It seems that he gathered around him some of the best minds of Safed, who acknowledged themselves as his disciples. Caro himself recognised him as an authority, quoting him as a rule with the epithet "our great master." Berab has left us a volume of Responsa, to which are appended commentaries on certain portions of the Talmud, but he is best known to history by his unsuccessful efforts to re-introduce the institution of "Ordination" (*Semichah*) among the Jews. This attempt was made in the year 1538, and bears evidence to the high position held in Jewry by the sages of Safed, both by their numbers and by the weight of their great learning: this fact alone could have emboldened Berab and his friends to embark upon their daring enterprise.[78] Ordination, as they intended it, was not the mere ceremonious laying on of hands in connexion with a candidate for Rabbinical office with some solemn speech attendant thereon. What Berab aimed at, was the re-establishment of the body of the Sanhedrin (that could exist only in Palestine), which

would wield supreme authority over the whole of
Israel in various ways, thus forming a new Jewish
spiritual centre. His great opponent in this matter
was R. Levi ben Chabib, a former resident of Safed,
living then at Jerusalem.

This is not the place to enter into the arguments of
both sides, which both parties drew from the Talmud.
There may have been also some petty personal
jealousies; some of the arguments are certainly of a
rather petty character, particularly on Berab's side.
Berab was something of what we might call a strong
man, of strenuous tendencies, and his treatment of
Ben Chabib was by no means tender. But there is
no doubt that Berab's aspirations were of great national
importance, and if realised would have served to
strengthen the bonds of union in Israel. The scholars
of Safed worked in harmony with Berab, twenty-five
of their number signing the epistle sent to the sages
of Jerusalem that contained the resolution of the
former to re-introduce Ordination. The resolution
was soon translated into action, Berab ordaining four
elders, representing the flower of Safed's scholarship.[79]
Caro, who was one of the four, and apparently figured
also among the signatories of the correspondence
with Jerusalem, is especially complimented by his Mentor-Angel for the zeal shown by him for the great cause.
He must also have entertained the hope that he might
succeed one day where Berab had failed; at least, he
received the heavenly promise that he would be the
instrument through which Ordination should be

restored.[80]   This is another of the Mentor-Angel's
unfulfilled prophecies.

The excitement of the Ordination controversy
subsided with the death of Berab, which occurred
shortly after 1540.   Caro, who devoted his time to
lecturing to his disciples, writing his books, and
attending to social work, or, as it is usually called
in Hebrew literature, the " needs of the congregation,"
was constantly growing in influence and authority.
He apparently felt trouble in his mind about this
interference with his studies, for we find that the
Mentor-Angel has to comfort him and make it clear
that the social work in which he was engaged was also
a part of his duties, which he had no right to ignore.[81]

His most formidable rival was R. Moses ben Joseph
Trani, who settled in Safed in the year 1518, and
became Rabbi of the Spanish congregation Beth Jacob,
and the head of the Yeshibah connected with it, in
1521, which offices he retained until his death in 1580.[82]
Like Caro, he was ordained by Berab, to whom he
stood in the relation of a colleague-disciple, and he
showed even more zeal for the honour of his master
than Caro.   Indeed, he resents in one place the in-
difference of Caro to the attacks made on Berab in
connexion with certain legal decisions.[83]   Trani wrote
several works, one of which was of a semi-philosoph-
ical nature on doctrinal questions, but he is chiefly
famous for the collection of his Responsa, which
show him to have been a Talmudist of the first order
and regarded as such by his contemporaries.   Though

generally, like all other Rabbis of the place, confined in his jurisdiction to his own congregation, he seems to have been regarded by the whole community as a specialist in real estate questions. "I have," he says, "been one of the first in everything relating to the holiness of the land in the city of Safed since the year 5335. God put it in my heart to build up the desolate places thereof. I have watched over them in most of their building enterprises, that no man should encroach upon the property of his neighbour, and other matters relating to questions of surveying and ancient lights, even with regard to the synagogues which were built all these years, when (the worshippers) coming from Turkey and other places divided according to their languages." [84]

Several cases occurred in which Trani had the opportunity to clash with Caro's opinions; the most important of these seems to have been one in connexion with the observance of the Sabbatical Year, the laws in regard to which were not considered entirely obsolete in the Holy Land. The great majority of scholars, however, were in favour of Caro's opinion, to enforce it as the norm for the practice. [85] This case arose in the year 1574, a year before Caro's death, but his recognition as a master of the Holy Land or, as he expressed it somewhere else, "the great codifier of the Holy Land," came long before. In almost all the Opinions of that generation, Caro's signature appears first, and his Yeshibah had, according to tradition, a seating capacity of seven hundred students. [86]

This is probably an exaggeration, but the attendance at his Yeshibah was undoubtedly very large, and included some of the greatest names of the time. As one of the Safed scholars expressed it, "We are all his disciples, drinking his waters, and bound to honour him." [87] Among these, Cordovero and Alsheich deserve special mention, both because of their connexion with the history of Safed and their influence on posterity.

R. Moses Cordovero was born in 1522 and died in 1570. Little is known about his private life except that he married a sister of Solomon Alkabez. In Talmud he was a disciple of Caro, who was apparently very proud of him and applied to him the verse, " My son, if thy heart be wise, my heart shall rejoice, even mine" (Prov. 23: 15). We know also that he acted as one of the Dayanim (Judges) of Safed and had a Yeshibah of his own. A Responsum of his incorporated in the Responsa Collection of Caro, testifies to his ability as a Rabbinical scholar, but his fame rests on his mystical work, in which he by far excelled all his predecessors.[88] At the early age of twenty, the Voice warned him to "heal the altar of the Lord which is broken down," under which he understood his neglect of a proper study of the mysteries of the Torah.[89] The " healing " came from his brother-in-law, Alkabez, in whom he perceived a holy angel come down from heaven, and who apparently figured at that period as the leading Cabbalist of Safed. Even Caro himself did not hesitate to seek instruction from Alkabez about a certain

obscure passage in the Zohar.[90]   At the age of twenty-
six (1548), we find Cordovero in the company of the
Associates (*Chaberim*).   This was a society consisting
of mystically-inclined students of Safed, apparently
presided over by Alkabez.   Very little has come
down to us relative to the activity of this society,
beyond the fact that its members used occasionally to
undertake excursions to visit the graves of the ancient
Rabbis supposed to be buried in the neighbourhood of
Safed, on which occasions they would discuss mystical
subjects.[91] But we possess in manuscript a list of moral
precepts drawn up by Cordovero, of which there is good
reason to assume that they were not meant exclusively
for the guidance of their author, but formed a sort of
hand-book for all the Associates.   The following extracts will convey some idea of the frame of mind and
the tender conscience of these men.

They are bidden not to divert their thoughts from
the words of the Torah and things holy, so that their
hearts become the abode of the *Shechinah;* not to be
betrayed into anger, as anger delivers man into the
power of sin ; not to speak evil of any creature,
including animals ; never to curse any being, but to
accustom oneself to bless even in moments of anger ;
never to take an oath, even on the truth ; never to
speak an untruth under any condition; to be careful
not to be included among the four classes excluded
from the Divine Presence, namely, the hypocrites,
the liars, the scoffers, and the tale-bearers ; not to
indulge in banquets except on religious occasions.

They are enjoined to mingle their minds with the minds of their fellow-men (that is, not to stand aloof from the world, but to share both in its joys and in its sorrows), and to behave in a kindly spirit toward their fellow-men, even though they be transgressors; to meet with one of the Associates for one or two hours every day for the purpose of discussing matters spiritual; to talk over with an Associate every Friday the deeds accomplished during the week, and then set out for the reception of Queen Sabbath; to pronounce Grace in a loud voice, letter by letter and word by word, so that the children at the table can repeat after the reader; to confess their sins before every meal and before going to sleep; to use the sacred language when speaking with the Associates, and to let this be always the language of conversation on Sabbath with other scholars as well. In another set of precepts drawn up by Alkabez, dating from this time and probably also meant for the guidance of these Associates, we have the ordinance that the students should rebuke or admonish each other, but the person admonished or rebuked must not make any reply in his defence before the lapse of three days.[92]

The most prominent among those for whose benefit these regulations were composed was the author himself, Cordovero, whose interviews with Alkabez seem to have been more frequent and of a more intimate nature than those of the other Associates. At a later period the relations of the latter to their master appear to have been almost forgotten, and they are quoted as the Associates of Cordovero. Indeed, it would seem that it was the great popularity achieved by the works of Cordovero that is responsible for the comparative oblivion into which the mystical writings of Alkabez fell, so that the greater part of them remained unpublished.[93]

Cordovero's *magnum opus* is the *Pardes* (the Garden), the clearest and most rational exposition of the Cabbala in existence, distinguished by the same qualities of methodical thought and logical argument which distinguished Caro's works in the department of things legal. The *Pardes* gave rise to a great number of works written by various mystics in Safed, in Italy, and in Germany.[94] The book is still considered a standard authority, even by modern scholars who have ever written anything worth reading about the Cabbala. Cordovero wrote besides this many other works, some of which are extant only in manuscript. The library of the Jewish Theological Seminary of America possesses a fine copy of his famous work *Alimah*, known from quotations by certain mystics. But these by no means fully represent his literary activity. R. Menahem Azariah, of Fano, in Italy, one of the greatest of Cordovero's students, states that the *Pardes*, in itself a big folio volume, forms only a thirtieth part of the works which Cordovero wrote, not counting many additions, appendixes, and a number of larger and smaller treatises which he composed.[95] His master, Caro, who survived him, gave the funeral oration at his death, in which he spoke of him as "the Holy Ark

of the Torah, to be hidden away in the grave," whilst
Loria is said to have seen two pillars of fire attending
the hearse, a compliment shown by Heaven only to
one or two men in a generation. Loria is also
reported to have applied to him, in allusion to his
name (Moses), the well-known phrase, "Moses is true,
and his teaching is true." [96]

The second of the disciples of Caro deserving
especial mention is R. Moses Alsheich, who survived his master for many years, being still alive in
the year 1593. The master of his early youth was
probably Joseph Taytasak. We possess from Alsheich a volume of Responsa in which his opinions
in matters of the law were solicited by various Rabbis
of repute. He also wrote Talmudical discourses
and a commentary to the *Midrash Rabbah* lost to us.
He lectured in two Yeshiboth in Safed (which Vital
attended in the capacity of a pupil), and performed
all the other functions of a Rabbi of that time.
He is, however, best known by his homiletical Commentary on the Bible, which was studied both by
preachers and laymen for centuries afterward, and is
still popular with preachers in various countries.
This Commentary is usually cited under the title,
"the Holy Alsheich." Loria gave the testimony
that most of his interpretations "hit the truth,"
though in spite of the efforts of Vital he did not admit
him into his mystical circle.[97]

Besides these and other Rabbis known more or less to posterity, we have in the contemporary literature any number of references to sages and saints of Safed flourishing about this time, in addition to a goodly number of Rabbis and students whose spiritual pedigree cannot be easily determined. The influence of these scholars was not confined to the schools. A religious atmosphere seems to have pervaded all classes of the Jewish population, so that the impression the Safed of the sixteenth century leaves on us is that of a revival camp in permanence, constituted of penitents gathered from all parts of the world. Life practically meant for them an opportunity for worship, to be only occasionally interrupted by such minor considerations as the providing of a livelihood for their families and the procuring of the necessary taxes for the government. Prayer was the main and universal occupation. For this purpose special teachers were appointed to instruct women and children in the liturgy and in the prescribed benedictions.[98] But the regular order of the service, with its fixed hours, morning, afternoon, and evening, did not satisfy their longing for prayer. For them the day began in the middle of the night, when the "learned" and the "men of action" would repair to the synagogues dressed in black, seating themselves upon the floor and reading a special liturgy, the burden of which was mourning over the destruction of the Holy Temple and the downfall of the people of God, and which concluded with a confession of the sins of Israel delaying the redemp-

tion.[99] The example set by them seems soon to have in-
fected the general Jewish public. The man who was
especially distinguished for his religious activity among
the masses was the mystic R. Abraham Halevi Beruchim.
His main work was of a missionary nature. He was
constantly preaching to the multitudes and exhorting
Israel to repentance. In the middle of the night he
would rise and walk through the Jewish quarter,
exclaiming in tears, " My brethren of the House of
Israel! Is it not known to you that our Strength,
the very Divine Presence, is in exile because of our
sins; that our Holy Temple is laid in ashes; that
Israel is subjected to the most bitter persecutions,
saintly men and women being daily martyred by
sword and by fire. . . .? And ye, my brethren, allow
yourselves to enjoy your sleep on your beds in quiet
and rest. Come, my brethren; come, my friends!
Rise, ye holy children, blessed by the Lord, and let us
supplicate the Lord our God, the King who sitteth on
the throne of Mercy." Thus he used to walk about,
knocking on the doors, giving the inhabitants no rest
until they rose and went to their places of worship, so
that at one o'clock in the morning the voice of prayer
or of the study of the Torah could be heard from all
the synagogues. On Friday afternoon, again, he
would go about in the market-place, in the high-roads,
reminding the people to be prompt in their preparations
for the coming day, so that they might not, by being
late, become involved in the sin of the desecration of
the Sabbath.[100] The eve of the New Moon offered

another opportunity for an additional service, when all the people fasted, and "men, women, and students" would spend the day in supplications, confession of sin, and in various ascetic practices. The eve of the seventh day of Passover, of the first day of the Feast of Weeks, of the Day of Atonement, and of the seventh day of the Tabernacle Feast were also distinguished by special readings from the Scriptures and the chanting of hymns, lasting nearly the whole of the night.[101]

R. Abraham Halevi was probably assisted in his missionary work by certain "saints and men of action" of whom it is reported that they used, on certain occasions, to preach on the subjects of meekness, sin, and repentance. Possibly they were members of the society Tent of Peace (*Succath Shalom*), mentioned by R. Eliezer Azkari, for which he wrote his devotional treatise, *Sepher Charedim*. In this he tried to show how "those that tremble at the commandments of our God" (Ezra 10:3) should consecrate the whole of man, in his various functions and different occupations, to the service of the Lord. The thought absorbing the minds of the "tremblers" and forming the object of their discussions at their meetings, was the delay of the advent of the Messiah, and the sins responsible for this delay, but it was also a part of their programme to cause "the many to turn away from sin" by lectures and exhortations. Like the Associates of Cordovero, the members of this society were also pledged to auricular confession, each of them giving at their weekly meetings a full and detailed account of his actions during the preceding week. The necessity of having to lay bare one's life before his fellow-men, and the shame following upon it in the case of an unworthy action would, so they thought, prove a preventive against sin. It should, however, be remarked that Vital, notwithstanding all his other vagaries and ascetic tendencies, protested against this institution, and declined to follow his friends in its practice.[102]

Besides the Tent of Peace, we have also on record the existence of a Society of Penitents, especially distinguished for its ascetic practices, which were of a very severe nature. Some of its members, we are told, refrained from food and drink during the day, performed their afternoon devotions in tears, and put on sackcloth and ashes. Others, again, observed every week a fast extending over two or three days and nights in succession.[103] R. Elijah de Vidas, in his attempt to show how much one can accomplish in the ascetic line, points with evident pride to these Penitents, saying : " I saw many of them rise in the middle of the night, when they would commence to study, which occupied them until the morning, and then fast the whole of the day. All this they were able to accomplish by special Divine aid, for man does not live by bread alone." [104] Of the Associates of Cordovero we read that some among them used to observe a fast extending over three or four days and nights, at the change of the four seasons of the year. It is further recorded that there were many pious scholars who refrained from wine and meat during week-days, whilst others observed on certain days of the year the same laws of levitical purity in respect to their food as the priests in olden times when eating the heave-offering and other sacrificial pieces.[105]

It should, however, be remarked that "doing penance" and chastisement of the flesh were not considered by them as synonymous with repentance. Repentance meant chiefly the absolute determination never to return to sin at the very risk of one's life, which must precede all regeneration of the heart. As Azkari himself expresses it, "Fasts and ascetic practices are vanity and the work of error without this preceding resolution," and he goes on to quote his contemporary, the Saint R. Jacob Gavinezo, who communicated to him the fact that a man committed a most atrocious crime after a continuous fast of three days. Like the sacrifice in the Temple, penance is only of value when preceded by purification of the heart, humility, and meekness.[106]

It is hardly needful to say that charity formed an important item in the Safed scheme of salvation. The injunction of the mystic is to give alms every day according to one's means.[107] This injunction, though originally intended for a small circle, was accepted by the general public, following the example of the saints of old, who used always to make some donation to the poor before beginning their prayers. The custom in Safed was to make a regular collection during the morning prayers in the synagogues. The men, however, with special aspirations to saintliness would tax themselves to the amount of twenty per cent of their income, and it is stated that even among the poor there were persons known to give two tithes. Others, again, would adopt boys and girls early orphaned, educating them in their own families, and bringing them into the holy state of matrimony when they approached the marriageable age.[108]

Yet Safed shows certain characteristics of its own which greatly redeem it from many an unpleasant feature which we are accustomed to associate with the modern revival camp. It is true that the strain was great, salvation being the absorbing topic of the community, and the terror of sin delaying this salvation ever present. No opportunity was allowed to pass for reminding men that Zion was still in ruins, and that man is a sinful creature and in need of grace, hence the injunction to confess sins before meals and before retiring to sleep, whilst the 137th Psalm, "By the rivers of Babylon we sat, etc.," was added to the Grace after meals.[109]

That this strain should produce certain psychological phenomena more interesting to the pathologist than to the theologian, is hardly necessary to state. The literature of the time, abounding in stories of all sorts of demoniacs, bears ample evidence to this fact.[110] We also have stories of men who through their importunate storming of Heaven for Salvation were, for some relapse from grace, suddenly hurled down to the very depths of hell, and doomed to perdition. The most tragic among these is the story of Joseph de la Reina, who flourished in Safed in the early decades of the sixteenth century. De la Reina is a sort of Jewish Faust, who, in his passion for salvation, did not hesitate to employ certain exorcisms and conjurations of a very daring nature. He succeeded in bringing the Evil One into his power, whose destruction is a preliminary condition to the advent of the Messiah. But in an unfortunate moment he was persuaded to show compassion to this fallen angel, allowing him to smell of the frankincense. The fiend then regained his former strength, and achieved full mastery over his captor, who, after realising his fall, abandoned himself to the most revolting immoralities, and ended his life by suicide. [111]

In spite of this strain, however, with all its hysteria and its dire results in some cases, it must not be thought that the Safed community was constantly on the mourning-bench and spent all its vitality in groaning and lamentations. Cordovero laid down the rule not to indulge in pretentious meals except on religious occasions, but these religious occasions were happily not infrequent, and the people were apparently not slow to avail themselves of the opportunities given to them. The Sabbath was such an opportunity, being held as a day of joy and recreation in every respect, physically and spiritually. Fasting was not only strictly prohibited on the Sabbath, but it was considered a religious work to partake of three meals, which, Caro's Mentor-Angel to the contrary notwithstanding, had to be distinguished by certain delicacies. Wine also was served at these meals, which even the Penitents would drink. The meals were further distinguished by a special set of hymns sung or chanted during the intervals between the various courses.[112] The prescribed ritual, again, in the synagogue was all joy and promise, containing no confession or the slightest reference to anything of a despondent nature. Indeed, the Sabbath should give man a foretaste of the blissful Messianic times when sin and sorrow shall have disappeared from the world.[113] Reluctant to part with these hours of serene peace and unalloyed joy, and anxious to prolong them as much as possible, the Sabbath received an extension both at the beginning and at the end. Thus they would, early Friday afternoon, dress in their best clothes and set out in groups to receive Queen Sabbath, with song and praise, reciting certain Psalms and singing certain hymns composed for the occasion. In like manner, they would refrain from work for several hours after the Sabbath sun had set, and spend them in chanting hymns and in feasting. They had even a special society whose members would meet to spend the end of the Sabbath, reaching way into the night, with song and dance. The New Moon was also observed as a partial holiday, affording an opportunity for relaxation and enjoyment, not to speak of festivals prescribed in the Bible, such as the Passover, the Pentecost, and the Feast of Tabernacles.[114]

All these things must have contributed more or

less toward mitigating the evil effects of an exaggerated asceticism. Nor must it be forgotten that joy forms a prominent feature in the programme of the mystic. His maxim was : the Divine light reaching man through the fulfilment of the commandment is only in proportion to the joy expressed by him when performing a religious action.[115]

Moreover, it must be borne in mind that Safed was just as famous for its scholarship as for its piety. Most of the leaders of the ascetic and mystical move-ments were at the same time distinguished scholars. Ranting in such intellectual society was just as much out of place as idle brooding and unprofitable gloom. The study of the Torah, to which they were so much devoted, was always considered a joy, and the Safed of the sixteenth century must have been a veritable Paradise on earth to any man with a tendency toward intellectual pursuits. If his interests lay in the regions of the visible, he would attend the lectures of Caro, Trani, or Sagis, and various other Rabbis at the head of the great Yeshiboth of the place. If he were mystically inclined, he would attach himself to Alkabez or Cordovero ; if he had a taste for homiletics, he would go to listen to the Biblical expositions of Alsheich, whilst he might also spare an hour for the lectures of R. Samuel de Useda on the Chapters of the Fathers (*Pirke Aboth*), whose work on this ethical tractate is still considered a standard commentary. He might besides this pay a visit with profit to the ancient R. David ben Zimra, who, though at the period of his second settlement in Safed, he must already have reached the age of ninety, was still a member of the General Board mentioned above, and interested in public affairs. An occasional walk with Vital might also have possessed its own attractions, for, besides being an adept in the Cabbala, he was, like so many devotees of nature-mysticism, likewise interested in alchemy, astronomy, astrology, magic, and all kinds of occult sciences. In the way of recreation one might attend recitals of the mystical bard, R. Israel Nagara, the author of the hymn book *Zemiroth Israel*, who, though somewhat "vividly erotic" in his metaphors, counted angels among his auditors, and probably came often to Safed on visits to his father, R. Joseph Nagara, a famous scribe of that city. [116]

Safed reached the zenith of its fame with the advent of Loria. [117] R. Isaac Loria was born in Jerusalem in the year 1534. He was a descendant of the famous German family Loria, on account of which fact he was also called Isaac Ashkenazi. It is not impossible that his ancestors came from the Rhine Provinces, from which most of the earlier scions of the Loria family hailed. Elijah Loanz (flourished about the end of the sixteenth century), who claimed some relationship with our Loria, was a native of Frankfort. One branch of this family settled in Poland, whilst the other seems to have emigrated to Palestine. The emigration of German Jews to Mohammedan countries was by no means confined to this case. The impulse to this expatriation from a land in which they had lived for many centuries and in which they had almost the claim of original settlers, came from the Epistle of a certain Joseph Zarphathi, whom fate drove from Germany to Turkey in his early youth. In this Epistle he described "the happy lot of the Jews under the Crescent as compared with their hard fate under the shadow of the Cross," and called upon them to escape from the German house of bondage and emigrate to Turkey. If the German Jews, he said, could realise but a tenth part of the prosperity awaiting them in Turkey, they would brave rain and snow, and would rest neither by day nor by night before reaching there. Another inducement that he offered them was that there is a route to the Holy Land lying open to them through Turkey. Though distance forbade emigration *en masse* from Germany, there can be no doubt that Zarphathi's Epistle was not quite without effect, for we soon find small congregations, both in Turkey and in Palestine, composed of Jewish emigrants from Germany. The Karaite Elijah Bashiatsi, of Adrianople, even complained of the bad influence of these newly-arrived Rabbinical students from Germany, alarming the community with their fringes and phylacteries, and their long gowns and their hoods, making themselves conspicuous and overawing the crowds.[118]

The birth of Loria was, as in the case of so many wonder-men, heralded to his father by the prophet Elijah, who said unto him: " . . . Be it known unto thee that the Holy One, blessed be he, sent me to bring thee the good message that thy wife will bear thee a son. Thou shalt name him Isaac ; he will deliver Israel from the power of the Husks (that is, the powers of evil and contamination which are at war with the powers of the good and the holy, and obscure them); and he will redeem many souls that are undergoing the agony of transmigration, and through him shall be revealed the teaching of the Cabbala to the world." He was further bidden not to begin the initiation of his son into the covenant of Abraham until aware of the prophet's presence in the synagogue. The father did as he was bidden, and the boy proved indeed a wonder-child. At the tender age of eight he was considered to be a marvel of Rabbinical learning, so that none of the Jerusalem scholars could compete with him in a Talmudical discussion. Unfortunately, the father, Solomon, died about this time, and left his widow in such needy circumstances that she was not able even to procure the necessary books which her son required for his studies. There was nothing left for them to do but emigrate to Cairo, where her brother, the wealthy tax-farmer Mordecai Francis, resided. Mordecai received them kindly, and made generous provision for his sister and those dependent upon her. Her son Loria he adopted as his own, and placed him under the care of R. Bezaleel Ashkenazi, the famous author of the *Shittah Mekube-zeth*, under whose guidance he continued his Rabbinical studies until he reached the age of fifteen, when he

married the daughter of his benefactor.[119] His introduction to the teaching of the Cabbala followed
some two years later. According to legend, it took
place in the following way : A stranger, whose
business transactions led him to Cairo, came one day
to perform his devotions at the synagogue in which
Loria was in the habit of worshipping. It so happened
that he took his seat opposite Loria and ostensibly
began to read his prayers from a written book which
he held in his hands. Loria, whose curiosity was
evidently aroused by the sight of the manuscript,
managed to take a glance at the volume, and was
surprised to see that its contents embodied the great
mysteries of the faith. Whereupon he approached
the owner of the book and questioned him as to his
person and his profession, and also demanded from him
some information as to the contents of the manuscript. The owner, who felt embarrassed by Loria's
importunate questioning, stated finally that he was a
mere Marrano, and even ignorant of the Hebrew
letters of the Torah, and confessed that he was
only simulating the reading of the volume in his
hands out of sheer shame before the other worshippers, who were all reading their prayers from the
prayer-books open before them. Loria then began to
urge him to sell him the manuscript, since it was of no
real value to its owner. This request was at first
refused, but afterwards our Marrano agreed to part
with his treasure on condition that Loria would
employ his good offices with his father-in-law, the

tax-farmer, to have the duties upon the wares which he was about to import to Egypt remitted for him.

The book, as it seems, proved to be the Book of Splendour, or *Sepher ha-Zohar*, ascribed to R. Simon ben Yochai, of the second century, and being, as is well known, the main classic of the Cabbalists. Loria then, for eight years, abandoned himself to the study of the Cabbala with all the energy and "fanatical enthusiasm" of which he was capable. The principal subject of his devotion was the Zohar, but it would seem that during the first six years of his study he did not always succeed in divining the real meaning of its supposed author, Simon ben Yochai. However, he received indications from "heaven" that to reach the desired end it would be necessary for him to submit to a more austere mode of living than had been his habit until then. He thereupon retired to a certain village, in the neighbourhood of Cairo, which belonged to his father-in-law, where he built for himself a cottage on the banks of the Nile. Here he lived during the whole week, returning to his family in the city only for the Sabbath. The other six days were spent in strict solitude, and in fasting, praying, and frequent ablutions, beside other kinds of voluntary self-chastisement. This continued for two years, when Loria, by reason of his holy life and complete absorption in meditation upon the holy mysteries, reached the degree of being worthy of the gift of the Holy Spirit, as well as of having communion with the prophet Elijah. Nothing is known of Loria's occupation during the next eight or ten years, preceding his emigration to Safed. We are told that this exodus was undertaken in obedience to a distinct command from Heaven, which announced to him that his tenure of life would be a short one, and ordered him, among other things, to leave the polluted land (Egypt) and go up to Safed in Upper Galilee.[120]

It will have been observed that no mention has been made of Loria's master in the department in which he was most to excel. Legend, which has served us as the source for the preceding description, is quite silent on this point. Nor was there any real need for a master in human shape. For, according to legend, it was the prophet Elijah himself who performed the functions of teacher in the case of Loria. It is further narrated that every night Loria's soul, released from all earthly ties, would ascend to heaven in the company of the "ministering angels," who watched over him until he reached the abode of the Celestials. Upon his arrival there, he would have his choice of attending any of the super-mundane academies, in which the souls of departed saints and great sages continue the occupations which formed their moments of bliss in the course of their earthly careers. But it may be humbly suggested also that Loria had, besides, a very fair library, in which, apart from the Zohar, were contained the works of various mystics who had preceded him. We know that he occasionally referred to them, assigning to each his proper place in the chain of mystical tradition. It is also possible that in the beginning he may have received some aid from R. David ben Zimra, at that time the Chief Rabbi of Cairo, who was also a great Cabbalist; as well as from his master, Bezaleel, who is recorded as having been learned in the mysteries of the Torah.[121]

More important is the indebtedness of Loria to Cordovero. This indebtedness is suggested by a passage in the "Writings" of Loria, in which Cordovero is cited as "our master and teacher."[122] The vagueness of the plural, however, as well as the uncertainty as to the genuineness of these "Writings", make it rather hazardous to base an important biographical fact upon them. But we are fully justified in doing so after the evidence of Sambari, who reports that "Cordovero was the master of Loria for a short time," whilst Conforte describes him as a disciple-colleague of Cordovero.[123] This evidence gathers strength from certain occasional remarks in a version of the life of Loria, in which the personal relations between the two masters are not entirely obliterated. Thus we learn that among the "men of wisdom and understanding whom Loria found in Safed upon his arrival there, were Caro, Cordovero, and R. Joseph Ashkenazi." The fact that these three sages were singled out by name, would suggest that Loria came into close relationship with them. From another place it is clear that it was practically Cordovero himself who designated Loria as his successor. Naturally, legend accounts for it by a miracle. Indeed, we are told that it was only to spare Cordovero's sensitiveness that Loria hesitated so long before revealing his greatness to the world.[124]　　But we may conclude that while Cordovero lived, Loria occupied the inferior position,—that is, that of a disciple in the presence of his master.

I lay no claim to be initiated in the science of the invisible, and am thus unable to determine with any exactness how far this indebtedness of Loria to Cordovero extended.　To cite a Biblical expression frequently used in such connexion, I am merely " looking through the lattice."　And what one can perceive by means of such dim vision is that all the Cabbalists laboured under an awful alternative— the dread of confusing the creature with his Creator, and the dread not less keenly felt of the *horror vacui*, or a God-less world, in addition to the well-known metaphysical, or rather physical, difficulty of the possibility of evolving a finite world from the Infinite. This dread called into being a whole system of emana- tions and immanations, of straight rays and reflected lights, of radiations and beams, crossing each other and commingling, and forming endless combinations, creating universes.　But these universes are, on the other hand, affected by a whole series of checks and balances, or defects and faults, disabling them from becoming identical with the life permeating them, but (just because of these defects) giving them tangible substance, by which process alone the creation of the world, as we see it, becomes possible. Still, this world, notwithstanding the endless grada-

tions and disguises and husks, is not only reached
by a Divine Essence, which created it, but is pervaded by it and is full of it. Cordovero's expression
with regard to the first immanations, that they are
identical and not identical, may be applied also to all
other developments in the scale of the universes.[125]
They are just effect enough not to be entirely confused
with their cause, but in such close proximity or con-
tiguity to the cause that they cannot be thought
separated from the cause. Some mystics were bold
enough to declare the world not only united with
God, but one with God. Even the lowest worm in
this scale becomes to a certain extent identical with
all the causes of worlds or emanations preceding it.
There is, accordingly, a constant blending of the
temporal and the eternal. Indeed, the action of the
first emanation, which assumes some room for imma-
nation, became possible only by the process of the
Divine Essence concentrating itself into itself, and
thus making a place for a world or the possibility of
emanations. This self-concentration of the Divine,
creating space for the universes, or for ideas or
attributes from which a universe might evolve, is
counteracted by a process of expansion, or an outflow of the Divine Essence, thus making Creation
God-full. The impossibility, however, on the part of
the universes, or the "vessels", to become a real
receptacle for the light emitted from Divine Grace,
inasmuch as the receptacle cannot be identical with
the thing received, caused a deterioration in the

descending *scala* of universes or worlds, which brought about the condition of chaos, in which the origin of evil is to be sought. The chaos is so thorough and so complete that evil cannot be entirely without good, indeed, it would have no existence; whilst the good, in the lower worlds at least, is not entirely free from evil. This is especially the case with this world of ours, the most substantialised. It is the world of the Husks, of mere appearances or disguises, obscuring the real realities, and but for the "sparks", or beams, of the holy and pure scattered in it, it would disappear into nothingness, and be swallowed up by its own unredeemable darkness. The elimination of evil, and the restoration of the world to Divine goodness, is the great problem under which creation is labouring.

Loria is usually described as the author of this system of Concentration, called in Hebrew *Zimzum*. Now, it is true that Cordovero, as far as I could see, only once uses this term in his *Pardes*.[126] But it should be remarked that R. Sabbatai Horwitz, the author of the *Shepha Tal* (Abundance of Dew), an avowed disciple of Cordovero, and considered the best expounder of his system, is constantly operating with Zimzum, at the same time giving the most lucid expositions of the Concentration theory to be found in any Cabbalistic book; but he never so much as mentions Loria. However, I am prepared to accept in good faith the testimony of R. Menahem Azariah of Fano, mentioned above, who spent a large fortune in procuring the writings of Cordovero and in giving them wide circulation, but who subsequently declared that the system of Loria bears the same relation to that of Cordovero as the latter sustains to the Biblical commentaries of Kimchi, which give only the simple meaning of the Scriptures and never touch on the mysteries of the Torah.[127]

Some light perhaps may be thrown on this point by a remark ascribed by legend to Cordovero himself, to the effect that Cordovero on a certain occasion expressed his opinion that there was no real disagreement between his system and that of his successor (Loria); only whilst he himself dwelt more on the aspect of the *Sephiroth* (Emanations), his successor enlarged more on the *Parzuphim*, as they are to be found in the *Idras* of the Zohar.[128] Parzuphim, a Greek term, signifies, when occurring in the regular Rabbinical literature, faces, visages, forehead, and features. The mystic seemed to use the term in the wider sense of the "full stature," comprising all parts of the human body, allegorised, sublimised, to represent attributes and ideas. Starting from the favoured notion of the mystics, conceiving man as a microcosm (or the world in miniature), virtually connected with and focussing all the different orders of creation, and pressing (rather unduly) the logical consequence involved in the Scriptural statement, "So God created man in his own image" and similar verses, the mystic reverses the process, and if he does not exactly create God in the image of man, he conceives even in the ideal universe "man in enlargement", and looks to his image for the illustration of all Existence and Generation. His language then becomes less abstract and his metaphors much bolder. He imposes on himself, it is true, absolute silence with regard to the Infinite, or the Unknowable, or the Super-Essential, who is transcendentalised beyond language and beyond thought. But more intrepid grows his phraseology when he reaches the first manifestation of the Most Hidden of all Hidden, which he terms the Original Man, or the Ideal Man (*Adam Kadmon*), the archetype of creation, endowed with certain qualities making it possible to establish likeness "between the image and him who fashioned it." The danger of this system, with its bold negations on the one hand, and its hazardous "anthropology" on the other, is evident enough and needs no further explanation. It should, however, be remarked that no one felt this danger more deeply and warned against it more emphatically than the Cabbalists themselves. It is sufficient here to refer to the compiler of the Idras, which, as just indicated, were the main source of Loria's inspiration. The Idras may, perhaps, be characterised as the mystical anatomy of the "Original Man". They dilate, naturally, upon the corporeal expressions of the Bible in connexion with the Deity, but add to them also limbs and organs of the human body not occurring in the Scriptures, describing them minutely and explaining them in a theosophic and mystical manner. But this lengthy discourse (especially the so-called Great Idra, claiming to have been promul-

gated in the circle of the ancient Rabbis) is prefaced by
a solemn warning by R. Simon ben Yochai, the alleged
hero of this gathering, not to take these metaphors
and terms literally. He enjoins them to rise and lift
their hands when he pronounces the anathema over
those not heeding his warning, with the Scriptural
words, "Cursed be the man that maketh any graven
or molten image an abomination unto the Lord, the
work of the hands of the craftsman, and putteth it in
a secret place. And all the people shall answer, and
say Amen" (Deut. 27 : 15).

Loria was apparently more given to this branch of
the Cabbala than to any other. This is, at least, the
impression one receives on examining the works or
the hymns attributed to him. There the anthropo-
morphistic element is more conspicuous, and the
terminology more concrete than in the works of his
predecessors, and it is not impossible that it was just
this novel feature in his teaching which proved attractive to the more daring spirits. But there must have
been, besides, something great and attractive about
Loria's personality that gave him this overwhelming
influence in a city so abounding in great scholars and
great mystics as was Safed. This will be more clearly
seen if we follow his career in his new home.

The whole ministry of Loria in Safed lasted at the
utmost six years.[129] With the exception of R. David
ben Zimra, whom he had known in Cairo, there is
nothing on record to show that he had any connexion

with the leading spirits of Safed before his settling in this city. But we find him soon, as shown before, in the society of Caro and Cordovero, the recognised heads of the Talmudic and mystical schools respectively. His relation to Cordovero was that, as we have already pointed out, of a disciple or disciple-colleague to his master. As to Caro, we are in possession of a Responsum showing that Loria solicited his advice in the decision of a civil case, which suggests a certain subordination on the part of Loria in purely Rabbinic matters. But this did not prevent Caro from being counted, according to legend, among the greatest admirers of Loria. Their relations must have grown more intimate when Loria's son became engaged to a daughter of Caro. Shlomel, to whom we owe the knowledge of this fact, reports in this connexion, in the name of Caro's widow, that when her husband came home from the banquet given in honour of this betrothal, he said to her, "My wife, I can hardly describe to you how much I profited in my knowledge of the secrets of the Torah coming from the mouth of Loria at this banquet. Not even an angel is in possession of such heavenly lore as he displayed this night, his soul being that of an ancient prophet." It should, however, be noted that Shlomel naïvely proceeds to say that Loria rather discouraged Caro in his efforts to become his disciple in the Cabbala, maintaining that Caro's soul was only fit to receive wisdom on the plane of Cordovero. As a proof of this, Loria is supposed to have given the fact, that as often as he began to reveal some great mystery to Caro, the latter would fall asleep, so that Caro himself became convinced that he was not sufficiently prepared for the revelations of Loria.[130]

The ascendency of Loria probably dated from the year 1570, when he succeeded Cordovero as the head of the mystical school. But whilst Cordovero was admired and revered as a saint and a scholar, Loria was looked upon as one of those superhuman beings who, by a special act of Providence, are permitted to visit us mortals for the especial purpose of our salvation. Their real home is heaven, and they come to us only on leave of absence. According to his biographers, his face was shining like the sun, and his thoughts were chaste and holy. In his knowledge of the Divine there was none like him since the glorious days of R. Simon ben Yochai. He was, moreover, master of all the sciences. He knew physiognomy and chiromancy, and understood the conversation of the trees, and the language of the birds, and the speech of the angels. Looking at the forehead of a man he could tell at a glance from what particular source his soul was derived, and the processes of transmigration through which it had passed, and what its present mission was on earth. He also could discern the souls of the wicked which (as a punishment) had taken up their abode in woods and in stone quarries, in the beasts of the field, in insects and unclean birds. He was able to tell men their past as well as predict their future, and to prescribe for them the rules of conduct calculated to make amends for their shortcomings in a previous existence.[131]

The name under which Loria usually appears in this new hagiology is ARI (Lion), forming the anagram of the Hebrew words signifying "the Divine Rabbi Isaac," whilst his disciples and other enthusiastic followers are termed "the Lion-Whelps." Probably they included among their number several of the old Associates of Cordovero who, indeed, under the leadership of Loria seem to have become more consolidated and to have figured more prominently as a compact body than in former days. It is true that we have indications that some of the disciples of Cordovero hesitated for some time in their recognition of the new master, putting him to the test in various ways. But all opposition seems soon to have ceased, so that Loria maintained the field.[132]

The most important acquisition to the Lion-Whelps was R. Chayim Vital who, it seems, had until then pursued his mystical studies entirely independent of the Cabbalists of Safed. At the time of Loria's appearance on the stage, Vital was living in Damascus, occupied in writing a commentary on the Zohar. He paid little attention to the rumours reaching him from Safed, that a great new master had arisen in Israel. These rumours, however, were strengthened by visions in dreams of the night, which, according to legend, Vital could no longer disregard, so that he determined to go to Safed and meet Loria. They had hardly met before Vital had occasion to learn that at last he had found a master. He soon became the most devoted member of Loria's school and the most active in the propagation of his teaching.[133]

The text-book of the school was the Zohar, which Loria would expound to his disciples after due preparation for it on their part. The Idra, referred to above, seems to have been the object of their particular inquiry and curiosity. But it must be remarked that even in the narrow circle of his trusted pupils, Loria was not very communicative in the revelation of what he considered to be the "mystery of mysteries." The few revelations he did make were made, according to the testimony of his disciples, only under protest, at their urgent solicitation and at the very risk of the life of the master, he having been apparently unwilling to reveal such great secrets to insignificant mortals. But even his disciples could not prevail upon him to give a presentation of his system in a book for the benefit of posterity. Nay, even the permission to take down notes of his lectures was given only grudgingly and, as it seems, was withdrawn subsequently.[134]

Next to the mysteries of the Torah, it was apparently the personality of Loria himself which exercised their minds. Loria, it is true, was vaguely known to the general population of Safed as "the Holy Man" and "the Divine Cabbalist." Occasionally he gave an edifying lecture in some synagogue. There is also a tradition that he was a member of the Board of Censors in Safed, composed of various Rabbis who

were responsible for the morals of the city, and that
he distinguished himself there by defending the honour of a woman who lay under grave suspicion.[135]
According to another account, he came also in contact
with the world through his business relations, to which
he gave up three days of the week.[136]   I do not think
that this report is correct.   It is more probable that
he had some competency granted to him by his rich
uncle and father-in-law.   Be this as it may, there is
no doubt that he was best known to the Associates,
numbering ten or twelve, who constituted the inner
circle of Loria's acquaintance and converted themselves
into as many Boswells.   None of his movements
escaped them.   They watched to see how he rose
from his bed and when; how he washed his hands,
how he cut his nails, how he read his prayers, how he
ate his meals, and more often, how he fasted and when;
how he said Grace after meals, how he addressed
himself to his fellow-men, and what his relations to
them were; how he prepared himself for the Sabbath,
and how many garments he wore on that day; what
songs he intoned during the meal, and how he cut
the bread, and what shape the table had at which
these meals were served.   This fitted in well with
their system, in which man, as already hinted, plays
the important part, especially the "superman," sur-
rounded by that Divine halo which makes him, to
use a Talmudical expression, a partner of the Holy
One, blessed be he, in the creation of the world.[137]
In the Talmud, this distinction of creating worlds is

bestowed on the man who administers justice.[138]   In
the Cabbala, this function of creating worlds, and not
less of destroying worlds (in the case of evil-doers),
is extended to all the actions of man by reason of his
soul being the *plexus* of the whole scale of worlds.
This makes a whole universe sensitive to all his
motions.   In the case of Loria arose a whole literature,
dealing with what is called Attentions, or Devotions,
including the rules of conduct observed by Loria.
The Attentions are for the most part of a mystical
nature, bearing upon Loria's interpretation of the
contents of the ritual and the mystical meaning which
he divined in the performance of every commandment;
but there are also Attentions of more general interest.[139]

Loria's first care was naturally for the young
"Lions", or the Associates, who were apparently in
need of a little taming and discipline, to effect which
he erected for them an "enclosure", or rather, square,
a block of buildings, providing chambers also for their
wives and children.   Isolation from the world, though
living in the world, forms a part of the programme of
every mystic.   But the experiment was not successful.
After a few months had passed, the women began to
quarrel, and imparted their grievances to their husbands, leading to unpleasantness among the Associates.   This mortified Loria very deeply.[140]

The Associates were divided into two classes,
probably in accordance with their knowledge of mystical lore, but this did not prevent Loria from considering
them as one body in the fullest sense of the word,

each of the Associates being held only as a member or a joint of the body, so that in loving himself he loved the whole organism. Loria further bade them to pray constantly one for the other, and especially to feel the distress of each other in the case of sickness and misfortune. The love of the organism, however, extended to the whole of Israel, and Loria prescribed, that before beginning prayers man should receive upon himself the affirmative commandment, "And thou shalt love thy neighbour as thyself" (Lev. 19: 17), so that he may pray for Israel, in Israel, and with Israel. And it was this overwhelming sense of his solidarity with Israel which urged him to read the Confession prescribed for Yom Kippur (Day of Atonement) in all its fullest details, explaining that though there may be sins which he himself had not committed, he felt himself to be a member of the great body of Israel whose individual members form only one great unit of souls.[141] Vital, the favourite pupil of Loria, prescribes as one of the conditions for the acquiring of the gift of the Holy Spirit, "Love all creatures, including non-Jews."[142] Loria himself was careful not to kill any living creature, be it even an insect or a worm. This was probably a result of his belief in the teaching of Metempsychosis, so prominent in Loria's system, which peopled for him the animate world with the souls of a fallen humanity, now appearing in the shapes of lower creation.[143]

Prayer, as may be expected, was to Loria one of the main functions of life, there being, according to him,

no prayer in which man, by reason of his close communion with God, does not become the receptacle of
new Divine light and a new outflow of Divine mercy.
Every word of the ritual, every letter in it, had, besides
its literal meaning, also its awful mysteries, occupying
a most prominent place in the writings attributed to him
or to his disciples. He saw in the lack of proper devotion during prayer the great obstacle in the way of
the redemption of Israel.[144] It is hardly to be wondered
at that such sublime prayer, accompanied by all the
"Attentions" as Loria prescribed them, should be
preceded by a series of ablutions, forming a part of the
mystical programme at all times. It is reported that
Loria said that physical purity, obtained by such
ablutions, is greatly helpful to man, and he would
perform them in the severest cold. On the other
hand, it is recorded that when his mother objected to
them on account of his delicate health, he would
defer to her wishes cheerfully.[145]

This trait of considerateness was an essential
feature of his character. He led, as we can imagine,
a very simple life, dressing very plainly and spending
little on himself, but he would accept the budget of
his wife without a protest, and grant all the expense
she considered fit.[146] It was also his custom to pay
for any object required for religious purposes the
amount asked, whatever it might be. Anger he
declared to be the source of all evil, considering it
as a sort of spiritual suicide, and though he was very
tender in the treatment of his disciples, he once

rebuked one of the Associates who showed too much
resentment against his brother for not being sufficiently
attentive to his studies.[147]   The man who is betrayed
into anger puts up a strange god in his heart, which
is a sanctuary, and where the Divine Presence should
dwell.   Hence, let no man be betrayed into anger,
either against a Gentile or a Jew, not even in the case
when he has been robbed or insulted, but let always
his mind remain calm.   "The Lord, his God, is with
him, and the shout of the King is in him."   It is
reported that the Loria Associates made it a rule not
to initiate anyone into the mysteries of the Cabbala
who was by temperament inclined to anger.[148]   There
is also a story about Loria that he would, on his
walks, usually place himself behind a certain student
of Safed.   It seems that his disciples rather resented
this humility of their master, and expostulated with
him.   His answer was to the effect that he could see
that the student felt especially honoured by walking
before him; since this was his desire, Loria thought it
his duty to satisfy it; just as we, according to the
Rabbinic law, are bound to provide a proper escort for
the poor of noble descent, if they have been accustomed to it all their lives.[149]

It is hardly necessary to say that Loria was chari-
table; he had appointed times every day when he
gave a certain amount of alms to the treasurer of his
synagogue, but he further considered it as a solemn
act, and would, as in the most important prayers,
stand on his feet when he gave his *Perutah*.   Often he

would give all the money in his possession, not looking to see whether anything remained in his pocket.[150]
This is certainly against all the rules of scientific charity.
I hope that we shall overlook this defect in his
character when we remember the remark of a French
philosopher of the eighteenth century, who said that
"magnanimity owes no account of its motives to
prudence."

He was especially strict in the fulfilment of the
command bidding us to pay the workman his wages
on the very day on which he has performed his labour
(Deut. 24 : 15), and it went so far with him that he
would not allow himself to read the afternoon prayer
before getting the necessary money to pay off debts of
this kind, saying, "How dare I approach my Maker
when such a commandment came within my reach and
I did not accomplish it?"[151]

In this connexion, the following story may be reproduced: As we have seen, many Jews in Safed were
engaged in the clothing trade. Among these was R.
Abraham Galanti, referred to above. One day Galanti
came to Loria asking him, as the phrase was, to "give an
improvement to his soul,"—that is, to tell him whether
Loria had not detected that he was backward in the
fulfilment of one of the commandments. Loria at first
declined to comply with his wish, as Galanti was one
of the scholars and saints of Safed; but after much
urging, he fixed his eyes on Galanti's forehead and
said to him, "that he was defective in the commandment
'Thou shalt not defraud thy neighbour, neither rob him'"

(Lev. 19 : 13). The mystical notion is that sin and passion leave their impression on the face of man, and disfigure the image of God. Galanti went home trembling in every limb, and deeply mortified that he should have disgraced himself so far as to be involved in the sin of dishonesty. He put on sackcloth and spread ashes on his head in accordance with the usage of penitents, and called a meeting of all the hands engaged in his factory. When they arrived, he said to them: "Know ye not that I am only flesh and blood, and therefore subject to error? Accordingly, I must ask that you should examine most carefully your accounts with me, to see that I do you no wrong." Their answer was: "We have no account against you. Since we have been in the master's employ we are wanting in nothing, and the Lord has sent us his blessing. There is none among us who would think of making a bill of his demands." Thereupon the Rabbi said: "It is through your negligence in this respect that I have become the victim of sin. I will, therefore, put money before you; take what you desire, and forgive any claims you may have against me." But they would not touch the money, except one woman, who stretched out her hands and took two *Perutoth*. Galanti then went to Loria, who said, as he came out to meet him, "Why did you feel so mortified?" Galanti answered, "Is it a small matter that I should feel that I may possibly have robbed somebody? Now, if I have found grace in your eyes, tell me if the mark of this sin is still upon my forehead?" Loria answered, "No sign of sin is visible any longer," and revealed to him that the mistake consisted in the fact that this woman who had taken two *Perutoth* was one of the best weavers in his factory, and should have been better paid than the other employees. "But they are very particular in heaven about such things," said Loria, "hence the ugly mark which I perceived on you." [152]

Sabbath was the day of days with Loria and the Associates, new heavenly light reaching our sublunar regions on that day. The preparation for the Sabbath began Friday morning, when Loria would read the portion of the week from a scroll of the Pentateuch. Then would come dressing the hair, ablutions, and arraying himself in white garments in honour of the Sabbath. Early in the afternoon, Loria would form a procession, together with the Associates, to the fields to receive there Queen Sabbath with the song, "Come, my Beloved." [153] It was on such occasions that Loria, who was otherwise, as we have seen, rather reserved in revealing the mysteries of the Torah, would become communicative and uncover Divine secrets which no ear had been worthy enough to listen to before. And not only would the living profit by this hour of grace, but also the souls of the departed would benefit, wandering about for eternities, and taking up their abodes in the different kingdoms, the mineral, the vegetable, and the animal. These would on such occasions come to Loria, asking for his prayers to lift them up into the higher regions. "He saw spirits everywhere, and heard their whispers in the rushing of the water, in the movements of the trees and grass, in the song or twittering of the birds, even in the flickering of flames."[154] The neighbourhood of Safed, to which legend, long before this period, had transferred from Judæa the earthly remains of prophets and ancient sages, became to Loria, who saw their souls hovering on the graves, a veritable Valley of Jehoshaphat in the hour of resurrection. He held intercourse with them, and united, in "concentrated prayer," his soul with theirs.[155] But, above all, it was contemporary humanity which harboured these souls, if such an expression be permissible with Loria. Indeed, recognising as Loria did, by the process of metempsychosis, in every person he met old acquaintances from history, with whom he had associated in a former existence, and believing further, as he did, that it was only with the advent of the Messiah that this transmigration of souls would cease, all limits of space and time practically disappeared for him. To him the "generations past and the generations to come formed with those who are alive one single whole." All souls were evolved from the "original soul" of Adam, derived from the different parts of his body, and they suffered by his Fall. All live eternally, and are swayed by almost the same passions and by the same ideals as they were before. A certain neighbour of Loria, of a quarrelsome disposition, was none else to him than Korah of old, whilst Loria himself was a spark of the soul of Moses.[156] R. Abraham Halevi, referred to above, was reported by legend to have perceived the Divine Glory during his prayers at the Holy Wall in Jerusalem. Loria thereupon discovered in him a spark of the soul of the prophet Jeremiah, who, according to a Rabbinical legend, had a similar vision on the same consecrated spot.[157]   R. Moses Alsheich, again, famous, as noted above, for his homiletical works, was pregnant with the soul of R. Samuel ben Nachmani, the famous Agadist of the fourth century.[158]   Loria himself and the Associates, in their present capacity as mystics, represented the reincarnation of the supposed heroes of the Zohar, headed by R. Simon ben Yochai and his son R. Eleazar.[159]   Men were not to him what they were, but what they had been once, and it was their former existence which determined his relations to them.   Thus it is reported that one morning his disciple R. Samuel de Useda entered the house of Loria, who was lecturing to the Associates.   Loria, upon perceiving him, at once arose before him and greeted him with the words, "Blessed be he that cometh," took him by the hand, placed him at his right side, and had a long conversation with him.   Vital, who was present, was curious to know why his master showed this young man so much honour, and asked him the reason.   He said : It was not before him that I arose, but before the soul of R. Phinehas ben Jair, who lived some eight hundred years ago, and was especially distinguished by his acts of charity and lovingkindness. Of this soul the young man became possessed to-day. Upon inquiry, Useda confessed that that morning, on his way to the synagogue, he had passed by a house from which the voice of lamentation and crying reached his ears. When he went in, he found the tenants all naked, robbers having taken away their clothes. He at once gave them all the raiment he had on, and returned home, where he clad himself in his Sabbath garments.[160]

Such things Loria saw best on the eve of the Sabbath by the aid of the Divine light radiating from the holiness of the day to come. When the prayers and the songs in the fields were over, Loria would return home, where he would be met by his mother, whom he kissed on entering the house. As it would seem, he was accompanied by Vital, who used to spend the Sabbath with him. Then would begin, as we can imagine, the *Kiddush* (Sanctification of the day over the cup of wine), and the meal, at which any number of concentrated "Attentions" were observed. We are also in possession of three mystical songs composed by Loria himself, sung at the three meals by which the Sabbath day was distinguished.[161]

The Sabbath emitted its rays, lighting up the whole week, sanctifying even such moments of human life as those in which material needs and common passions are very little favourable to spirituality. Loria, in common with other mystics, succeeded in spiritualising the whole life of man, just as the legalist finds nothing in human affairs which is either above or below the Torah. De Vidas, referred to before, the favourite pupil of Cordovero, wrote a book, *Reshith*

Chochmah, dealing with such topics as the fear of God,
the love of God, holiness, humility, sin, reward and
punishment, and repentance, but he did not disdain to
devote whole pages to such subjects as the intimate
relations or intercourse between the sexes, commerce
and trade, good manners and social etiquette, all of
which form a part of the sacred life.   The same thing
may be observed of the pupils of Loria.   The book,
Ez ha-Chayim (The Tree of Life), ascribed to Vital and
supposed to represent a compilation of the most
important of Loria's teachings, is prefaced among
others by this motto, "Depart from evil and do good"
(Psalms 34 : 14).   It is followed by a number of rules,
some of which we have already met with in the preceding remarks.   The first of them impresses upon
the mystic the necessity of the strict fulfilment of the
Law in all its minutiæ, whether Scriptural or traditional.[162]   "The Gates of Holiness," by Vital, gives
a set of rules for those who are in search of eternal
perfection, the absorption in the Divine, and is pervaded by the same spirit of loyalty to the Law, both
in its ceremonial and moral parts.

Thus the Safed of the sixteenth century, at least,
is free from all antinominian tendencies, which are the
supposed inevitable consequences of mysticism.   The
Safed Jew of that period saw no antagonism of principle
between Caro and Loria.   Caro was for him the authority,
Loria the model.   But just as Loria was amenable to
the discipline of the Law, so was Caro not unresponsive
to the finer impulses of love and admiration.

Loria died in the year 1572 (according to some, in 1574) after a short illness of three days.[163]   Vital took over the leadership, and it was under his direction that various writings and works were soon compiled and put into circulation, claiming the authority of Loria.   How far Loria would have felt himself responsible for all that was then written and said in his name, is a question not to be easily decided. Probably he would have disowned a great deal of what was afterwards known as the writings of Loria. I have already referred to his hesitation in giving publicity to what he considered to be the secrets of the Torah, but he must also have felt that his highly-coloured metaphors and rich imagery might become a stumbling-block to those who had not passed through all the grades of holiness, and were not satisfied with being brought near God on the "religious-fatigue" system, but preferred to have God brought down to them.   We have it also on good authority that before his death he said to his disciples, "Know for a truth that you have not a single Proposition (of the mystical lore expounded by Loria) that can be considered complete."   When they said to him, "Not even R. Chayim Vital?" he answered : Perhaps he knows a little more than you, but not much.[164]

The Propositions, however, concerned only a few exalted personages among the mystics, who made them the special subject of their studies and further development.   What filtered through these Propositions and reached those who laid no claim to this title, "was not metaphysic but moral, not immanence but sin," or rather the fear of sin. The Propositions placed man, as already hinted at, upon a pedestal, the eminence of which caused giddiness to many an exalted personage, who, deeming himself a god or a demi-god, lost his balance and fell beyond hope of redemption. The great majority of Israel remained mindful of the old warning, "Be not rash with thy mouth, and let not thine heart be hasty to utter anything before God : for God is in heaven, and thou upon earth · therefore let thy words be few" (Eccles. 5 : 2). Haste and rashness became especially discredited after the bursting of that theological bubble known in history as the Pseudo-Messianic claims of Sabbatai Zebi. The Propositions, with the over-emphasis of the God-likeness of man, were only allowed to stand so far as God-likeness demanded superior holiness on the part of man   With a proper instinct the people at large left the *Ez ha-Chayim* by Vital, with its Propositions, to the few, and it lasted nearly two centuries till it first appeared in print ; but his book "The Gates of Holiness," with its deeply ethical contents, became at once a popular tract, and passed through many editions. Likewise, the Jewish public took but little notice of R. Moses Chayim Luzzatto's "One Hundred and Thirty-Eight Doors of Wisdom", but it did appreciate at once his noble "Path of the Upright", preaching morality and holiness.   The book is constantly going through new editions, and in certain parts of the East there are special "Path of the Upright Societies" devoted to the study of this book. The Safed influence is especially marked on the devotional works of R. Isaiah Horwitz, R. Aaron Kaydanower, and R. Elijah Cohen, which works became the common spiritual good of the people. Their morality is austere, their tone sombre, and their demands on man's religious capabilities exacting. All this is traceable enough in the work of the Safed penitents. They certainly have not erred on the line of self-complacency and self-righteousness. They warn man not to behave "as so many fools do," who are so over-confident of their salvation because they are engaged in their trade the whole day, recite punctually the three prescribed prayers for the day, and neither steal nor rob nor commit any other acts of gross immorality, and harm nobody. These are cheap virtues, according to our moralists, of which even the Gentiles are not devoid, and which one's neighbours from motives of self-preservation would compel one to observe. What justifies man to entertain exalted hopes of the "world to come" is, according to the stern moralists, the minute observance of the Law in all its details "in great love," the constant increasing in the quality of saintliness, the possession of the quality to please God and man, and the readiness to give up his life in perfect joy for the sake of the love of God. On the other hand, they have, as indicated above, retained enough of the Safed emphasis of the God-likeness of man to disregard in the end the dualism of flesh and spirit, a conception un-Jewish in its origin, and now revived only under a mistaken notion of "spirituality." In spite of the ascetic teachings, with their depreciation of the "turbid body," to be threatened by the terrors of hell and cajoled by the joys of paradise, they were thus able to insist upon the holiness of the flesh (*Kedushath ha-Guph*) and upon its purity as much as upon that of the soul, as well as to accord to the flesh a share in the bliss to come, held out to man as a consequence of a holy and religious life, which a supercilious philosophy entirely denied.[165]

Caro passed away in 1575, Trani five years later (1580). The decline of Safed soon set in. Samson Bak, who travelled in Palestine in 1588, was compelled to leave Safed for Jerusalem on account of the distress which had overtaken the former city at that period. R. Isaiah Horwitz, who settled in Palestine soon after the beginning of the seventeenth century, describes the Jerusalem population as richer in numbers than that of Safed.[166]

The men who succeeded Caro and Loria were, for the most part, their disciples. R. Moses Galanti, an ordained disciple of Caro and an adherent of Loria, R. Yomtob Zahalon, described as the head of the city of Safed and of the Yeshibah, and R. Joseph Trani, the son of R. Moses Trani, who obtained in later life even more distinction than his famous father, seem to be the most prominent names of this period. At least this is the impression we receive from their Responsa collections, in which they figure as men of weight and authority. They still meet in the general board; and in a document giving the minutes of such a meeting dating from the first decade of the seventeenth century, we have the signatures of not less than twenty Rabbis, with some of whom we made acquaintance in the former pages. Mention is also made of a rabbi Joshua ben Nun, who is described as the Chief Rabbi and the head of all the heads of the colleges, and who was, besides, the administrator of all the charities of the city. The old devotion to the study of the Torah and the occupation with mystical literature are still continued. After they finished their prayers, the whole congregation formed themselves into groups, listening to lectures on such subjects as Bible, Halachah, Hagadah, or the Zohar, so that none left the Synagogue to go to business before he gave some time to study. The fifth day in the week (Thursday) seems to have been a special day of devotion, when they would all gather in one big synagogue to pray for Israel and to bless those who sent support for the poor of the Holy Land. The service would conclude with a sermon by Galanti and other men distinguished for their humility and saintliness. It is not impossible that this synagogue was the one built by a wealthy man in Constantinople in memory of Loria, and richly endowed by him.[167] None, however, was sufficiently great to make his authority felt in such a way as to give him any real prominence over his contemporaries. Even Vital's authority does not seem to have been quite undisputed. He afterwards left

Safed and died in Damascus in 1620, and the sons of Caro and Trani emigrated to Turkey. The Chmielnicki persecutions of the middle of the seventeenth century, which must have taxed the resources of Jewry to its utmost, probably withdrew a good deal of the support which Safed had received till then for its Talmudical Colleges; whilst the excesses of certain Cabbalists about the same period, who joined pseudo-Messiah movements, must have put a damper upon the zeal of the mystics and the study of mysticism which was the special glory of Safed.

Safed thus ceases to be a centre of attraction. It decays slowly, and Jerusalem comes to its rights. It lives on the past, profiting by the glory of Caro, Trani, Loria, and Cordovero. Even to-day the Synagogue of Caro and the Synagogue of Loria form the main sights in Safed. But it is not any longer the Safed of the sixteenth century.

APPENDIXES

APPENDIXES

The following two Appendixes bear upon the subject of the ninth essay "Safed in the Sixteenth Century"—A City of Legists and Mystics." In Appendix A are published, for the first time, from manuscripts, four lists of moral precepts and usages observed by the saints of Safed, in some cases by the community at large. They throw important light upon the spiritual history of the community in that century, and they are often referred to in the Notes on this essay. These four lists were composed by R. Moses Cordovero, Abraham Galanti, Abraham Halevi, and Moses of לוריאה (Lieria?). The first three are famous names, and occur often in our text, whilst Moses of לוריאה is known only by a reference to him in the Responsa of R. Abraham de Boton, in connexion with a money litigation, where he is called *Chacham*. Three of these lists are reproduced from a manuscript in the Library of the Jewish Theological Seminary of America, whilst the first was copied from MS. C 812, X 893, bearing the title *Likkute Shoshanim*, in Columbia University Library, containing only this list, but in a better text. On the other hand, there are missing in it the last five precepts, which were supplied from the Seminary MSS. They are indicated by square brackets.

Appendix B forms an attempt to furnish a list of the names of the sages and the saints of Safed in the sixteenth century, not all of whom could well be brought into the text. It is impossible to adhere rigidly to the date, and there occur names of persons who come to the front in the first two or three decades of the seventeenth century, after the disappearance of Caro, Trani, Cordovero, and Loria. But as they were more or less connected, either as disciples or followers of the authorities just mentioned, and certainly had already reached the meridian of life when the seventeenth century broke upon them, we have a right to include them in this list. Others, again, came to Safed only in their old age, or they may have stayed there only for a time, but they all contributed to the fame of Safed in that century. The sources used are the regular biographic and bibliographic authorities, such as Conforte, Sambari, Azulai, Michael, to which general references are given. In other cases, references are given to Responsa and to the Diary of Vital, and to the book גלגולים. In questionable cases, the doubt is indicated by a query. Of course, this list is to be considered as a mere attempt. It is impossible to obtain certainty in all cases, for there occur in the Responsa names connected with Safed for which there is really no authority that they ever lived in this place, their opinions having been obtained through correspondence with the Safed Rabbis.

LIST OF ABBREVIATIONS

OCCURRING IN APPENDIX B (PP. 302–6) AND IN THE NOTES ON "SAFED IN THE SIXTEENTH CENTURY" (PP. 317–28)

AN. JB. Letter by an anonymous traveller, published in the *Jahrbuch für die Gesch. des Juden.*, vol. 3. Leipzig, 1863.

AZ. or AZULAI. Chayim Joseph David Azulai.—שם הגדולים.

AZKARI. Eliezer b. Moses Azkari.—ספר חרדים (ed. Warsaw, 1879).

BERTINORO. Letters of travel by R. Obadiah, of Bertinoro, published in the *Jahrbuch für die Gesch. des Juden.*, vol. 3. Leipzig, 1863.

CALIMANI. R. Baruch b. Simchah Calimani.—Introduction to the Commentary of R. Moses Alsheich to the Pentateuch (Venice, 1601).

CARO I. R. Joseph Caro—Responsa.—אבקת רוכל.

CARO II. Responsa on דיני נשים (ed. Mantua, 1730).

CHABIB. R. Levi Aben Chabib.—Responsa (Venice, 1565).

CH. Y. חמדת ימים, ascribed to Nathan of Gaza; but see also כבוד חכמים by Menahem Mendel Heilperin (ed. Livorno, 1762–4).

CON. or CONFORTE. David Conforte.—קורא הדורות (ed. Cassel).

FRUMKIN. Arye Löw Frumkin.—אבן שמואל.

GHIRONDI. Samuel Mordecai Ghirondi, partial author of תולדות גדולי ישראל.

ג״ל. ספר הגלגולים (Przemysl, 1875).

Kahana. David Kahana.—אבן נגף.

Kaydanower. R. Zebi b. Aaron Samuel Kaydanower.—
קב הישר.

Mi. Heimann Joseph Michael.—אור החיים (Frankfort, 1891).

MM. מגיד משרים, by Caro (ed. Wilna, 1879).

MN. ספר הכונות ומעשה נסים (Constantinople, 1720).

Pardes. Moses b. Jacob Cordovero.—פרדס רמונים.

Rabinowitz. Saul Pinchas Rabinowitz.—מוצאי גולה (Warsaw, 1894).

Radbaz (usually abbreviated ר'ד'ב'ז). David b. Solomon Abi Zimra.—Responsa.

Samb. or Sambari. "Mediæval Jewish Chronicles" (ed. Neubauer, Oxford, 1887).—Containing also extracts of the Chronicles of Joseph b. Isaac Sambari, pp. 115–162.

Schwarz. תבואות הארץ, by Joseph Schwarz (ed. A. M. Luncz, Jerusalem, 1900).

SG. Moses ben Jacob Cordovero. ספר גרושין, Venice, 1600.

Sh. J. Baruch (Jacob b. Moses Chayim).—שבחי ירושלים (containing also a traveller's account of Palestine, in 1522, by an anonymous author. Livorno, 1785).

Shlomel. R. Solomon b. Chayim Meinsterl, better known as Shlomel.—שבחי הארי, together with the לקוטי ש״ם (Livorno, 1790).

Trani. R Moses b. Joseph of Trani.

Vital. R. Chayim b. Joseph Vital.—שבחי ר' חיים וויטאל (Ostrog, 1826).

אלה הדברים

אשר דיבר משה איש האלהי הרמ"ק זללה"ה אשר יעשה אותם האדם וחי בהם ויש בו ל"ו דברים.

א' אל יפנה לבו מלהרהר בדברי תורה ודברי קדושה שלא יהא לבו פנוי וריק מהרהורי מצוה בתורה ובמצות כדי שיהא לבו משכן לשכינה.

ב' שלא יכעוס כלל שהכעס מביא לאדם לידי כמה עבירות וצא ולמד ק"ו ממרע"ה וכבר ידעת מרז"ל בזוהר על ענין פגם הכעס בפסוק חדלו לכם מן האדם אשר נשמה באפו וגו' ובפסוק טורף נפשו באפו וגו' ואפילו יקומו כנגדו יהיה מן הנעלבים.

ג' לעולם יהא דעתו מעורב עם הבריות ויתנהג עמהם בנחת ואפילו על העוברים על התורה יתנהג בנחת.

ד' שלא לשתות יין ביום כלל ועיקר אלא בלילה ומזוג חוץ משבתות וימים טובים ור"ח שישתה ביום.

ה' למעט בבשר ויין בימי החול אפילו בלילה מפני שנותן כח לסמ'.

ו' שלא להרהר בדברים בטלים בשעת תפלה אלא בדברי תורה ועשיית המצוות ודברי קדושה.

ז' שלא לומר גנאי על שום אדם אפילו על שום בריה ובהמה.

ח' שלא יקלל שום אדם מישראל אפילו בשעת כעסו אלא אדרבה יברך ובזה יתברך ואברכה מברכיך.

ט' שלא ידבר בבית הכנסת אלא בדברי תורה.

י' שלא ידבר במילי דעלמא כלל ועיקר אלא בדברי תורה.

י"א לא תגע בגופו יד ולא יוריד ידו למטה מטיבורו.

י"ב שלא ישבע שום שבועה קלה כל שכן חמורה אפילו באמת.

י"ג שלא ידבר שקר ומדבר שקר ירחק ולא יוציא שקר מפי בשום צד ואופן.

י"ד להתחבר עם אחד מהחברים בכל יום לשאת וליתן
בענייני העבודה.

ט"ו לשאת וליתן עם החבר הנז' בכל ערב שבת מה שעשה
בכל ימי השבוע ומשם יבא לקבל פני שבת מלכתא.

י"ו לכוון בתפלתו כל מה שיוכל לפחות יכוון בשלש
ראשונות ובארבע כריעות ובארבע זקיפות שמי שאינו מכוין בהם
השכינה צווחת עליו נתנני ה' בידי לא אוכל קום.

י"ז להזהר להתפלל תפלת מנחה בטלית ותפלין ובחזרה.

י"ח לברך ברכת המזון בקול רם כדי שיאמרו בניו אחריו
אות באות מילה במילה.

י"ט ליזהר שלא לאכול ביום ראשון בשר ולא תבשיל של
בשר ולא יין וליזהר משחוק בו ביום יותר מיום אחר זולתי ביום
טוב ור"ח וסעודת מצוה.

כ' בכל לילה ישב על הארץ ויקונן על החרבן ויכוון לבכות
גם על עוונותיו שמאריכין קץ הגאולה.

כ"א שלא לקבוע סעודת רשות בביתו זולתי סעודת מצוה.

כ"ב בכל יום חול קודם ברכת המזון יאמר מזמור על נהרות.

כ"ג ליזהר משיחה בטלה כל מה שיוכל והיא אחת מעשרה
מילי דחסידותא דרב דלא שח שיחה בטלה מימיו.

כ"ד ליזהר שלא יהיה מאותם ארבע כיתות שאינם מקבלות
פני שכינה והם כת חנפים כת שקרנים כת לייצנים וכת מדברי
לשון הרע.

כ"ה ליתן צדקה בכל יום לכפר הטאתו שנאמר וחטאך
בצדקה פרוק.

כ"ו לכוון בקריאת שמע מאד בטהרת רעיונים יהיו הדברים
על לבבו.

כ"ז לשמוע קריאת התורה מפי ש"ץ כראוי ולא יטרידהו
שום דבר.

כ"ח ליזהר לשלם נדרו מיד ולא יאחר נדרו שלשים יום.

כ"ט ליזהר להתודות קודם אכילה וקודם שינה.

ל' שלא יאמר שהחיינו בין המצרים ולא יאכל בשר ולא

ישתה יין זולתי המתענה שמותר לו מפני התענית.

ל"א להתענות כפי כחו.

ל"ב להרהר בדברי תורה על כל לעיסה ולעיסה כדי שיהיה
המאכל כמו קרבן ושתיית המיים והיין כנסכים.

ל"ג לעסוק בכל יום במקרא משנה תלמוד קבלה פסק.

ל"ד ללמוד כל התלמוד שלשה פעמים כנגד שנים עשר חודש.

ל"ה להוריד דמעות בכל התפלות ולפחות בתפלה אחת מהן.

ל"ו להתענות שלשה רצופים ארבעה פעמים בשנה בארבעה
תקופות ואם יוסיף הרי זה משובח.

[לדבר בלשון הקודש עם החברים בכל זמן.]

[לאמ' על השלחן קודם ברכת המזון ב' פרקים ומזמור אחד.]

[ללמוד בכל ליל שבת משניות כפי כחו.]

[לחזור בכל שבוע כל המשניות שיודע.]

[לידע בכל שבוע ב' פרקים משניות על פה לפחות.]

ע"א
מנהגים טובים וקדושים הנוהגים בא"י
הועתקו מכתיבת יד החכם השלם כמוהר"ר
אברהם גלנטי יחי' היושב בצפת תוב"ב לי"א·

אלה הדברים אשר יעשה אותם האדם וחי בהם

א' ערב ר"ח כל העם מתענין אנשים ונשים ותלמידים ויש מקום
שבו מתכנסים אותו היום ויושבים שם כל היום כלו בסליחות ובתחנונים
ודויים ומלקיות ויש מהם שמשים על בטנו אבן גדול דמיון סקילה ויש מי
שמחנק בידיו בגרונו וכיוצא ויש מי שמשים עצמו תוך שק א' ומסחבים
אותו סביבות ב"ה.

ב' ליל ר"ח יש אנשי מעשה שמשכימין בחצות וקורין בספר
תהלות.

ג' מניחין טלית ותפלין בכל תפלת מנחה כמו בשחרית ונתפשט
מנהג זה בכל העם.

ד' ערב פסח אחר חצות מתקבצין בבתי כנסיות ובבתי מדרשות
וקורין בהלכות קרבן פסח בהרמב"ם ומתפללין מנחה גדולה ויוצאים

לעשות המצות שמורות ויש נוהגים וקוצרים וקוצרים החטים בידם ומקיימין לקט
שכחה ופאה תרומות ומעשרות וחלה ומברכין על אכילת מצה ליל פסח
במצה שנעשה עליה עשרה מצות.

ה' ימי חול המועד אחר הצות היום מתקבצין בבתי כנסיות
וקורין שיר השירים ומתרגמין ומפרשין אותו יום יום.

ו' ליל ז' של פסח עומדין בחצות לילה וקורין עד קריעת ים סוף
שבמדרש וויושע ומרננין ברנה של תודה עד הבוקר ואומרים בקשות
ובסיום הבקשות עומדין על רגליהם ואומרים בקול נעים מזמור בצאת
ישראל ממצרים.

ז' כל לילי ספירת העומר מכונים בכל לילה תיבה אחת
ממזמור אלקים יחננו ששיש בו מ"ט תיבות ואות אחת שבפסוק ישמחו
ויראו בכל לילה בשקורין מזמור זה אחר ספירת העומר כשמגיעין לאותה
תיבה שהיא כנגד אותה הלילה מרימים קול באותה תיבה להורות
כי תיבה זו היא של לילה זו ויש קבלה בידם שמי שמכוין בזה לא ינום
לילה אחת בבית האסורים אפי' שיהיה אסור בדיני נפשות.

ח' ערב שבועות ישנים שעה אחת או ב' שעות אחר שעשו צרכי
מועד לפי שבלילה אחר האכילה בבתי כנסיות כל קהל וקהל
בב"ה שלו ואינם ישנים כל הלילה וקורין תורה נביאים וכתובים ומשניות
וזהר ודרשות בקראי עד אור הבקר ואז כל העם טובלים בבקר קודם
תפלת שחרית כדאיתא בזוהר פ' אמור מלבד הטבילה שטובלין בערב
שבועות.

ט' כל ע"ש יוצאים לשדה או לעזרת ב"ה ומקבלים שבת כלם
מלובשים בבגדי שבת ואומרים מזמור הבו לה' בני אלים ופזמון של
שבת ואח"כ מזמור שיר ליום השבת.

י' ליום י"ו בתמוז בחצי היום מתקבצים בבתי כנסיות ובוכים
וקוננים ומספרים על שבאותו היום ובאותה עת נעשה בטול שבסבתו
אנו גולים בארץ הגוים.

יא' ערב ט"ב נוטל אדם קיתון של מים וישב בין תנור וכירים
ודומה כמי שמתו מוטל לפניו.

י"ב ביום ט"ב אינם יוצאים מב"ה כל היום כלו ושם קורין ספר
בן גוריון ושבט יהודה ואינם אוכלים בשר ערב ט"ב.

י"ג ליל יום הכיפורים אינן ישנין כל הלילה דוגמת מיקרי ירושלים לא היו ישנים כל הלילה ועוסקין בהלכות י"ה ובהלכות שביתת עשור ובשירות ותשבחות ובפיוטים.

י"ד ערב ר"ח מתענין אנשים ונשים ותלמידים.

ט"ו ליל הושענא רבה קורין כל הלילה בספר תהילים וסליחות בין ספר לספר.

י"ו אנשי מעשה כל ערב נ' רגלים קונין כבש אחד ומחלקין אותו לעניים.

י"ז אנשי מעשה עושין כמו נ' קילאוש סולת ועושין מצות שמורות ונותנין נ' מצות לכל אחד ואחד.

י"ח להתפלל עם הצבור ערב ובקר וצהרים.

י"ט להיות מעשרה ראשונים בבקר ובערב.

כ' שלא לדבר כל זמן תפלה וכל זמן שס"ת פתוח אפי' בדברי תורה.

כ"א לקבוע עתים לתורה ביום ובלילה ושלא לישן קודם קביעת עתים לתורה.

כ"ב יש אנשי מעשה שקורין על השלחן מזמור על נהרות בבל.

כ"ג לעבור על פשע ולסלוח לכל מי שמצער אותו בין בדבור בין במעשה וכ"ש שלא להוליך אותו בערכאות שמייקר שם ע"ז להשביחה.

כ"ד ליטול ידיו בקומו ממטתו קודם שיגע בשום דבר וקודם שידרוך על גבי קרקע להעביר רוח הטומאה.

כ"ה כשיוצא מפתח ביתו לשים ידו על המזוזה לזכור ייחוד ה' ומצותיו.

כ"ו להזהר בנדרים ושבועות כי בעון נדרים בניו של אדם מתים שנא' לשוא הכיתי את בניכם וכו' וכתיב כי לא ינקה ה' וכו' לשקר לא אמר אלא לשקר.

אלה דברי הברית אשר כרת ה' עם ישראל אשר יעשה אותם האדם וחי בהם והם סיג לתורה והם כנגד חשבון השם יהו"ד הקדש והמקיימם אלקי יעקב בעזרו.

כ"ז יש יחידי סגולה מקיימין מצות עשר תעשר כנ"ל בספרי דהיינו ב' עשורי' דהיינו חומש מכל ריוח שיבוא לידם ומניחין אותו בארגז

להיות מזומן לידם למצוה הבאה לתת בעין יפה הפקדון אשר הפקד
אתו וכדכתב ר' עובדיה ריש מ' פאה בפירושו למשניות ואפי' מי
שהוא עני ידענו שרגיל לעשות כן.

כ"ח יש נוהגין להקבלת שבת אהר מנחה מלובשים בבגדי שבת
קורין שיר השירים ואח"כ הפיוט של הקבלת שבת בואי כלה. ובליל
שבת קורין ח' פרקים ממ' שבת ובבקר ח' ובמנחה ח' דלהכי כיון
רבינו הקדוש לסדר כ"ד פרקים במ' שבה כנגד כ"ד קשוטי כלה.
ועתה יגדל נא כ"ח ה' אלהינו להיות על ימין המתאמת לעבוד את
יוצרנו ית' בסור מרע ועשה טוב. אבי"ר.

אלה הם חסדייות אחרות
נוהגים בצפת תבו"ב ויש מהם שנכתבו ג"כ
למעלה ואלן באו מן החסיד העליון כמ' אברהם
הלוי רוושב צפת תבוב"ב יצ"ו.

א' מנהג רוב בעלי תורה יראי שמים שמתפללין מנחה בטלית
ותפלין ויחידים מניחים כל היום ואפי' בדרך.

ב' רוב הקהלות מתענים ערב ר"ח ואפי' הנשים קרוב לאלף (לערב?)

ג' יש חברת בעלי תשובה שמתענים תמיד ומתפללים מנחה בכל
יום בבכיה ודמעה ומלקות ושק ואפר ויש מהם שמתענים בכל שבוע ב'
ימים וב' לילות ויש ג' ימים וג' לילות.

ד' רוב בעלי תורה כשקמים בחצי הלילה ללמוד יושבים לארץ
ומתעטפים שחורים ומקוננים ובוכים על חרבן הבית וכן עושים חברת
בעלי תשובה יום המשמר.

ה' רוב בעלי תורה לומדים משנה ע"פ יש מהם ב' סדרים ויש נ'
וכו'.

ו' כמה בעלי תורה יראי שמים טובלים לקרי שלהם. ועוד ע"ש
טובלין להבדיל בין קדש לחול ולובשים לבנים כל השבת.

ז' כמה כתות יוצאים ע"ש מבעוד יום לבושים לבנים ומקבלים
פני שבת וקורין מזמור הבו לה' בני אלים ופזמון לכה דודי ומזמור
שיר ליום השבת ואומ' בואי כלה.

ח' בכל ג' סעודות משוררים ומהללים ומזמרים וכן בר"ח וסי'

שי״ר ועוד למדים מס׳ שבת בג׳ סעודות ח׳ פרקים בכל סעודה.

ט׳ רוב המדינה מניחים פיאה רוחב אצבע מראש האזן ויש
מניחין רוח ב׳ אצבעות.

י׳ יש מהם שהולכים על כל חצר וחצר ועל החניות להזהיר
על השבת ולהכניסו מבעוד יום.

י״א יש מהן אוכלין חולין בטהרה ב׳ פעמים בשברת קודם
הפסח ובי׳ ימי תשובה.

י״ב יש מהם שמשיאים את בניהם ובנותיהם מי״ג ומי״ד שנים
הפך מן המניחים אותם כ״ה שנים ויותר בשביל הממון עד
שיעשה כמה עברות ומתחייב כמה מיתות.

י״ג יש חברה שהולכים כל מוצאי שבת לשורר ולרקד ולשמח
חתן וכלה.

י״ד רוב בעלי תורה אוכלין מצה שמורה ליל פסח ויחידים כל ז׳
ומחמירים כמה מיני חמרות.

ט״ו כל בעלי תורה לומדים ליל שבועות עד אור הבקר וליל
הושענא נ״כ וכמו כן והמון העם קמים ליל הושענא לסליחות.

י״ו בכל ב״ה נובים צדקה קודם תפלה בשירת הים.

י״ז יש מלמדים סובבים במדינה ללמד נשים וקטנים תפלה
וברכות.

י״ח כמה בעלי תורה לומדים כל ליל ששי.

י״ט כמה בעלי תורה חסידים שאין אוכלין בשר ושותין יין כל
השבוע שמתאבלין על החרבן ועל עונותיהן.

כ׳ כמה בני אדם שעושים ר״ח קרוב לשבת באכילה ושתייה
ומלבוש וכן מוצאי שבת שלחן ערוך ונר דלוק.

כ״א כמה בני אדם שאין נשבעין כלל ואפילו באמת ונזהרים
לדבר אמת.

כ״ב כמה חסידים מתענין ד״פ בשנה ג׳ ימים וג׳ לילות
בארבעה תקופות.

כ״ג מנדלים יתומים ויתומות בתוך בתיהם ומשיאים אותם סמוך
לפרקם.

כ״ד בר״ח ניסן מתקבצים ת״ח ועוסקין במלאכת משכן.

כ"ה בר"ח ניסן מתקבצים כמה כתות ומתעסקין בכל כלי המשכן
וקורין פ' ויהי ביום השמיני עד וירא וגו' ופ' ויהי ביום כלות
משה וקרבן נחשן ובכל יום קורין קרבן נשיא וכו'.

ואלו אחרים קבלתים מה"ר משה מליריאה יצ"ו

א' להניח טלית ותפלין במנחה והמחמירין כל היום והטעם
א' שמצוותן כך היא ב' שבעודן עליו לבו נמשך ליראת ה' ואהבתו
ג' התקונים כתיבת יד אומרים כי כל תפלה שאינה בה טלית ותפלין אינה
מתקבלת מפני שסמאל רודף אחריה ובהיות התפלה בטלית ותפלין
אין לו רשות ויכולת עליה ד' שהתורה והמצות שאדם עושה בעולם
הזה עושין לו מלכות לעולם הבא ומי שאינו מניח תפלין כל
היום אינו זוכה לעטרת זהב גדולה שמרדכי יצא מלפני המלך ית'
ששבעים שרים רודפים ומקטרגים תמיד על ישראל שנא' שרים
רדפוני חנם והמניח התפלין בכל תפלה ובכל היום הוא קושר אותם
שנא' לאסור מלכיהם בזיקים זהו ואת עורות גדי העזים הלבישה על
ידיו אלו תפלין של יד ועל חלקת צואריו אלו תפילין של ראש.

ב' להכניס שבת מבעוד יום לפחות שעה אחת קודם וזהו זכור
את יום השבת יום השבת לא נאמר אלא א"ת מכאן שצריך להוסיף
מחול על קדש ואם אינו מוסיף קובר את בניו שנ' וביו"ם השב"ת
שנ"י כבשי"ם ס"רת מתים ר"ל אם תראה תנוקות בני שנה שמתו
תמימים בלא עון תדע שאבותיהם מחללי' שבת אין לי אלא להוסיף
מחול על קדש בכניסתו ביציאתו מנין שנא' על כן בירך ה' את יום
השבת יום השבת לא נאמר אלא את את ואם מכניסו מבעוד יום יורש גן
עדן ולפי' ר"ת של פסוק זכור בגמ' גן ואם מחללו יורש גיהנם ולפי'
זכור את יום כך כתב.

ג' ללבוש בגדים לבנים בשבתות ובי"ט טעם א' זהוא מנהגו של
ר' יהודה ב"ר אלעאי שלובש לבנים ומתעטף לבנים ודומה למלאך ה'
ב' שהנשמות בשבתות וי"ט לובשי' לבנים בגדי אור וזהו על כן
באורים כבדו ה'. ג' אשריהם ישראל שמה שעושין למטה עושין
כנגדו למעלה בחול ה' מתלבש בדין שהוא שחור וכן השכינה
שנא' אלבש שמים קדרות שחורה אני ונאוה בשבת ה' ושכינתו

מתפשטים ומתלבשים ברחמים שהוא סוד בגדי לבן ולפי׳ חייבין ישראל
לשבת במקום ואם ח״ו אינו עושה למטה אינו עושה למעלה. (אמר
שמ״י והרמז לזה שבת במ״ק עם האותות עולה י״ב עת במ״ק עם
המלה עולה נ״כ י״ב ועל זה אמר הכתוב בכל עת יהיו בגדיך לבנים.)

ד׳ שעושין משמרה ערב ר״ח ומתקבצין בבתי כנסיות ובבתי
מדרשות ורוב היום בתפלה ודמעה ושק ואפר סמנם תשוב״ה
תענית שק וידוי בכיה הספד על שני סבות על חרבן בית המקדש
ועל עונות ועון שנא׳ והתודו את עונם ואת עון אבותם גטעם התענית
א׳ להרתיש כח החומר וזהו ויחבוש את חמזרו מלשון חומר ב׳
בזמן שבית המקדש קיים מקריב קרבן גּעכשיו מקריב חלבו וזהו
אדם כי יקריב מכם מכם ממש חלבכם ודמכם ג׳ שבזמן שאדם
הוטא מפריד הרחמין מן הדין ובזמן שהוא מתענה ועושה תשובה הוא
מחברם זהו ונרגן מפריד אלוף אלפו שהוא רחמים [פ״ו נמ׳]
אלקים. הרשע הוא מפרידם ומהזירהו הוא מחברם בחלב ודם
שהוא רחמים ודין.

ה׳ יש חסידים ואנשי מעשה שדורשי׳ בכל משמרה ומשמרה דברי
כבושין והכנעה וענינ׳ תשובה וחמר העבירות ובני אדם שבים לקונם.

ו׳ יש בני אדם יראי שמים שהולכים על כל הבתים לבקש על
המזוזות שמא הם פסולות ואם הוא עני נותנים אותו לו מכים הצדקה
גטעם המזוזה כי מזוזה בגימ׳ אל״ף דל״י וכו׳ וכן פי׳ ועשו לי מקדש
מזוז״ה קנ״ה דל״ה שד״י ושכנתי בתוכם לפי שסמאל הוא יושב לפתח
הטאת רובץ ובהיותו מניח המזוזה הוא ניצול.

ז׳ שרוב מדינה מניחים פיאה רוחב אצבע מראש האזן וטעם
מצוה זו לפי שבצאת המצוה בלבד הוא נכר בין בחיים בין במות
שהוא יהודי וזהו כל רואיהם יכירום ובחייו יכירו שהוא יהודי ופי׳
יהודי כי ליהודי ששם המפורש חתום בו שהוא כפולה ועוד כל מי
שאינו מניח פיאה כהות טומאה דנגמת פרות שולטין על נשמתו
פא״ת ראשיכ״ם ול״א תשחי״ת ר״ת פרות וטעמים גדולים יש ואסור
לגלותם אבל חסידים ואנשי מעשה מניחים פיאה רוחב הצדיה ומצוה
זו אינה כשאר מצות שהיא תמיד עמו ביום ובלילה מיום שנולד עד
יום מותו ובמותו הולכת עמו. (ופי׳ היינו יהודי אם תשים יו״ד תוך

ד הרי יהוד.)

ח' שנזהרים שלא לגלח שער הערוה ושער בית השחי וטעם
מצוה זו לפי הפשט שלא ילבש גבר שמלת אשה. עוד ששערות אלו
אסורות להשחיתם כי שערות קדושי' בם ולא אוכל לפרש והעובר מובטח
שביציאת נשמתו יתגלגל באשה וזהו שלא עשני אשה וזהו לא ילבש
גבר שמלת אשה שיתגלגל בגוף אשה העוברת על לאו זה.

ט' שבכמה חסידים ואנשי מעשה אינם מדברים משעה שיתחילו
להתפלל עד שיסיימו עלינו לשבח וטעם הדבר א' [שמשעה] שהתחיל
לדבר עם המלך אין ראוי לחזור לדבר עם העבד. ב' שהתפלה במקום
קרבן ופי' קרבן הוא על ידי עניינו אחד שמקרב אותיות ה' המיוחד
אחת אל אחת וזהו קרבן אל ה' ממש. הג' שמקרב ומערב הרחמים
עם הדין והדין עם הרחמים וזהו ה'. הוא האלקים היינו מדת הדין עם
מדת הרחמים והמדבר דברי חול מכניסם סמאל בקדושה הפך מעשה
מרע"ה שנא' בו ויך את המצרי זה סמאל שרצה לכנס בקדושה והרג
אותו וטמן אותו בחול מלשון ולהבדיל בין הקדש ובין החול.

י' שיש חסידים שהולכים ע"ש ב' שעות קודם היום על הבתים
ועל המבואות להזהיר בני אדם על שמירת שבת שכל המקים
שמירת שבת כאילו קיים כל המצות וזהו שב"ת תשב הסר תרי"ג
ישאר פ"ו שהוא אלקים שבר"א שמים וארץ ומנין שעובר על תרי"ג
מצות שנא' עד אנה מאנתם לשמוע מצותי ותורותי מצותי מצות עשה
ולא תעשה תורותי תורה שבכתב ותורה שבעל פה.

APPENDIX B

(For List of Abbreviations see pp. 290-1.)

AARON B. ELEAZAR (the Blind).   Mi., p. 147.

ABRAHAM ארומטי (ארואיטי).   See Manasseh b. Israel's *Nishmath Chayim*, III : 10 ; Caro I, 124.

ABRAHAM DE BOTON.   Con. 48 a.

ABRAHAM GABRIEL.   Con.;   Mi.; ל''נ, 88 b.

ABRAHAM GALANTI.   Con.; Samb.; Az.

ABRAHAM B. GEDALIAH B. ASHER.   Con.; Samb.; Az.; Mi.

ABRAHAM HALEVI ברוכים.   Con.; Az.; Mi. (p. 61.   See references, but confused there with Abraham Halevi the Elder.   Cf. Frumkin, 72).

ABRAHAM B. ISAAC LANIADO.   Mi., no. 145.

ABRAHAM B. ISAAC ZAHALON.   Mi.

ABRAHAM B. JACOB BERAB.   Con.

ABRAHAM LACHMI.   See Manasseh b. Israel's *Nishmath Chayim*, III : 10.

ABRAHAM SHALOM (the Elder).   Con. (see especially 33 b); Samb.; Mi.

ABRAHAM SHALOM (the Younger).   Con.; Mi. (p. 122).

ABRAHAM B. SOLOMON עלון.   See Preface to Zechariah b. Saruk's Commentary on Esther.

BENJAMIN HALEVI.   Con. (p. 49 b.) (?); Samb.; Mi. (pp. 280–281).

CHAYIM B. ISAAC החבר.   Con.; Samb.; Az.; Mi.

CHAYIM VITAL.   See text.

CHIYA ROFE (the physician).   Con.; Samb.; Az.; Mi.

DAVID AMARILLO.   See Solomon Adeni, Introduction to his Commentary מלאכת שלמה.

DAVID DE קאישטריש.   Con. 48 a.   See Notes.

DAVID COHEN.   Vital, 14 b.

DAVID HABILLO.   Con.; Samb.; Az.; Mi.

DAVID NAVARRO.   Con.; Samb.

DAVID B. ZECHARIAH ורנק.   See Mi., nos. 718 and 813.   See also Frumkin, 58.

DAVID ABI ZIMRA.   Con.; Samb.; Az.; Mi.

ELIEZER AZKARI.   Con.; Samb.; Az.; Mi.

Eliezer Ginzburg, son-in-law of רמ״א. See David Grünhut, טוב רואי, title page.

Eleazar b. Isaac ארחא. Con.; Az.; Mi.

Eleazar b. Yochai. Con.; Samb.; Az.; Mi.

Elijah Falcon. Con.; Samb.; particularly p. 152; Az., and *s. n.* Moses Alsheich; Mi. See Manasseh b. Israel's *Nishmath Chayim*, III : 10.

Elijah de Vidas. Con.; Samb.; Az.; Mi. See also text.

Elisha Gallico. Con.; Samb.; Az.; Mi. See also Zunz, Introduction to De Rossi, *Meor Enayim.*

Gedaliah Alkabez. See Az. Cf. Steinschneider, Catalogue, col. 1002.

Gedaliah Cordovero. Con.; Mi.

Gedaliah Halevi. Con. 48 a; identical with Vital's brother-in-law; see Vital, 3 a, and נ״ל, 87 b.

Isaac Alfandari. Con. 46 b.

Isaac ארחא. Con., especially p. 41 a.

Isaac de Boton. Con. 48 a.

Isaac Cohen. Vital, 20 a, 23 b; cf. Con. 41 a.

Isaac Gerson. Con.

Isaac Krispin. Samb. 152 (?).

Isaac Loria. See text.

Isaac b. Menahem בסמו. See Neubauer, Cat., no. 411.

Isaac Misod. Con. 36 a. Perhaps identical with Isaac b. David, called "Misod," mentioned by Trani, I, 32.

Isaac משען. See Az.; Abraham b. Asher and references; Con. (?).

Ishmael Halevi Ashkenazi. Vital, 14 b.

Israel Coriel. Con.; Samb.; Az.

Israel Saruk. Con. 46 b; Az., and sub Solomon Loria.

Issachar Sasson. Con.; Samb.

Jacob Abulafiah. Samb.; Az. MN 7 b and 12 a. See, however, Modena, *Ari Noham*, 19 b.

Jacob איש חם, etc. Samb. 151 (?).

Jacob אלטרף or אלטריץ or אלטרס. Vital, 14 b; Samb.

Jacob Berab. See text.

Jacob Berab (b. Abraham) (the Younger). Con.; Samb. 162.

Jacob b. Chayim. Pref. to באר שבע.

Jacob Falcon. Con.

Jacob גווילי. Perhaps a corruption of גוויניזו. See Samb.; Vital, 25 a, 151, and Azkari, 95.

Jacob Sasson. Con. 48 a.

Jacob Zemach. Con.; Az.

Jedidiah Galanti. Con.; Mi.

Jehiel Ginzburg. See תולדות משפחת גינצבורג, p. 187.

Jehudah b. Uri (of Heidelberg). See Caro II, 62 c.

Jeremiah of Candia. Con. 48 b.

Jonathan Galanti. Con. 48 a.

Jonathan Sagis. Con. 48 a; Vital, 23 b; ג"ל, 88 a.

Joseph Arzin. Vital, 23 b; ג"ל, 81 a. Cf. מאמץ כח, by R. Moses Almosnino, 18 b.

Joseph Ashkenazi. Con.; Samb.; Az. Cf. Kaufmann, *Monatsschrift*, vol. 42, p. 38 seq., and Bloch, vol. 47, p. 153.

Joseph Barzillai. Mi.

Joseph קלדירין. Con. 48 a.

Joseph of ליריאה (Lieria). Az.; Samb.

Joseph Sagis. Con.; Samb.; Az. (?).

Joseph Sajjah. Con.; Az.

Joseph Saragossi. Samb.; Az.

Joseph Skandrani. Con. 30 b; Az.; Mi., no. 1042.

Joseph b. Tabul. Con. 40 b and 48 a; Vital, 23 b. Probably identical with Joseph Maarabi.

Joseph Tibbon. Con. 41 a.

Joseph Vital. Samb.; Az.

Joshua b. Nun. Con.; Az.

Judah משען. Vital, 23 b; Con. 40 b; ג"ל, 88 a.

Lapiduth. Az. See Vital, 1 a.

Levi b. Chabib. Con.; Samb.; Az.; Mi. See also Frumkin, 30 a.

Menahem b. Abraham Galanti. Kaydanower, ch. 15.

Menahem ha-Babli. See Caro II, 35 b (?).

Menahem Gallico. Ghirondi, 252.

Misod Azulai. Con. Perhaps identical with Misod Maarabi. See Shlomel, 34 b, and Con. 40 b.

Mordecai ha-Cohen (author of a commentary on the Bible). Con.; Az.

Mordecai Dato. Con. 42 b; Landshut, עמודי העבודה, *s. n.*

MOSES ALKABEZ. Con.; Ghirondi, 242.

MOSES ALSHEICH. See text.

MOSES BARUCH. Con.; Az. See also Caro II, 17 a.

MOSES BASULA. Con.; Ghirondi, 250. Cf. also Mortara, p. 7.

MOSES CORDOVERO. See text.

MOSES GALANTI. Con.; Samb.; Az.

MOSES HALEVI טרינקי. Con.; Samb.

MOSES B. ISRAEL NAGARA. Con.; Samb.; Az.

MOSES JONAH. Con. 41 a; ג״ל, 89 a.

MOSES B. JOSEPH TRANI. See text.

MOSES OF ליריאה (LIERIA). Boton, לחם רב, no. 184.

MOSES B. MACHIR. Con.; Az.

MOSES MINTZ. ג״ל, 88 b; *Ez ha-Chayim*, 6 a. Cf. Mi., no. 531.

MOSES NIGRIN. Con.; Az.; cf. also Ghirondi, 226.

MOSES ONKENEYRA. Az. See Caro I, 124, spelled somewhat
    variously.

MOSES OF ROME. See שערי ג״ע.

MOSES SAADYA. Con.; Samb. See also Caro II, 17 a. Cf.
    Vital, 12 b, 15 b.

PHAREZ COLOBI. See text.

SABBATAI MANASSEH. Samb.; cf. Caro I, 124, and ג״ל,91 a.

SAMUEL BIAGI. See Manasseh b. Israel's *Nishmath Chayim*.

SAMUEL GALLICO. Con.; Az.

SAMUEL B. SHEM TOB ATIVA. Con.; Samb. See Frumkin, 51.

SAMUEL DE USEDA. Con.; Samb.; Az.

SAMUEL VERGA. Con.; Samb.; Az.

SHEM TOB ATIVA. Con.; Az.

SIMON ASHKENAZI. See *Peri Ez Chayim*.

SOLOMON אבסבאן. Con.; Samb.; Az. See also Jewish Quar-
    terly Review, IX, p. 269.

SOLOMON ADENI. See his Introduction to his Commentary מ״ש
    to the Mishnah (Wilna, 1887). For this reference I am
    obliged to Dr. L. Ginzberg.

SOLOMON ALKABEZ. See text.

SOLOMON COHEN. Con. 48 a.

SOLOMON SAGIS. Con.; Az.

SOLOMON סירילוו. Con.; Samb.; Az. Cf. Frumkin, 44.

SOLOMON B. YAKAR. Chabib, Responsa, 322 a.

Sulaiman b. אוחנא. Con.; variously spelled. See especially p. 42 a, and Cassel's note; Samb.; Az. ס ו, identical with the writer of the same name known by his notes to the Siphre and the Mechilta. Cf. Pardo's Preface to his commentary to the Siphre.

Tobiah Halevi. Con.; Samb.; Az.; Mi.

Yomtob Zahalon. Con.; Az.

Zechariah b. Solomon זעבשיל (father-in-law of Caro). Differently spelled by various authors. Samb.; Az.; Mi. (p. 364). Cf. also Frumkin, 59.

NOTES

NOTES

A HOARD OF HEBREW MANUSCRIPTS
I

[1] Published in The Times, London, August 3, 1897, and in The Sunday School Times, Philadelphia, about the same date.

A HOARD OF HEBREW MANUSCRIPTS
II

[1] Most of the contents of this article, written when the examination of the Genizah had been proceeding for several months, were published in The Jewish Chronicle, London, October 15, 1897, and April 1, 1898.

[2] See above, page 9 seq.

[3] See below, page 41 seq.

THE STUDY OF THE BIBLE

[1] Given as Inaugural Lecture on my appointment as Professor of Hebrew in University College, London, January 26, 1899.

[2] See Barth, *Etymologische Studien*, p. 14 seq.

[3] *Berachoth*, 61 a.

[4] Several more editions, embodying also fragments of Ben Sira that have come to light since the article was written, have been added. It should be noted that *doubts were also expressed since then against the authenticity of these fragments,* but those who raised these doubts were, with the exception of two or three students, hardly justified to speak about the matter. One of them even confessed that he did not study the question. His objections were probably on general principles to object to everything, whilst the doubts which came from the two or three serious students were refuted in ever so many brochures and articles in learned papers. The consensus of the great majority of scholars in America, England, France, Germany, and even Russia, who did study the question thoroughly and most carefully examined all the evidence *pro* and *contra*, is in favour of the authenticity of these discovered fragments.

⁵ See "The Wisdom of Ben Sira," edited by S. Schechter and C. Taylor (Cambridge, England), 1899. See especially *Introduction*, pp. 7 to 38, where the arguments advanced in these last pages are given more fully.

A GLIMPSE OF THE SOCIAL LIFE OF THE JEWS IN THE AGE OF JESUS THE SON OF SIRACH

¹ Lecture delivered at the Jewish Theological Seminary of America, in the series of Public Lectures, Academic Year 1904–1905.

² See above, p. 41 seq.

³ See above, p. 47.

⁴ See *Ben Sira*, original Hebrew, 51 : 23.

⁵ See *Mishnah Aboth*, IV, 13, and *Aboth d. Rabbi Nathan*, I, 31.

⁶ See 2 Maccabees, IV, 14.

⁷ See 2 Maccabees, VI, 19, and 1 Maccabees, I, 62, 63, and II, 42.

⁸ See *Bechoroth*, 29 a, of *Derech Erez Zuta IV*, of which the text is a paraphrase.

⁹ See Dr. Edersheim's Introduction to his commentary on Ecclesiasticus in the Speaker's Bible.

¹⁰ So Revised Version. Cf. also Ryssel in Kautzsch's Apocrypha, on this verse. The sense probably is that they pray for the prosperity of their work.

¹¹ See also *Syr. Version*.

¹² See *Kiddushin*, 82 a.

¹³ See original Hebrew, ed. Schechter–Taylor, and notes.

¹⁴ See *Baba Kama*, 110 b.

¹⁵ *Pesachim*, 57 a.

¹⁶ See *Bechoroth*, 26 b. It should, however, be remarked that according to Siphre, 145 a (ed. Friedmann), the majority of the priests were well off. I am inclined to think that this latter statement must be confined to certain places and certain ages.

¹⁷ See *Bechoroth*, 45 a.

¹⁸ See *Baba Kama*, 85 b.

¹⁹ The originality of Ben Sira can be maintained only by assuming, with Bötticher, Dillmann, and others, that the עשיר, the "rich" of Isaiah (53 : 9), is a corruption of עֹשֵׂי רע, "evildoers," or עֹשֵׁק, "oppressor." In this case Ben Sira would be the first to identify the עשיר עשיר with the רשע.

[20] See *Sukkah*, 49 b.

[21] See *Aboth d. Rabbi Nathan*, ed. Schechter, II, 15, text and notes.

[22] See Edersheim's commentary to these passages.

[23] See *Sanhedrin*, 23 a.

[24] See *Shabbath*, 11 a.

[25] See *Tosefta Berachoth*, 6, and references and the commentaries to it. Cf. *Aruch*, *s. v.* סער, and Friedmann in his work on the Agadah of Passover, p. 20 seq.

[26] See *Tosefta Berachoth*, ed. Zuckermandel, ch. 4.

[27] *Tosefta Berachoth*, ch. 7.

[28] See *Sirach*, XXXII, 11, original Hebrew, and *Ta'anith*, 5 b.

[29] See *Berachoth,* 63 b.

[30] See Leopold Löw, *Gesammelte Schriften*, III, 407.

[31] *Nazir*, 4 b.

[32] See *Sanhedrin*, 38 a.

[33] See *Aboth d. Rabbi Nathan*, II, 31.

[34] See *Ta'anith*, I, 23 a.

[35] See *Aboth*, I, 6, and *Aboth d. Rabbi Nathan*, I, 8.

[36] See *Siphre*, 93 b, and references given there.

[37] See *Yebamoth*, 61 a, and Graetz, *Geschichte*, III : 444.

[38] There is strong doubt about this verse. See Ryssel's commentary on *Die Sprüche Jesus*, etc., 26 : 18.

[39] See *Kiddushin*, 30 b.

[40] See *Kethuboth*, 59. See also *Tosefta Kethuboth*, 5. Cf. Maimonides, *Mishneh Torah, Hilchoth Ishuth,* 21, and commentaries.

[41] See *Midrash Rabbah* to Lamentations, I, 4.

[42] Jerusalem Talmud, *Peah*, III, 9, *Nedarim*, 40, and *Tractate Semachoth Zutarti*, ed. Horowitz, and reference given there.

[43] See *Nedarim*, 40 a.

ON THE STUDY OF THE TALMUD

[1] Paper read before the Hebrew class at University College, London, October 19, 1899.

[2] In connexion with this work I should like to call the attention of students to *Das letzte Passahmahl Christi und der Tag seines Todes*, by Professor D. Chwolson (St. Petersburg, 1892), a work which, for the depth of its Rabbinic learning and the

critical acumen displayed in it, has hardly its equal. It is, indeed, so far as I know, the first attempt to treat what one may
call the Halachic part of the New Testament with the thorough-
ness and devotion usually bestowed only on doctrinal points.

[3] Cf. מוונה״ץ, p. 45, הערות.

[4] *Lev. Rabbah*, I.

[5] See especially the Midrash *Lekach Tob*, ad loc.

[6] *Cant. Rabbah*, ad loc.

[7] Ibid.

[8] *Pesikta Rabbathi* (ed. Friedmann), p. 36, text and notes.

[9] *Shibbole Halleket*, 145 a.

[10] B. T. *Baba Mezia*, 45 a, and parallel passages.

[11] B. T. *Sanhedrin*, 39 a.

[12] Jer. T. *Sukkah*, 55 a.

[13] *Mishnah Yoma*, VIII, 9.

[14] *Cant. Rabbah*, I, and parallel passages.

[15] *Cant. Rabbah*, ibid.

[16] B. T. *Sanhedrin*, 95 a.

[17] B. T. *Chagigah*, 15 a, and parallel passages.

[18] B. T. *Berachoth*, 3 a.

[19] See Löw, *Gesammelte Schriften*, II, p. 58, note 1. A good
essay on the subject is still a desideratum.

[20] *Num. Rabbah*, XIV, and parallel passages.

[21] *Lev. Rabbah*, XXI.

[22] Jer. T. *Sotah*, 22 a.

[23] *Chapters of R. Eliezer*, XLIV, but see also B. T. *Yoma*, 22 b.

[24] See *Perek R. Meïr*.

[25] B. T. *Chagigah*, 15 a.

[26] *Pesikta* (ed. Buber), p. 162 seq.

[27] B. T. *Baba Mezia*, 59 a.

[28] *Torath Kohanim* (ed. Weiss), 91 b.

[29] See *Pesikta Rabbathi*, 124 b.

[30] B. T. *Sanhedrin*, 34 a.

[31] *Mechilta*, 3 a, 6 a, etc.

[32] *Tanchuma*, מטות.

[33] *Yalkut*, I, § 766. See Dr. Taylor's *Sayings of the Jewish
Fathers*, 2d ed., p. 160.

[34] See Jewish Quarterly Review, VI, pp. 419 and 634, for
references.

[35] *Yalkut,* ibid.; *Genesis Rabbah,* I, and *Cant. Rabbah,* VIII.

[36] *Cant. Rabbah,* VII; *Num. Rabbah,* II ; *Siphre* (ed. Fried-mann), 143 a ; and Rashi's Commentary to Cant. V, 9.

[37] B. T. *Chagigah,* II, and the Jerusalem Talmud, ibid.

THE MEMOIRS OF A JEWESS OF THE SEVEN-TEENTH CENTURY

[1] *Die Memoiren der Glückel von Hameln, 1645-1719, her-ausgegeben von Professor Dr. David Kaufmann* (Frankfort, J. Kauffmann, 1896).

[2] Diary, p. 24.

[3] Ibid. pp. 24 and 25.

[4] Ibid. pp. 26 and 27.

[5] Ibid. pp. 36 and 37.

[6] Ibid. p. 57 seq.

[7] Ibid. p. 58.

[8] Ibid. pp. 59 and 60.

[9] Ibid. pp. 61, 62, 63, and 66.

[10] Ibid. pp. 66 and 67.

[11] Ibid pp. 68 and 69.

[12] Ibid. p. 125.

[13] Ibid. p. 74.

[14] Ibid. pp. 108, 111, 113, and 116.

[15] Ibid. p. 121.

[16] Ibid. p. 57.

[17] Ibid. p. 235.

[18] Ibid. p. 80 seq.

[19] Ibid. pp. 145-148.

[20] Ibid. p. 24.

[21] Ibid. p. 34.

[22] Ibid. p. 264.

[23] See *Monatsschrift,* XXXIV, p. 145 seq.

[24] See Diary, p. 26.

[25] See ibid. p. 1 seq.

[26] Ibid. pp. 6 and 7.

[27] Ibid. p. 8.

[28] Ibid. p. 13.

[29] Ibid. p. 125.

[30] Ibid. p. 272. For similar passages, see pp. 93, 89, 121, 172, etc.

[31] Ibid. pp. 5, 6, and 13.
[32] Ibid. p. 141.
[33] Ibid. p. 133.
[34] Ibid. p. 185.
[35] Ibid. pp. 4-15.
[36] Ibid. p. 2.
[37] Ibid. p. 18.
[38] Ibid. pp. 17 and 82.
[39] Ibid. p. 136.
[40] Ibid. p 15.
[41] Ibid. p. 125.
[42] Ibid. pp. 18 and 19.
[43] Ibid. p. 277.
[44] Ibid. p. 274.
[45] Ibid. p. 275.
[46] Ibid. pp. 296-303.
[47] Ibid. pp. 312 and 321.

SAINTS AND SAINTLINESS

[1] Delivered in the Course of Public Lectures of the Jewish Theological Seminary of America, February 9, 1905.

[2] *Kethuboth*, 17 a. A fair collection of references to Rabbinic Literature regarding the expressions *Chasid* and *Chesed* is to be found in the *Sefer Chasidim*, Parma, p. 240, note 1.

[3] Rabbi Bachye ben Bakodah, חובות הלבבות, ch. 9; ש״פ, by Maimonides, ch. 4 and ch. 6. Cf. Schechter, Jewish Quarterly Review, X, pp. 8-12, quotations given there in the text and notes.

[4] See R. Moses Chayim Luzzatto, מסילת ישרים, ed. Wilna, p. 48, something of this definition.

[5] See Midrash to Psalms, 149.

[6] See Schultz, "Old Testament Theology," II, p. 80.

[7] See ibid.

[8] *Baba Kama*, 30 a.

[9], [10] See above, p. 9.

[11] See *Kuzari*, ed. Sluzki, p. 61; טוא״ח, 113, on חסידי אשכנז.

[12] See *Berachoth*, 30 b and 32 b.

[13] See *Sotah*, 40 a; T. J. *Berachoth*, 4 d.

[14] T. J. *Berachoth*, 7 d.

[15] T. J. ibid. See the end of the prayer of R. Tanchum.

[16] See *Midrash* to Ps., ch. 76.

[17] *Berachoth*, 3 b.

[18] See Bachye, חוה"ל, ed. Sluzki, 127 a.

[19] See שערי ציון, a liturgical collection very popular in the East.

[20] *Abraham Lincoln, Complete Works*, vol. II, p. 661.

[21] See *Kuzari*, ibid.

[22] See *Bezah*, 16 a.

[23] *Kuzari*, 62 b.

[24] See *Pesikta Rabbathi*, 117 b.

[25] See *Shabbath*, 150 b, and *Pesikta Rabbathi*, 116 b.

[26] See *Shabbath*, 12 b.

[27] See *Life and Conversations of R. Nachman of Braslaw*.

[28] See *Kuzari*, 59 a.

[29] *Yebamoth*, 20 a.

[30] See his commentary to Leviticus, 19:2.

[31] See below, p. 216.

[32] See *Mishnah Ta'anith*, IV, 3.

[33] See ראשית חכמה by R. Elijah de Vidas, especially the chapters on Holiness and Repentance. See also below, p. 245.

[34] See תולדות אדם, by Ezekiel Feivel ben Zeeb, containing the life of that Rabbi.

[35] See *Aboth*, V : 4.

[36] See *Little Sefer Chasidim* (page 13 a), by Rabbi Moses Cohen ben Eliezer, printed in Warsaw, 1866. Cf. Guedemann, *Geschichte des Erziehungswesens,* etc., III, p. 212.

[37] See אורחות צדיקים (Königsberg), p. 41 a.

[38] See לקוטי תורה, by Rabbi Mordecai of Czernobile, Lemberg, 1867, p. 6 b.

[39] See מדרש פנחס of Rabbi Pinchas, of Korzek, 26 b. To be quoted hereafter as *M. P.*

[40] See *M. P.* 27 a.

[41] See *Baba Kama*, 30 a.

[42] See שמירת הלשון, Warsaw, 1884, where all the Rabbinic references on this point will be found.

[43] *Makkoth*, 24 a. Cf. also Rashi's commentary.

[44] J. T. *Terumoth*, 46 c.

[45] See *Ecclesiastes Rabbah*, and *Sefer Chasidim*, 44.

[46] שערי הקדושה, Rabbi Chayim Vital, Warsaw, 1876, p. 9 a., to be quoted in this article as Vital.

[47] See Vital, 15 a.

[48] See *M. P.* 21 b.

[49] See Horodetzky, *Hashiloah*, XV, 167.

[50] See *M. P.* 21 b and 24 b.

[51] Vital, 17 a.

[52] Vital, 9 a.

[53] See *Aboth*, IV : 4.

[54] *Derech Erez Zuta*, 10.

[55] *M. P.* 22 a.

[56] See Vital, p. 13 a, who introduces this passage with אמרו, whilst the whole style proves it to be a Midrash. Cf. *Shabbath*, 31 a, but it forms no exact parallel passage.

[57] Guttman, דרך אמונה ומעשה רב, Warsaw, 1898, 7 a.

[58] *Sefer Chasidim*, Parma, 363.

[59] *M. P.* 28 a.

[60] הנהגות of Rabbi *Melech*.

[61] See below, p. 216.

[62] *M. P.* 26 a.

[63] See Horodetzky, *Hashiloah*, XV, 170.

[64] See *Kethuboth*, 50 a. See also commentaries.

[65] *Aboth*, V : 10.

[66] See *Baba Bathra*, 7 b.

[67] See לקוטי אמרים, ed. Wilna, 1896, p. 52 a seq.

[68] Guttman, ibid., p. 11 a.

[69] See below, p. 277, the story of Loria and Useda.

[70] See Chayim Meïr Heilman, בית רבי, Berditczev, 1892, II : 3 a.

[71] See *Little Sefer Chasidim*, 13 a. See also below, p. 238.

[72] See *Sefer Chasidim*, Parma, 477 and 478.

[73] See Kaydanower, ch. 7.

[74] See above, p. 157, and also below, p. 270.

[75] Ps. 16 : 8, 9 seq.

[76] See עמק המלך by Naphtali Bacharach, 121 c, to be quoted hereafter as Bacharach.

[77] See Bachye, חוה׳׳ל, 126 b seq.

[78] See Rabbi Judah Halevi, *Divan*, II, 91 a.

[79] See *Zohar*, ed. Krotoschin, to Num., p. 222 b. Ibid. to

Deut., p. 281 a. Cf. Luzzatto, מסילת ישרים, 29 a. See also *Sefer Chasidim*, Parma, p. 240, note 1.

[80] See בית רבי, I : 16 a.

FOUR EPISTLES TO THE JEWS OF ENGLAND

[1] Published in The Jewish Chronicle, London, 1901.

SAFED IN THE SIXTEENTH CENTURY
(For List of Abbreviations see pp. 290-1.)

[1] See Schwarz, p. 476; cf. Baedeker, Index. See also Rapoport, Introduction to קורא הדורות of Shalom Cohen (Warsaw, 1838).

[2] See Caro I, 1.

[3] See Graetz, *Geschichte d. Juden*, 2d ed., IX : 29 seq.; cf. also English Translation, IV : 400 seq.

[4] אור החיים, ch. V; cf. Kayserling, *Geschichte d. Juden in Portugal*, pp. 42 and 96.

[5] See Neubauer's "Mediæval Jewish Chronicles," I : 111. Similar sentiments may also be found in R. Isaac Arama's חזות קשה.

[6] Ed. Pietrkow (1902), p. 42.

[7] See *Responsa* of R. Asher (Rosh), VIII : 10.

[8] See Epstein, *Revue des Etudes Juives*, XLII, p. 18, and Büchler, XLIV, p. 241 seq.

[9] See Graetz, *Geschichte*, VII : 13; cf. Schwarz, 443. Of course, this brief outline has to be completed by the accounts of the travels of Benjamin of Tudela, and R. Pethahiah, and similar works.

[10] See Pharchi, כפתר ופרח.

[11] See Hebrew Appendix *Ozar Tob* to *Magazin*, I : 027; see also Graetz, *Geschichte* , VII : 182; cf. Hebrew periodical *Jerusalem*, edited by Luncz, II, p. 7.

[12] See Graetz, *Geschichte*, VII : 308-9, and *Jerusalem*, II, p. 12.

[13] See Carmoly, *Itinéraires*, 261, from an unpublished MS. (cod. Paris, 1070); cf. also Pharchi, 284.

[14] See *Jerusalem*, VI, p. 337.

[15] See Graetz, *Geschichte*, IX : 28; cf. the Hebrew translation, VII : 26, notes 2 and 4. The name points to a Spanish origin; cf. also Azkari, 24 a, and Azulai, *s. n.* The date of Saragossi's settling in Safed cannot be ascertained, but it must have been during the first two decades of the sixteenth century.

[16] See Bertinoro, 209 and 222; cf. Graetz, *Geschichte*, VIII : 278, and IX : 26, and Rabinowitz, 213 ; but see also Luncz in *Jerusalem*, I, p. 58. It should, however, be remarked that the travellers are not quite unanimous in their evidence as to the hostility of the Mohammedan population toward the Jews. On the other hand, it seems that matters with regard to taxes deteriorated later in Safed. Cf. Caro I, 1, and *Jerusalem*, V, p. 161.

[17] See Bertinoro, 222.

[18] See An. Jb., 277.

[19] See Shlomel, 42 d; see also Kaydanower, ch. 16, and טהרת הקודש, I, 43 a.

[20] See Sh. J, 16 b ; Shlomel, 43 a ; see also Responsa of R. Solomon Cohen, II, 38 ; Responsa לחם רב, by R. Abraham Boton, 148 ; מאמין כח by R. Moses Almosnino, 16 a.

[21] See in general about Caro, Graetz, *Geschichte*, IX, Index ; Rabinowitz, Index ; Cassel, *Joseph Karo und das Maggid Mescharim* (Berlin, 1888), and the authorities mentioned in Dr. Louis Ginzberg's article "Caro," J. Encycl. See Neubauer, Catalogue, no. 2578, containing a list of ten eulogies on the death of Joseph Caro, and as to the *untrustworthiness* of the Mentor-Angel, see Rabinowitz, p. 43, note 4.

[22] MM 17 a.

[23] Cassel, ibid., is almost the only writer who doubted the authenticity of this work. His arguments are in every respect weak, whilst there is contemporary evidence to the contrary. See Rabinowitz, 242 seq., Brüll, *Jahrbücher*, IX : 150, and Ginzberg, ibid.

[24] See MM 4 a, 13 c, 18 c, 23 d, 33 b, 49 a.

[25] See MM 3 c.

[26] See Horwitz, של"ה (ed. Warsaw), 162 a seq.

[27] See MM 22 c.

[28] See MM 11 c, 12 a, 17 a, 25 c, cf. Graetz, *Geschichte*, IX : 340 and 561, but see also Hebrew translation, VII : 415, and appendix at the end by Jaffe.

[29] See especially MM, pp. 25 c and 26 a about הרי"ט (ר'יוסף? טאיטאצק) ; cf. Kahana, 77, note 1.

[30] See MM 18 c and 28 a.

[31] See MM 4 a, 16 a, 37 a.

[32] See MM 6 b, 34 a, 50 a.

[33] See MM 28 a.

[34] See MM 35 c.

[35] See MM 2 b.

[36] See MM 30 d, 37 b.

[37] See MM 16 a, 18 d, 46 a.

[38] See MM 46 d.

[39] See MM 3 a, 14 a, 21 c, 24 c, 25 d, 34 d, 44 d.

[40] See MM 3 b.

[41] See MM 3 d, 21 b, c.

[42] See MM 52 b.

[43] See MM 29 d.

[44] See MM 3 b, 41 d.

[45] See MM 3 b.

[46] See MM 13 a, 18 c.

[47] See MM 8 a, 10 b, 19 d, 23 d, 26 b.

[48] See MM 8 b, c.

[49] See MM 50 d.

[50] See MM 4 d, 13 d, 14 a, 19 d, 20 d, 21 a, 27 a, 29 b.   About Nicopolis in particular, ibid., 17 b.

[51] See MM 25 c.

[52] See MM 12 d, 13 a.

[53] See MM 23 a.

[54] See MM 5 a, 6 b, 8 d, 14 c, 25 b and c, 27 a, b, c, 28 d, 30 a and b, 34 b, 42 c.

[55] See MM 3 d, 4 b and c, 8 c, 9 c, 16 d, 19 d, 24 d, 30 c, 46 c, 50 a and d.   About the possibility of references to Alkabez, see Rabinowitz, 245, note 1.   See also below, note 76.

[56] The following remarks about Molko are mostly based on Graetz, *Geschichte*, IX, Index.   See also English translation IV, Index, and Vogelstein and Rieger, *Geschichte der Juden in Rom*, II, Index.

[57] See Graetz, *Geschichte*, VIII: 253 and 562, and references given there, to which Sambari, p. 147, may be added.   See, however, Rabinowitz, 152, note 1.   His doubts are fully justified, as there is not a single real trace in all the contemporary literature coming from Palestine pointing to Molko's staying in that country.

[58] See references given to MM in note 55, especially the one to MM 50 a.

[59] See above, note 50. See also Horwitz, שלי"ה, I, 134 b, and Guttman, דרך אמונה ומעשה רב, Warsaw, 1898, 14 b.

[60] See Azulai *s. n.*; cf. also Ghirondi, p. 380 seq. See also Alkabez, Introduction to his ברית הלוי (Lemberg, 1863); cf. Brüll, *Jahrbücher*, IX, 150, and Rabinowitz, 245. See also Landshut, עמודי העבודה, *s. n.*

[61] See MM 50 d (headed עמוס), which is dated in the MSS. of the MM the second Adar רצו (March, 1536), and it is clear from the contents that Caro was still in חוץ לארץ at that period. For the fact that there were about one thousand families in Safed, I have only the authority of Graetz, *Geschichte*, VII : 302. See Trani, III, 48.

[62] See Trani, I, 28; Caro II, 16 c. Alsheich, Responsa, no. 27, and cf. Shlomel, 43 a.

[63] See Frumkin, 7.

[64] See Responsa of Berab, no. 22; Bacharach, 109 c; Boton, לחם רב, no. 92, and Vital, 13 b. There are also in the book תקון יששכר, by R. Issachar b. Mordecai b. Shushan, references to קהל האשכנזים and קהלות הספרדים.

[65] See Trani, III, 48.

[66] See Trani, I, 106; II, 115 and 131; Responsa by Alsheich, no. 27; Responsa by R. Joseph Trani, I, 82.

[67] See Sh. J., 16 b, and Bertinoro, 222.

[68] See Sh. J., 16 b, and Trani, III, 46.

[69] See Berab, no. 22; Trani, I, 171; II, 25; Radbaz, II, 638, and Responsa of R. Moses Galanti, no. 11.

[70] See Chabib, 292 d.

[71] See R. Chayim Alsheich's Preface to the Pentateuch Commentary of R. Moses Alsheich, ed. Venice, 1601, p. 6 a. Cf. Leo Modena's *Briefe* (ed. by Prof. Dr. L. Blau), Letter 147.

[72] See Berliner, periodical *Jerusalem*, II, 68 seq. The Jewish Theological Seminary Library possesses the most important productions of this press.

[73] See Sh. J., 16 b, and Shlomel, 43 a.

[74] See Responsa of R. Isaac de Latas, p. 54; cf. Graetz, *Geschichte*, IX, end.

[75] See above, p. 209.

[76] See MM 19 d; cf. ibid. 4 d. There can be little doubt that the Solomon mentioned there is Solomon Alkabez.

[77] About Berab and the history of the Ordination controversy, see Graetz, *Geschichte*, IX : 300 seq.; Rabinowitz, 218 seq.; and the references given there, especially to the אגרת הסמיכה forming an appendix to the Responsa of Chabib. It should never be forgotten that in judging Berab we are entirely dependent on material coming from an opponent, who in the heat of the controversy could with all his meekness not remain impartial to his antagonist, and therefore large deductions should be made from all that is said in the aforementioned appendix of the harshness of Berab's character and of the real motives for his action. Cf. also Frumkin, 38 seq.

[78] See Chabib, 186 d, 198 d, 302 b, and 305 c.

[79] See Chabib, 188 d. Of the four ordained, we have only the names of Caro and Trani. Graetz, *Geschichte* IX : 307, note, and Frumkin, 73, note 1, advance hypotheses as to the names of the other two. Yachya in his שלשלת הקבלה speaks of ten who received the Ordination, but the meaning of the passage is not quite certain.

[80] See MM 29 a; cf. Graetz, ibid. 311. Caro seems to have given up the matter altogether afterwards, there being not a single reference to the Ordination question, either in his חשן משפט, no. 61, or in his commentary to Maimonides' משנה תורה ה׳ סנהדרין, IV. Only in his בית יוסף to the חשן משפט, no. 295, there is a faint reference to it. Cf. Azulai's ברכי יוסף to חשן משפט, 64.

[81] See MM 16 d.

[82] About Trani, see Fin, הכרמל (octavo edition), II, 586 seq.

[83] See Trani, II, 67 ; cf. also I, 41 and 47.

[84] See Trani, III, 48.

[85] See e. g. Trani, I, 156, 189, 274, 336 ; II, 46 and 180; cf. Caro I, 24.

[86] See אהבת ציון, Anon., 26 d. Cf. also Caro I, 14, where he speaks of his lack of time, which is given to lecturing to the *Chaberim* both in the morning and in the evening.

[87] See Alsheich, Opinion incorporated in Caro I, 73.

[88] See Caro I, 92 ; II, 14 seq. Cf. R. Menahem Azariah of Fano, Preface to the פלח הרמון. Cf. also Azulai ; Conforte ; Sambari ; and Kahana, p. 80 seq.

[89] See *Pardes*, Preface.

[90] See ברית הלוי, 39 b seq.

[91] See SG, pp. 1 a, 23 a and b, 24 b; cf. Kahana, p. 80, note 2.

[92] See Appendix A. 292, 293. With regard to Alkabez see טהרת הקודש, II, 25 b.

[93] See אור הישר by Popers, 23 b. See also reference given above, note 60.

[94] See Kahana, p. 145, note 6, to which are to be added R. Menahem Azariah of Fano and R. Sabbatai Horwitz, the author of שפע טל.

[95] See Preface to the work mentioned in note 88. Cf. *Catalog der hebräischen Handschriften der kgl. Bibliothek in Modena*, S. Jona, p. 10 seq.; cf. also Kaufmann.

[96] See the authorities quoted above in note 88; cf. also Bacharach, 7 a and 33 c.

[97] Besides the usual authorities, such as Conforte (Index), Sambari (Index), and Azulai, *s. n.*, see also Calimani, and Alsheich's Preface to his Commentary to Proverbs. Cf. Leo Modena's *Briefe*, Letter 98. Most of the biographers give the relation of Loria as stated in the text. Cf. also Vital, 2 b. Rabbi Abraham Chazkuni, however, in his book זאת חוקת התורה, states in the name of Alsheich that he had a direct tradition from Loria regarding a certain mystic point, whilst according to Calimani he was one of the direct recipients of Loria's mystical teachings. See also Steinschneider, *Jerusalem*, III, no. 33 c, to a MS. חזות קשה by Alsheich on the precarious condition of the Jews of Safed. Unfortunately, the MS. was inaccessible to me.

[98] See Appendix A 298 : 17.

[99] See Appendix A 297 : 4; 293 : 20.

[100] See Conforte (Index), and Azulai, *s. n.* Cf. Bacharach 109 c; Ch. Y. II, 4a, and IV, 10 b; Kaydanower, 93, and Popers, 7 b.

[101] See Appendix A 294 : 1, 2; 295 : 6, 8; 296 : 13, 14, 15; 297 : 2; 298 : 15.

[102] See Azkari, Preface; cf. Kahana, p. 149.

[103] See Appendix A 297 : 3.

[104] See ראשית חכמה (ed. Cracow), 174 a.

[105] See Appendix A 294 : 36; cf. 298 : 11, 19, 22.

[106] See Azkari, 95 a seq.

[107] See Appendix A 293 : 25 ; cf. *Baba Bathra,* 10 a, ש"ע א"ח, no. 92, end.

[108] See Appendix A 296 : 27 ; 298 : 16, 27.

[109] See Appendix A 293 : 22 ; cf. 294 : 4.

[110] See Shlomel and Vital, where such legends are scattered over the books, parallels to which are to be found in Bacharach's and Kaydanower's works in various places.　Sambari, of whose chronicles the Jewish Theological Seminary Library possesses a good copy, is also replete with such stories.　Cf. also נשמת חיים, III, 10; see Kahana, pp. 146, 148, and 150.　Yachya in his שה"ק has also any number of such stories.

[111] The legend about Joseph is incorporated in the book לקוטי ש"ס (Livorno, 1790) ; Kahana, p. 11, note 5.

[112] See Appendix A 293 : 21 ; 297 : 8.

[113] Cf. *Shabbath,* 12 a and b, and the references given there on the margin to the codes of Maimonides and Caro.

[114] See Appendix A 293 : 19; 295 : 9 ; 297 : 7, 8 ; 298 : 13, 20.

[115] See אורחות צדיקים incorporated in the Hebrew book mentioned above in note 111, 69 b.

[116] See Azulai, *s. n.*; Ch. Y., II, 55 b.

[117] The main sources for Loria's biography are the legendary accounts, of which two versions exist.　The one is that first published in the *Sammelwerk* נובלות חכמה (see Zedner, 356), and republished any number of times both as appendix to other works as well as by itself under the name of שבחי האר"י.　This is the version made use of by almost all writers on the subject. The second version, strongly related to it, but in a somewhat more connected form as well as more precise in its dates, is the ספר הכונות ומעשה ניסים published first in Constantinople in 1720, and then in Safed by R. Samuel Heller in the year 1876.　See also אור האמת by Moses Mordecai Lebtob, pp. 214–216, where the first two or three pages of this version are reproduced. Sambari's account of the life of Loria is omitted by Neubauer, but the Jewish Theological Seminary Library possesses a photograph copy of the whole work as preserved in the Paris MS., and a copy of the omissions relating to Safed from the Oxford MS. This account of Sambari is almost identical with the second version.　Much material is also to be found in Bacharach, 6 a, 7 b,

10 b to 14 a, 33 a to 34 a, 77 a, 109 c, 116 b and c, 126 a and d, 138a, 141 c, 142a and b, 143 a, 146 b, c, and d, 152 to 154. Bacharach's story is, as is well known, based on Shlomel. Kaydanower has also various legends about Loria (see chs. 2, 5, 7, 9, 12, 16, 22, 31, 34, 46, 48, 77, 80, 87, and 93), which agree on the whole with the second version. Ch. Y. also made use of this version. This version, hardly known to any modern writer except Bloch, in his *Die Kabbalah auf ihrem Höhepunkt und ihre Meister,* (Pressburg, 1905), is extant in various MSS. It is hardly necessary to say that all these legends are greatly exaggerated, and sometimes even written "with a purpose." Cf. Modena, ארי נהם, ch. 25 ; but on the whole, the legends fairly represent the estimation in which Loria was held by his contemporaries. Cf. also Calimani, Conforte Index, Sambari Index, and Azulai, *s. n.* See further, Graetz, *Geschichte*, IX, Index, and Kahana. The account in the text is mostly based on the Constantinople edition, to be quoted as MN, the initials of the *Maaseh Nissim* version. Cf. also Dr. Ginzberg's article "Cabala," Jewish Encyclopedia, and the literature given there about the various mystical systems, to which has to be added Bloch as above. The reader who will study the question will find that we are still in want of a good exposition of Loria's Cabbala, its strange and bewildering terminology, and how far it is to be considered a development of Cordovero's system. The best essay on this subject is undoubtedly the just mentioned article by Dr. Ginzberg, and the book of Mieses mentioned by him ; but even in these articles we have more of the system of Cordovero as expounded by R. Sabbatai Horwitz than that of Loria as conveyed by his disciple Vital.

[118] See Graetz, *Geschichte*, VIII : 211-213. See also ibid., p. 292, note. Cf. Frumkin, pp. 15, 58, 61-68. From the Responsa of R. Samuel de Modena, 2, it is clear that the German-Jewish settlements in the Turkish Empire preceded those of the Spanish Jews. Cf. Solomon Rosanis, דברי ימי ישראל בתוגרמה, p. 163 seq. Graetz's statement in *Geschichte*, IX : 24, that the Jewish settlement in Jerusalem counted in the year 1522 fifteen hundred families rests on a mistaken reading of his authority, where Graetz, by some oversight, added the word מאות, which is not to be found in the text. The sense in the

Sh. J. is plain enough, that the German community counted fifteen families. Cf. Schwarz, pp. 453 and 457. See also Epstein, משפחת לוריא, pp. 33 and 35. It is interesting to see that our Loria's son was named Solomon Loria, probably after his grandfather.

[119] See MN 2 a. Cf. Azulai, *s. n.*, and Ch. Y., 13 b. According to Conforte (40 b), however, Loria was the pupil of R. David Abi Zimra and the colleague of R. Bezaleel, a view which is supported by Vital, 9 a, רדב״ז רבן.

[120] See MN 2 a-b. The MS. has the following important additional matter: ויתן לו הספר ההוא וילך ויתבודד בביתו בחצירו ששה שנים . . . ולפעמים אומרים לו . . . צריך סינופים אחרים קשים מהראשונים וכראותו כן יצא מחצירו והלך כן להתבודד במצרים הישנה סמוך לנהר נילוס ב׳ שנים אחרים ובכל ערב שבת הולך לביתו. Sambari has the following words: במצרים הישנה בכפר אחד שנ׳ המקייאץ שבצוען מצרים הנקרא אל״רודא ע״י חמיו שהיה עשיר גדול וזה הכפר היה ברשותו. See Shlomel's chronology (p. 33 d), which is somewhat different. It is to be observed that the MS. contains no statement as to the date of Loria's leaving Egypt, so that it may be fixed with Graetz, *Geschichte*, IX : 587, not later than 1568. This would allow ample time for his making the acquaintance of Cordovero, who died in 1570, and becoming his regular disciple. Kahana's arguments against Graetz (p. 150) are not convincing. We have always to remember that the tendency was to reduce Loria's residence in Safed to a minimum, so as to make him entirely independent of Cordovero.

[121] See Shlomel, 33 b, and Preface to the עץ החיים. About the mystical writings of R. David Abi Zimra, and those of R. Bezaleel, see Azulai, *s. n.*

[122] See Kahana, p. 203, note 1.

[123] See Sambari, 151, and Conforte, 40 b.

[124] See MN 1 b. The MS. adds Joseph Ashkenazi.

[125] See *Pardes*, 77 a.

[126] *Pardes*, 26 a.

[127] Introduction to the פלח הרמון, 3 b.

[128] See MN 2 b and 3 a. More fully in the MS. 3 a-b. וכובש
נביאתו מפני הרמ״ק . . . וביום שנפטר אמר להם . . . שבימי
היו צינורי קדושה חתומים כתבתי דברי בסיתום גדול בבחינת
ספירות אבל אחרי מותי יתגלו יותר הצינורות ויפרש האיש ההוא
דברי בבחינת פרצופים כדאיתא בס׳פ ד״צ אידרות. See also
Preface to עה״ח. Cf. Graetz, *Geschichte*, IX : 589. See also
Bloch (as above, note 117), p. 35.

[129] See above, note 120, and below, note 163, as to the date
of Loria's death.

[130] See Shlomel, 44 b, and Bacharach, 6 c. It is to be noticed that
Vital maintained a sceptical attitude toward the relations of Caro's
Maggid. See Kahana, p. 268, text and notes, and Rabinowitz,
243. It is not impossible that the distrust was mutual.

[131] See Shlomel, 34 b seq. See also Preface to עה״ח.

[132] See MN 3 a and 5 b. The author of the קול בוכים was a
disciple of Cordovero.

[133] See MN 3 a b.

[134] See MN 4 a b. The MS. 5 a has that Loria said : לכן עצתי
שכל אחד מכם יכתוב לו מה שישמע ממני . . . אמנם לא ניתן
רשות לכתוב זולת למה רח״ו. The question whether Loria wrote
anything, and how far these so-called traditions in his name are
to be relied upon is still a very mooted one. See Kahana, p. 202,
text and notes, and references given there. The general impression one receives from the various legendary accounts
quoted above is that he declined to write anything, and that he
was reluctant to impart any mystical knowledge even by word
of mouth.

[135] See Azulai, *s. n.* See MN 3 a with regard to Loria's
serving on a board.

[136] See Modena, ארי נהם, p. 66.

[137] See such works as the ספר הכונות in its various editions
and arrangements (Zedner, 379), and the נג״ד ומצוה by R. Jacob
ben Chayim Zemach (Zedner, 299).

[138] See *Shabbath*, 10 a.

[139] See above, note 137, to which has to be added the פע״ח
by Vital.

[140] See Shlomel, 141 b. הסגר seems to mean a block of buildings with a synagogue attached to it. According to the Ch. Y.,
34 c, it means a College or a Yeshibah. See also Vital, 15 a.

[141] See Graetz, *Geschichte*, XI: 587 seq., and references given there. See also כונות (ed. Jessnitz, 1723), 1 a.

[142] See above, p. 168.

[143] See כונות, 2 d; cf. Kahana, p. 203, note 5.

[144] See כונות, 11 c.

[145] See כונות, 1 b.

[146] See נגיד ומצוה, 45 b.

[147] See כונות 6 c. Cf. אורחות צדיקים, 67 a.

[148] See Azkari, p. 48. See also the statement of the traveller Samson Bak, *Jerusalem*, II, p. 145.

[149] See כונות, 3 a.

[150] See ש״ע האר״י הלכות צדקה.

[151] See כונות, 1 a.

[152] See Ch. Y., IV, 53 a and b.

[153] See כונות, 3 b seq., 24 b seq. Bacharach, 11 d.

[154] See Shlomel, 39 c, Bacharach, 11 a, and Ch. Y., I, 37 b.

[155] See Shlomel, 39, and Bacharach, ibid.

[156] See גלגולים (Przemysl, 1875), 86 a and b.

[157] See Azulai, *s. n.*, and Kaydanower, ch. 93. Cf. *Pesikta Rabbathi*, 131 b seq., and the Second Esdras, ch. 10, *r. v.*

[158] See Azulai, *s. n.*

[159] See Shlomel, 39 a, Bacharach, 10 d. Cf. Graetz, *Geschichte*, IX: 588. See also ג״ל, 50 seq.; 61 seq; 87 d seq., about various contemporaries of Loria. Cf. also Steinschneider, Catalogue Munich, 2d ed., Berlin, 1895, pp. 250–1.

[160] See Shlomel, 35 b.

[161] See כונות, 1 b, and Ch. Y., I, 48 b, 51 b, and 59 b.

[162] See Preface to the עה״ח.

[163] The date of Loria's death is given by most bibliographers as the year 1572. Against this we have, however, the evidence of Conforte, 41 a, who fixes it in the year 1573, for which he is attacked by Azulai and others. Sambari, p. 151, fixes it in the year 1574, which is also confirmed by the traveller Samson Bak. See *Jerusalem*, II, p. 146, text and notes.

[164] See the statement of R. Moses Galanti, the Younger, in the preface to the book מגן דוד, by R. David Abi Zimra (Amsterdam, 1679).

[165] Horwitz is the one who dwells more on the mystical exposition of the ideal man than any of the authors of ספרי מוסר

who became popular with the large masses, and a careful reading of the first seventy pages of his שֶׁלֹ״ה (ed. Warsaw, 8°) will show that it is chiefly the קדושת הגוף and the hope conse-quent upon it which he is aiming at. Cf. especially page 19 b; 20 a seq.; 28 a seq.; 30 b seq.; 33 a seq.; 47 a seq.; 59 a seq.

[166] See *Jerusalem*, II, p. 143, and Frumkin, 117.

[167] See Azulai under these names. Cf. also Shlomel, 36 a and 41 d. See also the Responsa of R. Joseph Trani, I, 82. Cf. also Sambari, 161, with regard to the Loria Synagogue.

INDEX

INDEX

𝕿𝖍𝖊 𝕷𝖔𝖗𝖉 𝕭𝖆𝖑𝖙𝖎𝖒𝖔𝖗𝖊 𝕻𝖗𝖊𝖘𝖘

BALTIMORE, MD., U. S. A.